1984

Conversational Organization

INTERACTION BETWEEN SPEAKERS AND HEARERS

LANGUAGE, THOUGHT, AND CULTURE: *Advances in the Study of Cognition*

Under the Editorship of: E. A. HAMMEL

DEPARTMENT OF ANTHROPOLOGY
UNIVERSITY OF CALIFORNIA
BERKELEY

Michael Agar, Ripping and Running: A Formal Ethnography of Urban Heroin Addicts

Brent Berlin, Dennis E. Breedlove, and Peter H. Raven, Principles of Tzeltal Plant Classification: An Introduction to the Botanical Ethnography of a Mayan-Speaking People of Highland Chiapas

Mary Sanches and Ben Blount, Sociocultural Dimensions of Language Use

Daniel G. Bobrow and Allan Collins, Representation and Understanding: Studies in Cognitive Science

Domenico Parisi and Francesco Antinucci, Essentials of Grammar

Elizabeth Bates, Language and Context: The Acquisition of Pragmatics

Ben G. Blount and Mary Sanches, Sociocultural Dimensions of Language Change

Susan Ervin-Tripp and Claudia Mitchell-Kernan (Eds.), Child Discourse

Lynn A. Friedman (Ed.), On the Other Hand: New Perspectives on American Sign Language

Eugene S. Hunn, Tzeltal Folk Zoology: The Classification of Discontinuities in Nature

Jim Schenkein (Ed.), Studies in the Organization of Conversational Interaction

David Parkin, The Cultural Definition of Political Response: Lineal Destiny Among the Luo

Stephen A. Tyler, The Said and the Unsaid: Mind, Meaning, and Culture

Susan Gal, Language Shift: Social Determinants of Linguistic Change in Bilingual Austria

Ronald Scollon and Suzanne B. K. Scollon, Linguistic Convergence: An Ethnography of Speaking at Fort Chipewyan, Alberta

Elizabeth Bates, The Emergence of Symbols: Cognition and Communication in Infancy

Mary LeCron Foster and Stanley H. Brandes (Eds.), Symbol as Sense: New Approaches to the Analysis of Meaning

Willett Kempton, The Folk Classification of Ceramics: A Study of Cognitive Prototypes

Charles Goodwin, Conversational Organization: Interaction between Speakers and Hearers

In preparation

P. L. F. Heelas and A. J. Lock (Eds.), Indigenous Psychologies: The Anthropology of the Self

Conversational Organization
INTERACTION BETWEEN SPEAKERS AND HEARERS

Charles Goodwin

Department of Anthropology
University of South Carolina
Columbia, South Carolina

ACADEMIC PRESS
A Subsidiary of Harcourt Brace Jovanovich, Publishers
New York   London   Toronto   Sydney   San Francisco

To Helen, Chil, and Candy,
with love

ACADEMIC PRESS, INC.
111 Fifth Avenue, New York, New York 10003

United Kingdom Edition published by
ACADEMIC PRESS, INC. (LONDON) LTD.
24/28 Oval Road, London NW1 7DX

Library of Congress Cataloging in Publication Data

Goodwin, Charles.
    Conversational organization.

    (Language, thought, and culture)
    Bibliography: p.
    Includes index.
    1. Conversation. 2. Discourse analysis.
I. Title. II. Series.
P95.45.G6   001.54'2'0141   81-3573
ISBN 0-12-289780-3   AACR2

Contents

3. Notes on the Organization of Engagement   95

4. Modifying Units of Talk to Coordinate Their Production with the Actions of a Recipient   127

5. Designing Talk for Different Types of Recipients   149

6. Conclusion   167

Transcription Conventions

Speech

```
         1 2                      3        4        5   6 7          8
         ↓ ↓                      ↓        ↓        ↓   ↓ ↓          ↓
JANE:   It- It was (– – – – – – – – – – + – –) so: : (0.3) °incredible.
                                                    [
MEG:                                        I (love) it. = I do.
                                            ↑     ↑      ↑
                                            9     10     11
```

1. A dash marks a cut-off.
2. Italics show that the talk so marked is being emphasized in some fashion.
3. Dashes within parentheses indicate tenths of a second within a silence.
4. Each full second within a silence is marked with a plus sign.
5. A colon indicates that the sound preceding it is noticeably lengthened.
6. Numbers within parentheses constitute an alternative way of showing the duration of a silence.

7. A degree sign shows that the talk so marked is spoken with noticeably lowered volume.

8. Punctuation marks indicate intonation as follows:
A falling contour is marked with a period.
A rising contour is marked with a question mark.
A falling–rising contour is marked with a comma.

9. A bracket connecting the talk of different speakers shows that over-lapping talk begins at that point.

10. If words are placed within parentheses, a possible but not certain hearing of that talk is indicated.

11. An equals sign indicates that no break occurs between two pieces of talk by either the same or different speakers.

Gaze

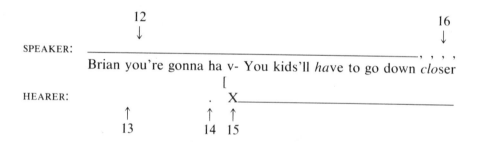

The gaze of the speaker is marked above the utterance; that of the recipient(s) is marked below it.

12. A line indicates that the party so marked is gazing toward the other.

13. The absence of a line shows that that party is not gazing toward the other.

14. A dot or series of dots marks the movement that brings gaze to another.

15. A capital X connected to a specific point in the talk with a bracket shows the place where gaze reaches the other.

16. Commas mark a movement withdrawing gaze.

Preface

To engage successfully in conversation, participants are required not only to produce sentences but also to coordinate, in a meaningful fashion, their talk with the talk of others present. Such activity constitutes a pervasive—but intricate—form of human social organization, one that makes full use of both the linguistic and the cultural competence of the parties engaged in it. It is therefore not surprising that the analysis of conservation has begun to attract the attention of scholars from a number of different disciplines. The present study takes as its point of departure the work of Harvey Sacks and his colleagues on the sequential organization of conservation, and investigates some previously unexamined features of this process.

Within conservation, talk proceeds through a series of turns at talk. The most basic social identities relevant to the turn are those of speaker and hearer. This analysis focuses on how the turn is constituted through the mutual interaction of speaker and hearer. Perhaps the best way to make clear what is meant by this is to provide a brief overview of the material to be covered.

In Chapter 1, relevant research is reviewed and methodological preliminaries, such as the transcription system, are presented. Data for the analysis consist of videotapes of conversation recorded in a range of settings.

Chapter 2 investigates the work participants do to bring about a state of affairs in which the talk of the speaker is being addressed to, and attended by, a hearer. Among the phenomena given special attention are ways in which displays of hearership affect the talk in progress, the use of phrasal breaks—such as restarts and pauses—to request gaze, and the ordering of mutual gaze within the turn.

It is also possible to produce talk without speaker and hearer displaying explicit mutual orientation. In Chapter 3, alternative types of engagement frameworks are investigated. Particular attention is paid to the organization of disengagement and also to how participants work with each other to move from one type of engagement to another.

Chapter 4 examines the ability of speakers to add new sections to units in their talk so that the talk can be precisely synchronized with relevant actions of the hearer. This process is found to be operative in the production of units on many different levels of organization and may lead to changes in the sentence being constructed within the turn.

Chapter 5 investigates ways in which speakers differentiate recipients, as well as some of the consequences this has for the production of their talk. As speakers move their gaze from one type of recipient to another, they change the sentence in progress so that it remains appropriate to its recipient of the moment.

Each chapter thus investigates a particular phenomenon implicated in the organization of action between speaker and hearer within the turn at talk. The issues posed are quite basic:

— How is a framework of mutual orientation achieved within the turn?
— What constitutes a display of hearership and how is it relevant?
— What engagement alternatives are open to participants and how do these alternatives affect the talk of the moment?
— How are the separate actions of speaker and hearer coordinated with each other within the turn?
— How do speakers make visible the appropriateness of their talk for its recipients and what consequences does this have for the structure of the talk?

An examination of the ways in which these issues are dealt with by participants serves to make visible some of the constitutive features of the turn, as well as to reveal many intricate, finely coordinated processes of interaction that occur with it.

The phenomena being investigated should be of interest to researchers concerned with social interaction and language in a number of different fields including sociology, linguistics, anthropology, psychology, and communications. The study as a whole is relevant to work in nonverbal communication, and some of the analysis in Chapter 2 complements work done in psychology and psycholinguistics on speech errors.

Acknowledgments

Most of the analysis, with the exception of Chapter 3, was done as part of my work toward a doctorate in communications at the University of Pennsylvania. I owe a tremendous debt to the people who taught me there, and would like to thank in particular Klaus Krippendorff, William Labov, Ward Goodenough, and Erving Goffman. In addition, I had the great privilege of being able to work with Harvey Sacks on some of this material. Others whose aid and suggestions were most valuable include Anita Pomerantz, Emanuel Schegloff, and John O'Neill. Two people, Candy Goodwin and Gail Jefferson, require very special mention. Without Candy's constant aid and collaboration and Gail's inspiration, teaching, and criticism, this work would not have been possible. I want to thank all of these people for what they have given me.

A slightly different version of the analysis that constitutes the beginning of Chapter 2 was published as "Restarts, Pauses, and the Achievement of Mutual Gaze" in *Sociological Inquiry*, Vol. 50, numbers 3–4, Special Double Issue on Language and Social Interaction, Don Zimmerman and Candace West (eds.), 1980. Portions of Chapters 4 and 5 (specifically the analysis of the sentence "I gave up smoking cigarettes one week ago today actually") have appeared as "The Interactive Construction of a Sentence in Natural Conversation" in *Everyday Language: Studies in Ethnomethodology*, George Psathas (ed.) (New York: Irvington Publishers, 1979). These materials have been incorporated into the present work with the permission of Jossey Bass, Inc. and Irvington Publishers.

I wish to thank Randee Falk and the editorial staff of Academic Press for the help and suggestions they gave for the final revision of this work. In addition, special thanks are owed to Joan Toms Cureton, Ginger Hollis, and Cheryl Fowler for their typing and to John Ballou for his drawings. Final preparation of the manuscript was assisted by a productive research grant from the University of South Carolina.

1

Introduction

Preliminary Definitions

Some of the phenomena to be investigated in this study will here be provisionally defined. The present definitions are provisional because I believe that precise definitions of these phenomena can only be obtained by empirical investigation of their properties.[1]

CONVERSATION

Goffman (1975:36) has noted that two different approaches can be taken to the definition of conversation. One can try to capture the sense in which the term can refer to casual talk in everyday settings, or alternatively the term can be "used in a loose way as an equivalent of talk or spoken interaction." It is in this latter sense that the word "conversation" is used in this study.[2]

Despite the broad scope of the term when it is used in this fashion,

[1] Vološinov (1973:45) notes that "at the outset of an investigation, it is not so much the intellectual faculty for making formulas and definitions that leads the way, but rather it is the eyes and hands attempting to get the feel of the actual presence of the subject matter."

[2] For a similarly broad definition of conversation, see Schegloff (1968:1075–1076).

conversation is still but a special case of what Goffman (1963:24) has called focused interaction: "the kind of interaction that occurs when persons gather close together and openly cooperate to sustain a single focus of attention." As such, it stands in contrast to unfocused interaction, the kind of communicative situation concerned with "the management of sheer and mere copresence."

Placing conversation in this typology raises some analytic difficulties. Because Goffman bounds the area of his investigation in terms of copresence, conversations between nonpresent parties—for example, phone calls—are excluded from it.[3] Nevertheless, the distinctions he makes are valuable.

Goffman also notes (1975:33) that though conversation is defined in terms of talk, it can include behavior other than talk. In the present study, conversation is taken to include nonlinguistic as well as linguistic behavior, and both will be investigated; however, talk is seen to occupy a central place in the organization of conversation.

TURN-TAKING

A basic empirical finding about conversation, one that has been discovered independently by different investigators (see, for example, Allen and Guy 1974:30,177; Argyle 1969:201–202; Duncan 1974; Goffman 1964:135; Jaffe and Feldstein 1970:9; Sacks, Schegloff, and Jefferson 1974; Yngve 1970:1–2), and that can be seen by even casual inspection of almost any fragment of conversation, is that talk within it proceeds through a sequence of turns. Miller (1963:418) gives this phenomenon the status of a language universal but notes that it does not seem intrinsically necessary.

In the abstract, the phenomenon of turn-taking seems quite easy to define. The talk of one party bounded by the talk of others constitutes a turn, with turn-taking being the process through which the party doing the talk of the moment is changed.

A number of problems with such a definition emerge when actual conversation is closely examined. For example, both simultaneous talk and silence between the talk of different parties are regularly found. Such phenomena raise relevant theoretical questions about the proper definition of the turn's boundaries as well as the process through which it is exchanged.

---

[3] Elsewhere Goffman (1953:113) notes that "the criterion of immediate presence provides a heuristic delimation of scope, not an analytical one. From the point of view of communication face-to-face interaction does not seem to present a single important characteristic that is not found—at least within certain limits—in mediated communication situations."

However, providing a better description of either the turn or turn-taking requires careful investigation of actual data. Such analysis is beyond the scope of the present attempt to provide preliminary definitions. Though the definition that has been given will eventually be found inadequate, it does at least locate a phenomenon that can be made the subject of further investigation. When research into the structure of turn-taking is discussed, other definitions of the turn will be examined in terms of their ability to accurately characterize the phenomena being studied.

TYPES OF PARTICIPANTS

The term "participant" will be used to refer to anyone engaged in a conversation. For example, on a busy street, several different "withs" (Goffman 1971:19–27) may be simultaneously engaged in conversation. A party is a participant to the conversation in his "with" but not a participant to conversations in other "withs."[4] Someone not part of a relevant conversation will be called a nonparticipant. Although in many cases—such as the street example—the distinction between participant and nonparticipant is quite clear, in other cases—for example, when a new member is joining a casual group—the distinction may be ambiguous and may even itself be one of the events at issue in the interaction. I wish to leave the manner in which the distinction is formulated in such cases a matter for empirical investigation. I also wish to use the term "participant" in a broad enough sense to include someone who is momentarily disattending the conversation.

A party whose turn is in progress at a particular point in time will be called a speaker. In that pauses may occur within a turn, a party may be a speaker even though he is not saying anything at the moment.[5] Because the term "speaker" is defined in terms of the turn, in some circumstances—such as simultaneous talk—whether a party is a speaker

---

[4] Goffman (1953:116–117) examines in more detail some of the theoretical issues raised by such a situation. He notes that whereas directed information will be confined to a single conversational cluster, undirected information—for example, one's choice of clothes and companions—will be available to all in one's physical presence. These issues are given more extended treatment in Goffman (1963) where some of the same distinctions are examined with respect to differences between focused and unfocused interaction.

[5] Throughout this analysis I will use the masculine pronoun to refer to speaker and hearer as generic entities. I am only too well aware of the sexist implications of such use and in fact tried to write portions of the analysis so that such pronouns were not used. I found, however, that not only did the writing become more awkward and difficult to follow but that some of the distinctions I was trying to make in the analysis were obscured or lost altogether. As there is no neuter singular pronoun in English, I have therefore reluctantly decided to continue with such use of these pronouns.

may be subject to dispute (for analysis of this and related issues, see Jefferson 1973).

Duncan (1974a:302) has defined an "auditor" as "a participant who does not claim the speaking turn at any given moment." This definition seems inadequate in a number of respects.[6] First, Schegloff (1968:1092–1093) has noted that

> conversation is a "minimally two-party" activity. That requirement is not satisfied by the mere copresence of two persons, one of whom is talking. It requires that there be both a "speaker" and a "hearer." . . . "Hearership" can be seen as a locus of rules, and a status whose incumbency is subject to demonstration . . . .

Second, a number of different types of nonspeaking participants must be differentiated. Goffman (1975:3) makes the following distinctions.[7]

> Broadly speaking, there are three kinds of listeners to talk: those who *overhear*, whether or not their unratified participation is inadvertent and whether or not it has been encouraged; those who are ratified participants but (in the case of more than two-person talk) are not specifically addressed by the speaker; and those ratified participants who *are* addressed, that is, oriented to by the speaker in a manner to suggest that his words are particularly for them, and that some answer is therefore anticipated from them more so than from the other ratified participants. (I say "broadly speaking" because all sorts of minor variations are possible—for example, speaker's practice of drawing a particular participant into an exchange and then turning to the other participants as if to offer him and his words for public delectation.)

In describing participants to the turn, it is useful to distinguish three different levels of organization.

First, the activity of conversation provides a set of positions for the participants, the most salient being speaker and hearer. These positions have an ongoing relevance to the conversation in that different kinds of actions such as speech and silence are appropriate to each.

Second, distinct from the positions provided by the activity are the actions of individual participants displaying incumbency or nonincumbency[8] in these positions. How participants display their occupancy of

---

[6] It must, however, be emphasized that Duncan's work itself does not suffer from any of the weaknesses being noted about this definition. He in fact provides (for example, 1974b) detailed analysis of some of the ways in which the hearer participates in the turn at talk.

[7] For other discussion of different types of listeners see Bales (1970:6) and Philips (1974:162–163); for an early statement on the importance of conceptualizing an utterance as being addressed to a recipient with specific characteristics see Vološinov (1973:85–86).

[8] It must be recognized that displays of nonincumbency can be as carefully and relevantly constructed as displays of incumbency. For example, a speaker might begin an utterance addressed to a specific party and inappropriate to others present. Before the recipient of

the positions provided by the activity of conversation, especially the position of hearer, is one of the topics to be investigated in this study.

Though events on this level of organization are performed by single individuals, they are nonetheless social and include a projection about the other as well as a display about the self. Consider the case of one party, A, addressing an utterance to another, B, who is, however, attending a different speaker, C. In order to adequately describe A's action, one has to include the projection of B as an addressee; that description is unaffected by whether B displays hearership to A. The actions of B relevant to the position of hearer can be described separately. Further, a display of hearership on B's part includes a projection of the party he is attending as speaker.[9]

The term "hearer" can thus refer to three quite different objects. First, it might designate the complementary position to "speaker" provided by the activity of conversation. Second, it might refer to the addressee of an act by a speaker. Third, it might designate a party performing acts in his own right relevant to the position of hearer. If these distinctions are not kept in mind, confusion results, since, for example, a party may be an addressee without acting as a hearer.

A third level of organization is provided by events that can only be described in terms of the actions of more than one individual.[10] For example, the exchange of turns in conversation requires action by at least two parties, one who changes his behavior from speaking to hearership and another who moves from hearership to speaking. The actions of either alone are insufficient to provide for an exchange of turns. Within the turn, events such as the address of the speaker toward the hearer and the orientation—or lack of it—of the hearer toward the speaker are defined on this level of organization. What Goffman speaks of as "rat-

---

the utterance has been made clear, one of the inappropriate parties may begin to attend the speaker as a hearer. The speaker might then emphasize who his addressee is (for example, with an address term) while avoiding the inappropriate hearer. The latter, upon recognizing that the utterance is not being directed to him, might then actively turn his attention elsewhere. In such a situation, both nonhearership and nonaddress have been carefully displayed.

[9] Units that provide projections of the matching identities of both self and other have been termed "identity relationships" by Goodenough (1965:6).

[10] John Smith (personal communication) has reported that the distinction between an act toward another by one individual and an act defined in terms of the behavior of several individuals has raised conceptual problems in ethology. Thus the analysis of a "display" is appropriate to a social act by a single individual, a greeting, for example, but cannot be applied to a social act defined by the actions of several individuals, for example, a handshake.

For a definition of "display," see Smith (1974:332). My own use of this word is not meant to imply the technical, evolutionary sense it has as a term in ethology.

ification" also fits here.[11] The identity assumed by one party is ratified, not by his own actions, but by the action of another who assumes a complementary identity toward him. For example, it is quite common in conversation that while a speaker is addressing an utterance to one party, another, who has not been attending him, will also begin to orient to him. In such circumstances, speakers frequently address a subsequent part of their turn to the new party, thus ratifying him as a hearer. The term "collaborative action" has been given to events on this level of organization by Sacks and his colleagues, who have provided extensive investigation of their structure in conversation (Jefferson 1973; Sacks *et al.* 1974; Schegloff and Sacks 1973).

It should be noted that the terms "speaker" and "hearer" are being used here in a slightly different way than they are usually employed in linguistics. Whereas the present emphasis is on the complementary positions they describe in a particular social arrangement, in linguistics the social character of these terms is usually not given much attention. Rather, the speaker is conceptualized primarily as an entity capable of constructing sentences and, as such, is not generally distinguished analytically from his listener, who is assumed to possess a similar competence in order to be able to comprehend sentences. Thus Chomsky (1965:3) refers to "an ideal speaker–listener."

UNITS OF TALK

Linguistics and allied fields such as kinesics have provided a rich technical vocabulary for describing the units regularly found in conversation. This vocabulary is not, however, without its problems. To begin with, it has been developed within two separate linguistic paradigms, structuralism and generative grammar. These paradigms make very different assumptions both about the nature of the phenomena being examined and about what a proper theoretical description of that phenomena consists of. Therefore, classifications of phenomena formulated within these different theoretical frameworks are not likely to be consistent. For example, Scheflen (1974:19) defines a sentence as follows: "A syntactic sentence is not identified according to a grammatical structure; it is instead that unit of speech that is marked off by certain traditional behaviors that accompany the stream of speech." Such a definition of the sentence would not be accepted within the framework of transformational grammar. Indeed, Lyons (1972:61) argues that from the

---

[11] A discussion of the reciprocal quality of ratification is found in Goffman (1964:35) and Goffman (1967:34).

perspective of contemporary linguistics, "sentences never occur in speech." Rather,

> as a grammatical unit, the sentence is an abstract entity in terms of which the linguist accounts for the distributional relations holding within utterances. In this sense of the term, utterances never consist of sentences, but of one or more segments of speech (or written text) which can be put into correspondence with the sentences generated by the grammar [Lyons 1969:176].

For my analysis I will find it necessary to examine the details of actual speech as well as abstract linguistic units which do not stand in a one-to-one relationship with the sounds in the speech stream.[12] I will use the term "utterance" to refer to the stream of speech actually produced by a speaker in conversation, and the word "sentence," as well as related terms such as "phrase" and "clause," to refer to abstract entities capable of describing distributional relationships within and between utterances.

Bloomfield (1946:170) defines a sentence as "an independent linguistic form, not included by virtue of any grammatical construction in any larger linguistic form." Although the structural independence of the sentence can be called into question,[13] this definition remains useful.

In defining "utterance" as the actual stream of speech, I mean to include the entire vocal production of the speaker—that is, not only those sounds which could be placed in correspondence with elements of sentences, but also phenomena such as midword plosives, inbreaths, laughter, crying, "uh's," and pauses. I also do not wish to separate a speaker's speech into subordinate utterances in terms of sentence-like properties. Rather, I wish to leave units on these different levels of analysis conceptually distinct and admit the possibility of an utterance containing several sentences as well as the possibility of a sentence being constructed through several utterances. The utterance can, however, be divided into subsections in terms of units appropriate to its own level

---

[12] For example, the word "put" occurs twice in the following fragment of speech but only once in the sentence produced through that speech:

↓   ↓
He pu:t uhm, (.7 sec pause) Tch! Put *crab*meat on the bo::ttom.

Were I unable to distinguish these different levels of organization, or were I committed to a theoretical framework that recognized the analytic validity of only one, my ability to adequately analyze the structure of conversation would be seriously compromised.

[13] The work of Sacks and his colleagues on the sequential organization of conversation has provided some analysis of structures organizing separate sentences relative to each other (see, for example, Jefferson 1973; Sacks 1978; Schegloff 1968). Within linguistics, ties between different sentences have been examined by Gunter (1974), Hiz (1969), and in the work on discourse analysis to be discussed in what follows.

of organization such as the "phonemic clause" or "breath-group."[14] For clarity, I also wish to restrict the use of the term "utterance" to vocal phenomena and not, as Grice (1969:147) does, include the possibility of "sentence-like" nonvocal phenomena such as hand signals.

The definition given the sentence also differentiates "discourse analysis" from the analysis of conversation. George Lakoff (1972:130) defines a "discourse" as "essentially a string of English sentences." In view of the distinction discussed earlier between utterance and sentence, the study of discourse, as it is conducted within the framework of contemporary linguistics, emerges as quite different from the study of conversation. And, in fact, most work on discourse in linguistics has not examined sequences of actual talk, restricting itself to the study of hypothetical sentences. The structure of speech acts, rather than turn-taking, has emerged as the central theoretical problem in this analysis.[15] Moreover, in part because of the particular definition given discourse, analysts of it have not generally viewed events smaller than the sentence as within the scope of their inquiry, whereas analysts of conversation have devoted considerable attention to such phenomena (see, for example, Jefferson 1974; Sacks 1972a, Sacks *et al.* 1974). The analysis of discourse is thus not the same as the analysis of conversation. However, as the work of Labov (1972a, 1972b; Labov and Fanshel 1977) has demonstrated, much fruitful work can be done from a perspective that makes use of both approaches. In addition, some linguists working from a perspective somewhat different from that of discourse analysis have made important studies of certain phenomena that tie together units larger than the sentence. See, for example, the work of Halliday and Hasan (1976) on cohesion, Gunter's (1974) work on intonation, and van Dijk's (1977) approach to text analysis.

The units of talk considered until this point have all been vocal. However, the definition of conversation provided at the beginning of this chapter was left broad enough to include other types of behavior. Indeed, this interdependence is so strong that the boundary between language and nonlanguage emerges as a difficult theoretical problem. For example, Lyons (1972) notes that the concept of "non-verbal communication" should properly include intonation and stress, which are nonetheless essential components of "verbal" signals, and that the term "paralin-

[14] A definition of the phonemic clause is provided by Boomer (1965:150). For a definition of the breath-group, see Lieberman (1967:26–27). These units will be discussed in greater detail when research into the turn and related phenomena such as the utterance is examined.

[15] A good sample of the work available on this issue can be found in Cole and Morgan (1975). For a critique of this approach from a sociolinguistic perspective, see Hymes (1971:62).

guistics'' may well include many gestures, facial expression, and eye movements. In order to deal with such issues, Lyons finds it useful to distinguish the different types of behavior that can be found in talk in terms of overlapping, rather than mutually exclusive, categories. The classification he develops is more accurate and useful than the more frequently made distinction between verbal and nonverbal behavior. However, since many of Lyons's distinctions are not relevant to the present analysis, they will not be described in detail here.

Birdwhistell (for example, 1970) provides very detailed description and analysis of the different kinds of nonvocal behavior that can occur in talk and examines the relationship of that behavior to speech. He has stated (1970:xiii) that his goal "was to develop a methodology which could exhaustively analyze the communicative behavior of the body." In the present work, my primary analytic concern is not with nonvocal phenomena per se, but with rather limited aspects of the structure of the turn at talk. I will therefore examine only a very small part of the nonvocal behavior that occurs in conversation, principally whether a participant is gazing toward a specified other. My decision to limit myself to this very narrow aspect of nonvocal behavior emerges in large part from my recognition of the complexity and intricate order Birdwhistell has demonstrated to be operative in this area.

Phenomena To Be Investigated

The analysis in the present study will focus specifically on interaction between speaker and hearer within the turn. It will be argued that one way in which a nonspeaking party can indicate whether he is acting as a hearer is by gazing at the speaker. Hearership can of course be demonstrated in other ways (this technique would obviously not be applicable to telephone conversations), but this is the only method that will be systematically investigated here. A speaker can use gaze to indicate that the party being gazed at is an addressee of his utterance. Other techniques available to the speaker for indicating that his utterance is directed to some specified recipient will also be examined, especially in Chapter 5.

Chapter 2 will investigate some of the ways in which speaker and hearer achieve a state of mutual orientation at the beginning of the turn. It will be shown that speakers who do not obtain the gaze of a hearer may perform specific actions, such as the production of restarts and pauses. After such phrasal breaks, nongazing hearers generally begin to move their gaze toward the speaker; if they do not, the speaker may continue to produce phrasal breaks until he obtains an appropriate response. The data support the possibility that the actions of speaker and hearer together constitute a particular type of summons–answer sequence. When the criteria for choice between alternative actions capable of requesting the gaze of a hearer are investigated, it is found that the gaze of the speaker is also relevant to this process. Thus the task of achieving mutual orientation within the turn both provides organization for the bodies of the participants and leads to the production of a range of phenomena in the stream of speech.

It is also possible to produce talk without speaker and hearer displaying explicit mutual orientation; in Chapter 3, alternative types of engagement frameworks will be investigated. First, some of the ways in which disengagement is organized will be examined, and it will be shown that, although during disengagement the participants are explicitly displaying nonorientation toward each other, each is in fact paying close attention to what the other is doing. Analysis will then turn to how participants move from a state of talk to a state of disengagement. After disengagement has been entered, talk is still possible, but this talk has both a different sequential organization at its boundaries and a different structure of coparticipation in its course than talk produced during full engagement. The presence of such engagement alternatives has implications for processes of reengagement, including the phenomena examined in Chapter 2, and also permits participants to negotiate about the type of orientation they are prepared to give a particular piece of talk. Thus the coparticipation status that a strip of talk is seen to have might be the product of an active process of interaction between speaker and hearer as it is being spoken. The organization of engagement integrates the activities of the participants' bodies into the organization of their conversation, and in so doing has numerous consequences for the structure of their talk.

Chapter 4 investigates the ability of participants to add new sections to their emerging vocal and nonvocal actions. Such ability is found to constitute a resource for the achievement of social organization within the turn, enabling one participant to coordinate the units he is producing with the relevant actions of a coparticipant. Specific phenomena examined include the lengthening of sound articulation within a phoneme, the addition of phrasal breaks of various types to an utterance, the addition of new words and phrases to a sentence, the addition of sentences to a turn, and, finally, the addition of new sections to the nonvocal actions of the participants. Reasons displayed by a participant for the addition of a new segment to a unit are also examined.

Chapter 5 will investigate one way in which possible recipients to a turn might be distinguished from one another. It will be argued that some actions in conversation (for example, reports) propose as their hearer a recipient who does not yet know about the event being described by the speaker, whereas other actions (for example, a request for information) propose a recipient who has knowledge of the event being talked about. These two types of recipients are mutually exclusive in that an action appropriate to one is inappropriate to the other. Situations will be examined in which both types of recipients are present—for example, the situation in which a speaker describes an event in the presence of both someone who has not yet heard about it and someone who himself participated in it. Analysis will focus on the problem of how the speaker can construct a turn capable of providing for the participation of both types of recipients. It will be found that the speaker has available to him a number of techniques that enable him to change an utterance appropriate to one type of recipient into one appropriate to the other. The use of these techniques produces a range of characteristic phenomena within the turn, including changes in the intonation of the utterance, changes in the type of action being constructed by the utterance, and changes in the state of knowledge proposed for the speaker as well as his recipient. In this chapter, some demonstration is provided that the speaker has the ability, not only to add new sections to his utterance, but also to change its emerging meaning so that it maintains its appropriateness for the recipient of the moment.

This study thus investigates some specific aspects of the interaction of speaker and hearer in the construction of the turn at talk. First, particular states of mutual orientation between speaker and hearer are described and are demonstrated to be relevant to the structure of the turn. Second, the participants are shown to possess specific techniques for achieving and maintaining appropriate states of mutual orientation, and the structure and operation of these techniques is described. Third, the use of these techniques is shown to both provide organization for the bodies of the participants and produce specific phenomena in their talk.

Relevance of This Research to Other Lines of Study

The research reported here is relevant to several different lines of study in the social sciences.

First, it is perhaps most relevant to the study of human interaction.

Simmel (1950:21–22) has argued that "if society is conceived as interaction among individuals, the description of the forms of this interaction is the task of the science of society in its strictest and most essential sense."[16] Conversation is among the most pervasive forms of human interaction. However, as Goffman (1963:13) has noted: "The exchange of words and glances between individuals in each other's presence is a very common social arrangement, yet it is one whose distinctive communication properties are difficult to disentangle." Conversation has been studied as a form of human interaction by a number of different investigators, including Goffman, Sacks and his colleagues, and Duncan (see, for example, Duncan 1974a). The organization of gaze in interaction has also received considerable attention (see, for example, Argyle and Cook 1976; Kendon 1967). The present research examines some previously uninvestigated aspects of these phenomena.

Second, the work to be presented here is relevant to several methodological and theoretical issues in linguistics. For example, the present research investigates an aspect of communicative competence relevant to the production of language—the interaction of speaker and hearer in the construction of the turn at talk—that has been almost totally ignored in traditional linguistics.[17] Moreover, as the work in Chapters 4 and 5 will show, these phenomena are implicated in the process of sentence construction. Methodologically, most contemporary linguists do not use actual speech as a source of data for the analysis of linguistic structure. They base this position in part on the argument that the phrasal breaks, such as restarts, found in actual speech give evidence of such defective performance that the data are useless for the study of competence (see, for example, Chomsky 1965:3–4). In Chapter 2 it will be found that, when the actions of the hearer are taken into consideration, such phenomena may in fact demonstrate, not only the competence of the speaker, but also his orientation toward the production of coherent, unbroken sentences. Moreover, many of the phenomena investigated here could not have been studied if actual talk were not looked at carefully. The situation is perhaps not that actual speech restricts the analyst to in-

---

[16] A similar position is taken by ethologists in the study of nonhuman societies. For example, Cullen (1972:101) states that "all social life in animals depends on the coordination of interactions between them."

[17] Some analysis of the assumptions a speaker makes about his recipient have been provided in the study of speech acts (for example, Searle 1970) and deixis (for example, Bar-Hillel 1954). However, in such studies the hearer has been analyzed merely as an addressee and the process of interaction between speaker and hearer has not been investigated.

adequate and degenerate data, but rather that, if he refuses to look at actual talk, an important range of phenomena may be inaccessible to observation and study.

Third, some of the work to be reported here is relevant to a line of research in psychology and sociology which has investigated phrasal breaks, such as restarts and pauses, in utterances (see, for example, Allen and Guy 1974; Bernstein 1962; Cook, Smith, and Lalljee 1974; Dittman 1974; Goldman-Eisler 1961, 1972; Mishler and Waxler 1970). Details of this work will be examined where relevant in Chapter 2; for the present, it is sufficient to note that analysis has focused entirely on the speaker, and that it has been assumed that his phrasal breaks are manifestations of performance difficulty. The current study thus complements this line of research by investigating interactively phenomena that have there been studied from an individual perspective.

Fourth, the research reported here is relevant in a number of different ways to the study of human communication. Cherry (1971:12) has stated that "conversation . . . is the fundamental unit of human communication." Though types of interaction in which no words are exchanged are just as fundamental,[18] conversation is certainly among the most basic forms of human communication. Analysis of the procedures through which conversation is organized thus contributes to our understanding of how human beings communicate with each other.

In addition to its importance in its own right, the analysis of conversation is also relevant to a number of theoretical issues in communications research.

First, many communications researchers have assumed that a unit smaller than the exchange of turns cannot be investigated as a communications process. For example, Coulthard and Ashby (1975:140) state that "the basic unit of all verbal interaction is the exchange. An exchange consists minimally of two successive utterances: one speaker says something and a second says something in return. Anything less is not interactive." Similarly, Rogers and Farace (1975:226) argue that "the smallest unit of relational analysis is a paired exchange of two messages," where message is defined as "each verbal intervention by participants in dialogue."

---

[18] Such a position has been consistently taken by Goffman, who conceptualizes conversation as but one type of focused interaction and assigns equal theoretical importance to unfocused interaction (see, for example, Goffman 1963). Similarly, though the work of Sacks and his colleagues has been directed specifically to conversation, they state explicitly that "this is not because of a special interest in language, or any theoretical primacy we accord conversation [Schegloff and Sacks 1973:290]."

Second, the turn has been employed to locate relevant units in many category systems constructed to study interpersonal communication (some examples are provided by the statements quoted in the last paragraph). However, in such studies the structure of the turn itself has remained unanalyzed, with the result that analytic units are being specified in terms of a structure whose own properties are unknown (on this issue, see Sacks 1963; Sacks *et al.* 1974:701–702).

Third, but related to the point just made, a consistent problem in the study of interpersonal communication has been the location of appropriate units for analysis. In general, the objects that participants within interaction in fact construct, such as actual utterances, have not been made the primary subject of analysis. Rather, these objects have been transformed into other objects through the use of a category system, such as the ones proposed by Bales (1950), Rogers and Farace (1975), Sluzki and Beavin (1965), or Soskin and John (1963).[19] Analysis has then focused on relationships between these categories rather than on the actual phenomena. In contrast, this study focuses on the objects actually being constructed within the interaction, such as specific sentences.

Fourth, Krippendorff (1969a) has distinguished three different analytic models for the study of communications processes: an association model, a discourse model, and a communications model. Each of these models makes different assumptions about the phenomena being studied and requires data with a different structure (the types of data required for different types of communications analysis are discussed more fully in Krippendorff 1969b). Communications models are more powerful than discourse models, which in turn are more powerful than association models. Conversation provides data of the type required by communications models, specifically a detailed protocol of ordered exchanges through time. This study provides some analysis of how the messages being exchanged by communicators are both changed by and manifestations of the constraints organizing their communication.

---

[19] A good review of the different category systems that have been employed to code verbal interaction is found in Rogers and Farace (1975).

Goodenough (personal communication) has criticized category systems of this type because they take for granted what should be one of the main objects of study: the ability of the observer (or participants) to recognize discrete phenomena in the data and the organization of such perceptions. Thus, the ability of the observer employing Bales's category system to distinguish agreement from disagreement is not treated as part of the phenomena under investigation but rather used as a tool to study other phenomena. These matters have, however, received explicit analysis from Sacks and his colleagues. For example, Sacks (1973b) and Pomerantz (1978) have analyzed the construction of displays of agreement in conversation and the consequences that the perception of a statement as an agreement, rather than a disagreement, have on the subsequent sequencing of the conversation.

Previous Research on the Turn and Its Constituents

Both the structure of the turn and the structure of recognizable units in the stream of speech have been examined by investigators in a number of different fields.

THE TURN AND TURN-TAKING

Despite the abstract simplicity of the notions of turn and turn-taking, and the ease with which such phenomena can be recognized in conversation, providing a precise description of the turn is a difficult and elusive task. A review of attempts to describe its structure will not only provide a more accurate definition of the turn, but will also summarize most of the research on the turn relevant to this study.

In that the description of the turn is as much an empirical as a theoretical issue, in order to evaluate various proposals about its structure, it might be useful to examine them with respect to actual data. For this reason a transcript of a fragment of actual conversation has been included in what follows. The complete transcription system can be found on pages 46–53; for present purposes it is sufficient to note that numbers in parentheses mark periods of silence to the nearest tenth of a second and that a left bracket joining utterances on different lines means that these pieces of talk are being produced simultaneously. Line 1 is being shouted to someone who is driving down the street.

(1)[20]

1.	MARSHA:	BYE BYE ENJOY YOUR *BRO*CCOLI PIE::.
2.		(0.4)
3.	DIANNE:	*Bro*ccoli pie::,
4.		(0.6)
5.	MARSHA:	She's going to her *s*ister's house.
6.		(0.3)
7.	MARSHA:	(She thought–) She just couldn't wait to get over
8.		there and get rid of this *ha:*ssle right? And then
9.		she *h*eard she was having *b*roccoli pie and she was
10.		really ticked off she didn't want to go,

---

[20] As will be seen later in the chapter, dealing with transcribed material makes strong demands on the reader. In order to present the transcribed data extracts in as clear and uncluttered a fashion as possible, citations giving the source of each extract (i.e., the setting and tape number it is drawn from) appear, not in the text itself, but rather in a separate appendix, where they are listed according to chapter and example number.

11. DIANNE: *Bro*:ccoli *p*ie I think that sounds grea:t.
12. MARSHA: I: said as*par*agus might sound a little bit better.
13.   but I wasn't sure (but–) I'm not big on broccoli.
                                                          [
14. DIANNE: *Jeff* made
15.   an asparagus pie it was s::*so* : *goo*:d.
                                          [
16. MARSHA: I love it.
17. MARSHA: Yeah I love tha:t.
                             [
18. DIANNE: *He* pu:t uhm,
19.   (0.7)
20. DIANNE: Tch! Put *crab*meat on the bo::ttom.
21. MARSHA: Oh: ::
                 [
22. DIANNE: (You know) with chee::se, =
23. MARSHA: Yeah.Right.
           = [[
24. DIANNE: And then just (cut up) the broc–'r the as*par*agus
25.   coming out in *s*pokes. = It w as *so g*ood.
                                               [
26. MARSHA: Right.
27. MARSHA: °°(*Oh*: *Go*:d that'd be fantastic.)

It can be observed that the talk in this fragment does proceed through
a sequence of turns. The two parties alternate in their production of talk,
and while one is speaking the other is generally silent. Nonetheless, the
delineation of the unit being exchanged—the turn—poses problems. Are
Lines 5 and 7, in which the same party speaks after a period of silence,
different parts of the same turn or two different turns? The same situation
occurs in Lines 18 and 20, but there the sentence begun in Line 18 is
not completed until Line 20. Are these cases different or the same? Is
the silence in Line 4 part of any particular turn and if so which one? Is
this silence the same type of object as the silence in Line 19? Line 14
occurs simultaneously with the end of Line 13. Whose turn is in progress
at that point? All of Line 26 is produced simultaneously with part of
Line 25. Does Line 26 constitute a turn?
   Though the unit being examined has not always been called a turn,
questions such as these have occupied the attention of linguists, communications researchers, and anthropologists, as well as researchers explicitly investigating conversation. Thus, Harris (1951:14) defines the
utterance as "a stretch of talk, by one person before and after which

there is silence on the part of the person."[21] According to such a definition, Lines 18 and 20, as well as Lines 5 and 7–11, would be different
units. In contrast, Bernstein (1962:38), by defining an utterance to extend
"from the time subject commenced to talk until he finished," would
group each of these pairs of lines into a single unit.

Taking a slightly different approach, some researchers have attempted
to specify the boundaries of the turn in terms of talk on the part of the
other party rather than silence on the part of the speaker. Thus Fries
(1952, cited in Jaffe and Feldstein 1970:10) defines the utterance as "all
the speech of one participant until the other begins to speak." However,
this definition runs into problems when simultaneous talk is considered.
According to the definition, Dianne's utterance in Line 15 ends before
she has finished pronouncing her sentence. Norwine and Murphy's definition of "talk-spurt" (1938:281, cited in Jaffe and Feldstein 1970:12)
encounters similar problems.

Jaffe and Feldstein (1970:19) avoid the conceptual ambiguities of their
predecessors and produce a set of rules and categories so clear that it
enables a computer to code some turn-relevant features of audio records
of conversation without human intervention. Their approach is to ignore
the content of what is said, examining the process of exchanging turns
purely in terms of the sequence of sounds and silence of the different
participants. Thus, their definition of possession of the floor marks its
boundaries in terms of both speech by the next speaker and silence by
the previous speaker:

> The speaker who utters the first unilateral sound both initiates the conversation and
> gains possession of the floor. Having gained possession, a speaker maintains it until
> the first unilateral sound by another speaker, at which time the latter gains possession
> of the floor. The conversation terminates at its last sound [Jaffe and Feldstein 1970:19].

The very success of their project raises the question of whether constructing an internally consistent set of categories capable of unambiguously coding any relevant data presented to it is in fact what is at issue
in defining the phenomena being investigated. Jaffe and Feldstein themselves admit that, rather than revealing the order in terms of which the
data are structured, their category system sometimes—for example, in
dealing with simultaneous speech—imposes order on the data by fiat.

> [Other patterns] especially those involving simultaneous speech, are so complex that
> some rule is called for to bring order out of the chaos. The "speaker switching rule"

---

[21] Frake (1972:91) proposes a similar definition: "The constituents of exchanges are
utterances: stretches of continuous speech by one person."

used in defining possession of the floor . . . resolves, by fiat, all these complex patterns that defy classification [1970:114].

The precision of their categories thus obscures, rather than clarifies, the phenomena being investigated through use of those categories. Simultaneous speech has been approached as a phenomenon worthy of study in its own right by other investigators (see, for example, Jefferson 1973), and they have found it to be not chaotic but, rather, precisely ordered.

Similar problems arise with the way Jaffe and Feldstein classify silence in conversation. Silence between the talk of different parties is assigned to the turn of the party who was speaking before the silence (Jaffe and Feldstein 1970:19). However, as Sacks and his colleagues (Sacks *et al.* 1974:715) have pointed out, silence after a question is regularly heard as being part of the next speaker's—the answerer's—turn. (Consider, for example, the silence after a teacher asks a student a question.)

It is conceivable that the problems with Jaffe and Feldstein's system are mere weaknesses, which could eventually be eliminated by successively refining their definitions. However, this does not appear to be the case. Closer study reveals that any category system that unambiguously divides a stretch of observed conversation into a single set of distinct objects will suffer similar problems.

Consider the categorization of the silence that occurs in the following fragment:

(2) JOHN:　Well I, I took this course.
　　　　　　(0.5)
　　ANN:　In h　ow to quit?
　　　　　　[
　　JOHN:　　　　which I really recommend.

There is general agreement among investigators that silence should be classified differently according to whether it occurs within the turn of a single speaker or between the turns of two different speakers. (See, for example, Goffman 1975:10; Sacks *et al.* 1974:715. Even Jaffe and Feldstein 1970:19, who did not include the content of speech in their analysis, found it necessary to distinguish different kinds of silence in these terms.) For convenience, a within-turn silence is frequently referred to as a "pause," whereas a between-turn silence is called a "gap."

When Ann begins to talk, the silence in this fragment is placed between the turns of two different speakers. It thus constitutes a gap rather than a pause. However, John's talk a moment later continues the production of the unit in progress before the silence began. The silence is now placed within the ongoing talk of a single speaker. As such it is a pause rather than a gap. Thus, the same silence yields alternative classifications at different moments in time and from the perspective of different participants. This is not to say that either the silence or the rules for producing it are ambiguous. The types of objects—pauses and gaps—constructed by the alternative structural descriptions remain conceptually distinct. Further, at the point where Ann begins to talk, the data provide no evidence to support the classification of the silence as a pause rather than a gap. Though John subsequently demonstrates that he has not finished talking and that the silence should therefore be categorized as a pause, this does not change the reading of the situation available at the time Ann began to act.[22]

In short, no single classification of this silence is available to the analyst, who, instead, must deal with it as an event emerging through time and thus capable of ongoing transformation. Much the same point can be made with respect to the definition of the turn. When Ann begins to talk, John may be seen as having constructed a complete turn. (Ann's action of beginning her talk where she does provides some evidence that participants within the conversation itself see the turn as having been completed.) However, when his later talk is produced, his earlier talk becomes but the beginning of the turn eventually constructed. (Note that the talk in the later unit is a subordinate element of the earlier unit and thus cannot be seen as the beginning of a new unit.)[23] At the time Ann begins to talk, her turn is positioned as the next turn after John's. However, when John resumes talking, Ann's talk becomes placed in an "interruptive" position, beginning not after but in the middle of another party's talk.

This example provides some insight into why obtaining an accurate and analytically relevant definition of the turn has proved so elusive.

First, almost all of the definitions considered have been concerned with the problem of accurately defining the boundaries of the turn. However, it appears that in actual conversation the boundaries of the turn are mutable. Different boundaries can be specified for the same unit at

---

[22] For clarity, the issue here has been oversimplified. In fact, it might be argued that, when John produces his second piece of talk, the participants are proposing competing definitions of what is occurring. As Jefferson (for example, 1973) has demonstrated, participants have available to them techniques for negotiating such issues.

[23] Bloomfield's distinction (1946:170) between "included position," "a linguistic form [that] occurs as part of a larger form," and "absolute position," a linguistic form "not included in any larger (complex) linguistic form," is relevant here. John's second piece of talk is in included position with respect to his first and thus cannot be seen as the beginning of a new sentence.

different points in the sequence. Even the issue of whether or not some turn follows another may have different answers at different points in time. Thus, a definition of the turn as a static unit with fixed boundaries does not accurately describe its structure; rather, the turn has to be conceptualized as a time-bound process.

Second, some of the data considered (for example, Ann's beginning to talk where she does) suggest that the location of turn boundaries is not simply a problem for the analyst but one of the issues the participants face in arranging the exchange of turns. If this is correct, then the delineation of the turn is not properly an analytic tool for the study of conversation, but rather part of the phenomena being investigated and as such should be approached empirically (for more complete discussion of this issue, see Sacks *et al.* 1974:728–729; Schegloff and Sacks 1973:290).

Third, insofar as the boundaries of the turn mark points of speaker change, an accurate definition of the turn is not independent of a specification of the process through which turns are exchanged. It thus does not seem possible to first define the turn and then work out how it is to be exchanged. Rather, intrinsic structural elements of the unit being exchanged—its boundaries—seem implicated in the process of exchange itself.

The organization of turn-taking in conversation has been most extensively investigated by Sacks, Schegloff, and Jefferson (1974). The turn-taking system they describe provides a way to deal with the problematic aspects of the turn noted earlier and to specify its structure more adequately. Because this work constitutes the point of departure for the present study, it will be examined in some detail.

The system that Sacks, Schegloff, and Jefferson describe consists of two components and rules that operate on those components. A first component describes the type of units that can be utilized to construct a turn. A key feature of such turn-constructional units is that they "allow a projection of the unit-type under way, and what, roughly, it will take for an instance of that unit-type to be completed [Sacks *et al.* 1974:702]."[24] Many different types of speech units—from single words to sentences—have this feature. The property of recognizable completion has several consequences. First, it specifies where in the turn transition to a new turn can occur. Second, it specifies the limits of the speaker's current right to talk. Initially, a speaker is entitled to one such unit; at the

---

[24] The orientation of conversationalists to the projectability of turn-constructional units is empirically evident in actual sequential materials. On this issue, see Sacks *et al.* (1974:702–703, footnote 12).

completion of that unit, a place occurs where speaker transition becomes relevant. A second component, which allocates next turn, includes two groups of procedures: In one group, current speaker selects next speaker; in the other, next speaker self-selects.

The system also contains Rule-set 1a–c and Rule 2. The former, operating at an initial transition-relevance place, provides for three possibilities: (*a*) that if a "current speaker selects next" allocation technique is used, then transfer to the party so selected occurs at this place; (*b*) that if such an allocation technique has not been used, then self-selection is permitted, but not required, at this place; and (*c*) that if another does not self-select, then current speaker may, but need not, continue. Rule 2 provides that, in those cases where current speaker continues into a new turn-constructional unit, the rule set reapplies at the next transition-relevance place and others that follow it until transfer to a new speaker occurs.

In specifying how turns are exchanged, these rules also describe significant aspects of the structure of the turn itself. For example, they avoid the problems of approaches that conceptualize the turn as a static structure by explicitly providing (for example, through Rule 2) discrete but mutable boundaries. These rules also lead to alternative classifications of silence, as well as the possibility of one type of silence being transformed into a different type. For example, a gap can be transformed into a pause if the silence is ended by further talk by the same speaker (Sacks *et al*. 1974:715, footnote 16).

On a more general level, both turn-taking and the turn itself can be characterized as being "locally managed, party-administered, and interactionally controlled [Sacks *et al*. 1974:727]." Turn-taking is locally managed because the system deals with single transitions at a time in a comprehensive, exclusive, and serial fashion.[25] It is party administered because control over its operations and products is vested in the participants to the conversation themselves (p. 726). Finally, and of particular relevance to the present work, by virtue of the options it gives both speaker and hearer, this system provides for the interactive construction of the turn:

> A speaker can talk in such a way as to permit projection of possible completion to be made from his talk, from its start, allowing others to use its transition places to start talk, to pass up talk, to affect directions of talk etc.; and . . . their starting to talk, if properly placed, can determine where he ought to stop talk. That is, the turn as a unit is interactively determined [pp. 726–727].

[25] Such a view of turn-taking stands in contrast to many other approaches (for example, Taylor 1970) which have sought structure in conversation (or in the groups conversing) by trying to find repetitive multiturn sequences.

The structure of the turn-taking system also provides for the interactive organization of a number of more specific types of phenomena in particular types of turns. For example, stories routinely contain many sentences before they come to their completion. However, the turn-taking system only allocates one turn-constructional unit (of which the sentence is a particular type) to the speaker at a time. The systematic production of stories without interruption is possible only if Rule 1b, granting others the right to begin talk at each transition-relevance place, can be suspended until the end of the story. Such a suspension requires the agreement of the hearer since it is he who would invoke Rule 1b. This dilemma shapes the production of stories in conversation into a particular format. First, the speaker produces a single-unit turn containing an offer to produce a multisentence turn (a turn of this type is frequently referred to as a "story preface"). The hearer then provides an acceptance (or rejection) of the offer and only then does the speaker proceed to construct his multisentence turn. The preface routinely provides information enabling the hearer to recognize when the story has been completed so that the suspension of Rule 1b can be lifted at the appropriate moment. The particular structure stories take in conversation is thus organized in part by the orientation of participants to the features of the turn-taking system.[26]

The features of the turn-taking system can also provide for the systematic production of a particular class of restarts. Consider the following:

KEN: You wanna hear muh–eh my sister told me a story last night.

By producing a correction here, the speaker is able to begin a new unit without overrunning the completion point of his initial unit (for more detailed analysis of this phenomenon see Sacks 1974:342).

In turns that contain more than a single turn-constructional component, the distribution of components within the turn is frequently organized by the properties of the turn-taking system. Many adjacent turns in conversation take the form of particular types of utterance-pairs, for example, question–answer, greeting–greeting, accusation–denial, complaint–rejection. Despite differences in particular pair types, all such pairs have many organizational features in common (for example, the first element in the pair sets constraints on what can be done in the turn following it) and therefore can be analyzed as a single class. For convenience, the members of this class are referred to as "adjacency-pairs"

---

[26] The interactive structure of stories in conversation receives extensive analysis in Sacks's unpublished lectures of spring 1970 and fall 1971. The use of story prefaces to provide for the production of multisentence turns is analyzed explicitly in the lecture of April 9, 1970. A published synopsis of some of this work, including the points discussed here, can be found in Sacks (1974).

(Schegloff and Sacks 1973). The first element in a pair is called a "first pair part" and the second, a "second pair part."[27] A turn may contain many components in addition to a first or second pair part.[28] However, in such multicomponent turns, the first pair part will be placed in a particular position—at the end of the turn—since it invokes Rule 1a. Similarly, if a turn contains a second pair part, it will be placed at the beginning of the turn. A speaker can thus employ a first pair part—for example, a tag question—to specifically mark that his turn has come to completion and that someone else now has the obligation to talk.

The structure of turn-taking is thus implicated in the organization of many different types of conversational phenomena from corrections (Jefferson 1974a) to stories (Sacks 1974) and even, as Jefferson (1979) has shown, the syllable-by-syllable production of laughter. Most relevant to the present study is the interactive organization turn-taking provides for the structure of the turn.

The position turn-taking occupies in conversation permits a more precise definition of conversation itself. Although not all conversation occurs in "single conversations,"[29] turn-taking does seem to be central to conversational activity (Schegloff and Sacks 1973:292). Other forms of talk, such as debates, meetings, and ceremonies, can be distinguished from conversation in terms of explicit differences in the structure of their turn-taking.[30] Indeed, it appears that these speech-exchange systems represent systematic transformations of the turn-taking system for conversation (Sacks *et al.* 1974:729). The organization of turn-taking as analyzed by Sacks and his colleagues thus permits more accurate and precise definitions of both conversation and the turn than those provided at the beginning of this chapter.[31]

Other investigators have provided different analyses of how turn-taking

[27] Some analysis of the properties of adjacency pairs can be found in Schegloff and Sacks (1973). These phenomena are discussed in more detail in Sacks's spring 1972 class lectures and his 1973 Summer Institute of Linguistics lectures.

[28] See, for example, Goffman's (1975:3) discussion of "back pairs."

[29] Conversational activity that does not occur in the unit of a single conversation includes talk between "members of a household in their living room, employees who share an office, passengers together in an automobile, etc., that is, persons who could be said to be in a 'continuing state of incipient talk' [Schegloff and Sacks 1973:325]." Such talk differs from a single conversation in that it does not require exchanges of greetings or closings and permits extended lapses between talk. Analysis of some features of this situation is provided in Chapter 3.

[30] For an analysis of the organization of talk in courtrooms from such a perspective, see Atkinson and Drew (1979).

[31] Such definitions could not, however, have been constructed without extensive theoretical investigation of actual empirical materials. Rough definitions of the type provided earlier are thus quite appropriate as guides for further research as long as their provisional character is kept in mind.

might be achieved in conversation. Jaffe and Feldstein (1970:17) provide the simplest version of what is perhaps the most common hypothesis, the proposal that turn-transition is cued by a discrete signal on the part of the speaker:

> An explanation for the switch of roles is still required, however. We look to the cues operative at the boundary between time domains. The utterance of each speaker is presumably terminated by an unambiguous "end of message" signal, at which point the direction of the one-way channel (and the transmitting and receiving roles) are simply reversed.

In essence, conversation is argued to be like short-wave radio communication, with the production of some equivalent of "over" at the end of each turn signaling to the recipient that he should now take the floor. A common candidate for such a signal is a pause.[32]

The turn-taking system proposed by Duncan (1974a, see also Duncan and Fiske 1977) is essentially of this type. In this system, the speaker cues his recipient that he is about to relinquish the floor by producing a "turn-yielding signal" (Duncan 1974a:302). On the basis of empirical observation, Duncan describes six specific turn-yielding signals: rising or falling (but not sustained) pitch at the end of a phonemic clause, elongation of the final syllable of a phonemic clause, the termination of a hand movement used during the turn, a number of stereotyped expressions such as "you know" which may be accompanied by a drop in pitch, and the termination of a grammatical clause. Though the hearer may take the floor after one or more of these signals, he is not required to do so (Duncan 1974a:303). The more signals displayed at a specific moment, the greater the probability of the hearer taking the floor (p. 308). However, the speaker has the ability to neutralize any floor-yielding signals he is displaying with an "attempt-suppressing signal." This signal consists of the speaker maintaining gesticulation of his hands during the turn-yielding signals (p. 304). Duncan's work thus provides detailed and important analysis of many phenomena occurring at points of speaker transition.

However, because of its focus on a set of discrete signals, Duncan's turn-taking system does not organize in terms of a small set of specific rules the range of conversational phenomena that the system of Sacks and his colleagues does. For example, it confines its analysis to the termination points of turn-constructional units and does not examine

---

[32] However, turns are regularly exchanged without any silence whatsoever occurring between them (for examples, see Sacks *et al.* 1974:731); the Jefferson transcription system specifically uses an equal sign to mark turn-transition without any intervening silence.

either their projectability or the ability of the speaker to delay or avoid their reaching termination. Different types of turn allocation techniques, such as adjacency pairs, are not included, and no sharp distinction is drawn between a current speaker selecting a next at a specific point (so that the selected party is located as the one who has the floor even if he is silent) and self-selection by the next speaker. Sacks's system provides for the systematic possibility of overlap (for example, two parties may invoke Rule 1b simultaneously) at the positions where it characteristically occurs (transition points), whereas, for Duncan, such a situation means that "the turn-taking mechanism may be said to have broken down, or perhaps to have been discarded, for the duration of that state [1974a:320]." Neither is gap between turns analyzed by Duncan, who states that it did not occur in his data. It would, however, seem that insofar as gap is one of the basic sequential possibilities arising at turn-transition (a structural alternative to both smooth transition and overlap), it cannot be ignored in any general theory of turn-taking. Because of its power and generality, and because it provides a more accurate description of the detailed phenomena actually found in conversation (for example, gap and overlap), the approach to turn-taking of Sacks and his colleagues will be followed in this study.

In other work Duncan (1974b) provides detailed and interesting analysis of some processes of interaction between speaker and hearer occurring within the turn and notes how these processes might segment the turn into subordinate units. Though the particular phenomena examined (auditor back channel behaviors and speaker cues that elicit such behaviors) will not be investigated in the current study, their importance to the analysis of the interactive organization of the turn is recognized.

UTTERANCE UNITS

In addition to research on turn-taking as a phenomenon in its own right, some of the phenomena that occur within the turn have received extensive attention from investigators in a number of disciplines. The unit that has perhaps been most studied is that which has come to be called the phonemic clause: "a phonologically marked macrosegment which, according to Trager and Smith, contains one and only one primary stress and ends in one of the terminal junctures /,//,#/ [Boomer 1965:150]." This unit has been important not only in the analysis of the natural units into which the stream of speech, the utterance, is divided, but also in the investigation of intonation, kinesics, and the psychological study of speech encoding. Though the phonemic clause fell into some disrepute when Chomsky's positions initially gained ascendence in linguistics, a closely related unit, the "breath-group," was subsequently reintroduced into linguistics within the framework of transformational grammar by Lieberman (1967). Lieberman's work has not been generally accepted (for a critique, see Gunter 1976), and recent work by Goffman (1981) indicates that the structure of the utterance, including its intonation, is far more complex than the work done on the phonemic clause would indicate. Nevertheless, the unit has been quite important to a number of very diverse approaches to the study of a range of phenomena occurring within the turn. Research on its structure will therefore be examined in some detail.

Analysis of the phonemic clause stems from Pike's (1945) work on intonation. Pike distinguishes two different patterns of intonation that can terminate units. Rising intonation indicates "uncertainty or finality" and is found "in hesitation and after almost all questions [Pike 1945:32]." Falling intonation marks "finality" and "occurs most often at the end of statements [Pike 1945:33]." These terminal contours thus divide utterances into two different classes, roughly corresponding to statements and questions. Building on Pike's work, Trager and Smith (1951) distinguished three terminal junctures characterized by falling [#], rising [//], and sustained [/] pitch. These are of course the three terminal junctures that, with the requirement that there be one and only one primary stress, define the phonemic clause.

In introducing the "breath-group" within the framework of transformational grammar, Lieberman argued that, if extra articulatory effort is not expended, both pitch and amplitude naturally fall at the end of a unit of talk. A unit with such a terminal contour is called an unmarked breath-group. It stands in contrast to the marked breath group in which the tension of the muscles in the larynx is increased during the last 150–200 msec. of phonation with the effect that the terminal contour does not fall.

Although Lieberman's breath-group is not identical to the phonemic clause, the two units have much in common. First, both lines of research are in agreement that it is possible to clearly demarcate comparatively large units in the stream of speech. Second, in both, the intonation contour at the end of these units, roughly the final 150–200 msec, is found to be particularly important. Third, differences in the ending intonation contour are categorized in approximately the same fashion. A primary distinction is made by all investigators between falling and non-falling intonation, with some investigators further subdividing nonfalling into sustained and rising. Fourth, despite very different theoretical points of departure, investigators in both traditions agree that falling intonation at the end of a unit marks finality and is found at the termination of declarative statements (see, for example, Pike 1945:33 and Lieberman 1967:38–39), whereas nonfalling intonation either marks a question or indicates that the utterance being produced has not yet come to completion (see for example, Pike 1945:32 and Lieberman 1967:60, 168).[33]

The study of such phenomena is quite relevant to the analysis of turn-constructional units. Indeed, Duncan's work utilizes the phonemic clause explicitly (1974a:301), and the first of his turn-yielding cues—a phonemic clause ending on either raising or falling intonation (1974a:303)—is based directly on the work of Trager and Smith. However, the work on the phonemic clause is not sufficient to provide an adequate characterization of turn-constructional units; for example, it fails to take into account the projectability of such units. Nevertheless, this work constitutes one of the major studies of the natural units constructing the turn.

One important reason for paying close attention to the phonemic clause is that it has been used as an analytic resource in disciplines other than linguistics; it has been found to organize nonvocal as well as vocal phenomena within the turn and to be relevant to the study of speech encoding. The study of kinesics is based explicitly on the methods of structural linguistics (Birdwhistell 1973:97). Scheflen (1964:320) reports unpublished work of Birdwhistell demonstrating that the junctures marking the phonemic clause are regularly accompanied by similar movements of the body. In brief, "if pitch is raised, the eyelids, head, or hand will be elevated slightly. When pitch is lowered, such bodily part is lowered [Scheflen 1974:20]."

The relevance of the phonemic clause to the psychological study of speech encoding was investigated by Boomer (1965), who found that pauses in speech most frequently occur after the first word of a phonemic clause. Boomer argued that this provided evidence that speech encoding is organized in terms of the phonemic clause rather than proceeding word by word as some earlier studies (for example, Maclay and Osgood 1959) had implied. This work led to a second line of investigation relating speech to body movement through the phonemic clause. Building on Boomer's work, Dittman (1974:174) found that body movement, as well as pauses in speech, occurred near the beginning of the phonemic clause (see also Dittman and Llewellyn 1969). In addition, the phonemic clause was found to organize the actions of the hearer as well as those of the speaker. Dittman and Llewellyn (1967:342) report that hearer's listening

---

[33] Rising intonation is not, however, a definitive question marker since, on the one hand, it can occur in the absence of a question (for example, to mark nontermination), and, on the other, questions constructed with special particles, such as wh-words, are terminated with falling intonation (on this issue, see Lieberman 1967:132–133). For further problems with the notion of a "question" see Schegloff (1979).

responses occur at the boundaries of phonemic clauses rather than within them. Such a finding is obviously relevant to the description of the turn at talk, as it provides an approach for specifying the distribution of one party's talk within the turn of another. The structure of the phonemic clause was also used to differentiate two different types of pauses: juncture pauses, which occur at its boundaries, and hesitation pauses, which occur within the clause (Boomer 1965:151, 153–154).

Work in both kinesics and psychology thus provides some demonstration that a number of different aspects of talk, including both vocal and nonvocal phenomena, may be organized in terms of a single unit, the phonemic clause or breath-group. Similar findings have been made with respect to units on other levels of organization. Condon and his associates (for example, Condon and Ogston 1966; Condon and Ogston 1967; Condon and Sander 1974) have shown that the boundaries of body movements of both speaker and hearer coincide with syllable and other boundaries in the stream of the speaker's speech. Condon and Sander (1974) even found that the movements of 1-day-old infants were precisely synchronized with the articulatory segments of human speech (whether English or Chinese, live or taped) but not with disconnected vowel or tapping sounds. The stream of speech thus seems to provide a (perhaps innately recognized)[34] reference signal capable of synchronizing the behavior of separate participants. (An analogy that comes readily to mind is the music that trapeze artists use to coordinate their separate actions. However, in conversation, the signal used to synchronize the action of the participants, the stream of speech, is itself a product of their coordinated action, much as if the music in the circus was not a preformulated melody but rather an emergent product of the coordinated actions of the performers and simultaneously a resource employed to achieve that very coordination.) This work provides a strong demonstration that language is not simply a mode of expression for the speaker but rather constitutes a form of social organization, implicated in the coordination of the behavior of the different parties present.

Condon and Ogston (1967:227–229) note that speech and body movement become more independent in sequences larger than the word. The method they use for finding a relationship between speech and body movement—congruent boundaries for these different types of action—must therefore be used with caution when analyzing units as large as the phonemic clause. For example, Lindenfeld (1971) has sought to determine just how much relationship exists between syntactic units and

---

[34] This work provides a direct challenge to the common argument that language behavior is not manifest until about the child's first year. Condon and Sander (1974:101) note the implications their work has for theories of language acquisition.

units of body movement. She argued (1971:228) that body movements whose boundaries coincided with syntactic boundaries were related to speech whereas body movements whose boundaries fell in the middle of syntactic units were not. However, when language and body movement are considered with reference to the process of turn-taking, an alternative possibility emerges. Specifically, in order to indicate that though a possible turn-transition place is being marked syntactically the floor is not being yielded, the speaker might position his body movement so that it bridges a syntactic boundary, beginning shortly before the termination of one turn-constructional unit but not ending until a new unit is under way. (In such a case the body movement would constitute what Duncan [1974a:304] has analyzed as an "attempt-suppressing signal.") From this perspective, a close relationship between kinesics and syntax would be demonstrated precisely in the lack of congruence between syntactic and kinesic boundaries. Some of Lindenfeld's own examples—including the following (1971:231)—are consistent with this line of analysis:

There was nobody I could talk ⌐ to and ⌐ no . . . no . . . etc.

I didn't go for ⌐ that . . . And uh ⌐ every . . . one, etc.

In both of these examples, the speaker begins his body movement just before the next transition point of his turn and continues the movement until a new turn-constructional unit has been begun. Such positioning is quite consistent with the argument that the speaker is placing his body movement so as to indicate that he is not prepared to yield the floor at the syntactic boundary in his utterance marking the termination of a turn-constructional unit.

The analysis of the natural units into which the stream of speech is divided thus supports Goffman's conceptualization of talk (for example, the definitions of conversation cited at the beginning of this chapter) as an interactionally sustained form of social organization, achieved through the coordinated action of multiple participants and including within its scope nonvocal, as well as vocal, phenomena.

Gaze

The aspect of nonvocal behavior to be examined most intensively in this work is gaze. The glances of individuals toward other individuals, and especially their mutual gaze upon each other, has in fact been the subject of considerable study in the social sciences. Simmel (1969:358) argues that "the totality of social relations of human beings, their self-assertion and self-abnegation, their intimacies and estrangements, would be changed in unpredictable ways if there occurred no glance of eye to eye." Of special importance to the present study is the fact that gaze is not simply a means of obtaining information, the receiving end of a communications system, but is itself a social act (see, for example, Simmel 1969:358–359 and Goffman 1963:92). Within conversation, the gaze of the participants toward each other is constrained by the social character of gaze and this constraint, rather than purely informational issues, provides for its organization and meaningfulness within the turn. Thus, the gaze of a speaker toward another party can constitute a signal that the speaker's utterance is being addressed to that party.[35] Similarly, the gaze of another party toward the speaker can constitute a display of hearership.[36] Such social attributes of gaze provide for its ordered distribution within the turn. The structure of this distribution will be one of the main subjects investigated in Chapter 2.

The movement of gaze within conversation makes relevant some consideration of how participants arrange themselves for conversation. Scheflen (1964:326–327) notes two basic patterns: side-by-side or face-to-face, this latter being referred to as a vis-à-vis arrangement. He argues that these different arrangements are typical of different kinds of activities; the vis-à-vis provides for interaction between the participants whereas side-by-side arrangement involves mutual orientation toward some third party or object. In conversations with more than two participants, both arrangements are typically found—for example, two side-by-side listeners vis-à-vis a speaker. Participants sometimes orient different parts of their bodies in different directions so that the same party can be in vis-à-vis arrangements with two different others. The exact orientation of participants toward each other within a vis-à-vis requires more precise specification. Sommer (1959:250–251) found that people

---

[35] See, for example, Sacks et al. (1974:717) and Philips (1974:162). Bales (1970:67) notes that a speaker who wishes to address a group as a whole must avoid letting his glance "pause on any one person long enough to encourage the belief that he speaks to that particular one." Schegloff (1968:1088) reports a case where a speaker on a bus addressed an utterance to another party without turning his gaze to that party. This led to an elaborate search by others on the bus for the addressee of the utterance. This study will explicitly examine the orientation of participants in conversation toward the gaze of the speaker as a form of address, as well as the constraints this imposes on their action (for example, the utterance of the speaker must be one that can be appropriately addressed to the party he is gazing at).

[36] For example, Argyle and Cook (1976:121) note that "glances are used by listeners to indicate continued attention and willingness to listen. Aversion of gaze means lack of interest or disapproval."

who had a choice preferred to seat themselves corner-to-corner rather than face-to-face.[37] Ekman and Friesen (1974:276–277), reporting much the same preference, note that such a seating arrangement is implicated in the organization of gaze, since it makes gazing at the other a marked act. They also note other aspects of the arrangement of the participants that are relevant to the organization of the conversation. For example, the order in which a speaker generally addresses different recipients may be constrained by the details of their seating arrangement. However, although phenomena related to arrangement of participants are important subjects for further research, they are beyond the scope of the present study.[38]

Kendon (1967) has provided the most extensive analysis of the function of gaze within conversation. He reports a particular distribution of gaze over the course of an utterance (a term he uses in roughly the sense of turn at talk). A speaker looks away at the beginning of his utterance but gazes steadily toward his addressee as the utterance approaches termination, whereas a hearer at this point looks away from the speaker.[39]

---

[37] That is, positions such as B and A in the following diagram were preferred over positions such as B and H:

[38] It may, however, be reported that the data are generally consistent with the findings of Sommer and of Ekman and Friesen, but that very frequently the physical structures available for seating made achievement of the preferred arrangement difficult or impossible. For example, most picnic tables have benches along the side but do not have chairs at the end. Thus, when participants were seated at picnic tables, only face-to-face or side-by-side positions were available to them, though they could—and did—modify this somewhat by turning their bodies in appropriate directions. In a dyadic conversation that was not constrained in such a fashion (the participants were seated in individual lawn chairs), the participants arranged themselves in just the positions described by Ekman and Friesen.

[39] Analysts investigating gaze from an individual, rather than interactive, perspective have found that, after being asked a question, a subject turns his head to the side in characteristic directions (for example, left versus right) depending on the content of the question (for example, whether it deals with verbal or mathematical material). The argument here is that lateral orientation is controlled by frontal centers in each hemisphere of the brain and that "when the effects of the two centers are equally balanced, attention is directed straight ahead [Kinsbourne 1972:539]." However, the brain is asymmetrical with respect to certain cognitive functions, with language processes occurring predominantly in the left hemisphere, in contrast to spatial and temporal processes, which are localized in the right hemisphere. It is proposed that when a person engages in processes requiring the use of a specific hemisphere, for example, a verbal task, "the verbal activation overflows into the left-sided orientation center, driving attentional balance off center and to the right [Kinsbourne 1972:539]." In such experiments, the person asking the stimulus question is seated behind the subject. Gur (1975) investigated what happened when subject and experimenter were seated face to face. She found that the same subjects who would

Thus, when turn-transition occurs, the new speaker is gazing away from his recipient, as is expected of a speaker near the beginning of his utterance. The sequencing of gaze at turn-beginning studied in Chapter 2 of this study is consistent with the pattern described by Kendon and supports his findings.

Kendon also finds (1967:26) that the hearer gazes at the speaker more than the speaker gazes at the hearer. The pattern of gazing is also somewhat different for each position. Hearers give speakers fairly long looks broken by comparatively brief glances away, whereas speakers alternate looks toward their recipients with looks away from them of about equal length (pp. 27,33). The looks of the speaker toward the hearer occur at the ends of phrases (p. 40). At points of hesitation, the speaker looks away from his recipient, gazing back at him when fluent speech is resumed (p. 41); for more extensive analysis of the relationship between gaze and hesitation and the possible relationship of such phenomena to underlying processes of speech production, see Beattie (1978b, 1979). Mutual gaze between speaker and hearer is found to be quite short, in most cases lasting less than a second (p. 28).

According to Kendon (pp. 52–53), an individual's perceptual activity within interaction functions in two different but interrelated ways: as a means of monitoring and as a means of regulation and expression. These functions account in some measure for the positioning of gaze within interaction. Thus, the places where a speaker gazes at his recipient— utterance endings and phrase boundaries within the utterance—are choice points, places where the future action of the speaker is contingent on the subsequent action of his hearer. By looking at his recipient at these points, the speaker can both monitor the recipient's response and signal that a response is desired (p. 4).

Kendon also suggests (p. 60) that the characteristic gaze patterns at utterance ending may be used to signal the willingness of each party to effect turn-transition and thus help facilitate a smooth exchange of turns. Such a function for gaze in the process of turn-taking has not been supported by subsequent analysis (see, for example, Rutter *et al.* 1978

---

turn their eyes in different task-related directions when not facing another would, when facing the questioner, move "their eyes predominantly in only one direction, either right or left, regardless of problem type [1975:751]." This supports the possibility that "an experimenter's presence before the subject affects the lateralization of underlying cerebral activities in lawful and meaningful ways [p. 752]." Gur concludes that "situational variables interact with variables related to cerebral activity in producing gaze aversions as well as in determining their direction [p. 756]." By focusing on a particular situational variable, processes of interaction between speaker and hearer implicated in the construction of the turn at talk, the present work complements this line of investigation. For a more complete summary of such work see Argyle and Cook (1976:21–23).

and Beattie 1978a, as well as Kendon's [1978] comments on their papers). Indeed, Rutter and Stephenson (1977) find that overlap is both more frequent and longer in face-to-face conversation than in situations where the participants cannot see each other. Beattie and Barnard (1979) find that, although the absence of a visual channel in telephone calls does not cause problems for speaker transition, filled pauses assume greater importance.

Other analysts have suggested different explanations for the intermittent character of gaze in activities such as conversation. For example, Eibl-Eibesfeld (1974:28) attributes it to an innate fear of being stared at, although Argyle and Dean (1965) have argued that mutual gaze satisfies affiliative needs. In the face of such conflicting statements, Kendon (1967:59–60) argues that the primary import of eye contact is not the gratification of some particular "need"; rather through eye-contact a party knows "that he is affecting [the other] in some way and that he is, thereby, making progress in whatever he is attempting to do."

In this study, gaze will be investigated in terms of specific tasks posed in the construction of the turn at talk. A great many other factors—such as dominance, embarrassment, the maintenance of an appropriate equilibrium of intimacy, various emotional characteristics, and distance between the participants—have, however, also been found relevant to gaze. This research is too extensive to discuss in detail and is not directly relevant to the analysis in this work. An excellent summary of it can be found in Argyle and Cook (1976).

Data

Data for the analysis to be reported here consist of approximately 50 hours of videotape of actual conversation recorded by myself and Marjorie Goodwin in a range of natural settings. The term "actual conversation" is meant to contrast the data used in this work with, on the one hand, data consisting of reports about conversation[40] (as might, for example, be obtained by questioning people about what they do in con-

---

[40] The conceptual problems of using reports as data about the phenomena being reported on are well known. The report may be inaccurate in the sense that the description fails to correspond the phenomena being described—for example, a male is described as a female or, as Sommer and Becker (1974:261) found, a subject tells an interviewer that he performs some action which actual observation shows he does not perform.

Scheflen (1974:47, see also p. 15) notes another, more serious problem. Because "many features of an emic system have not been coded in the language of a people," informants may be unable to codify relevant aspects of the phenomena being reported on. For such

versation) and, on the other, with hypothetical versions of it (as are employed, for example, by many linguists studying discourse). The term "natural" is meant to distinguish the samples of conversation used in this work from samples obtained in conditions, such as experiments, where attempts are made to control in principled ways parameters of, or variables within, the talk being sampled.[41]

The importance of using natural data for research of the type undertaken here has been emphasized by a number of investigators. For example, Condon and Ogston (1967:221) argue that

> the need to control the variables in experimental method tends to modify the process under investigation. In human behavior, it is quite often not even clear what the variables are, such that they could be controlled. What is required to some extent is a method which could investigate and make relatively rigorous, predictable statements about a process without disrupting the process too severely.

They note further that "naturally occurring processes are, theoretically, as determined as the events in a controlled experimental situation."

---

events (which include conversation), reports will fail to provide relevant information about the phenomena being described within them.

Yet another problem has been noted by Sacks and his colleagues (see, for example, Garfinkel 1967; Garfinkel and Sacks 1970; Sacks 1963, 1966; Schegloff 1972). The same phenomenon can be accurately described in many different ways (for example, a single individual might be accurately described as "Fred," "my husband," "a guy," "a Caucasian male," "an engineer," "a Philadelphian," *etc.*). The problem of accurate correspondence between a description and the phenomenon being described is thus subordinate to the analytically prior problem of specifying the procedures governing the selection of some appropriate description from the set of correct descriptions. In view of this, it is argued that the process of description itself, rather than the object being described, should be the primary focus of analysis. The principles providing for the construction of appropriate descriptions have been found to be lodged within the interactive circumstances of their production, a point demonstrated in some detail in Schegloff's (1972) analysis of how terms to describe a specific phenomenon, place, are selected. Sacks (1972:331–332) argues that the independence of a description from the object it describes is in fact a great advantage to the social scientist since he can study descriptions as phenomena in their own right without having to wait for the other sciences to provide definitive characterizations of the objects in the world being described (such a position seems quite close to that of cognitive anthropologists such as Goodenough and Frake who focus analysis on how the perception of phenomena is organized by a culture [for example, the principles used to classify plants] rather than focusing on the objects so perceived [i.e., the plants themselves]).

In sum, the use of reports to analyze the objects being described within the reports poses some rather serious conceptual problems. This is especially true for the study of conversation since reports are among the phenomena constructed within it. They therefore should be part of the subject matter under investigation.

[41] The present work is thus similar to what Birdwhistell (1970:18) refers to as "the natural history approach": "In kinesics we engage in experimentation in the British sense. That is, we look at phenomena to trace what is happening, rather than attempt to control the variables and make something happen in an artificial situation. This is the natural history approach."

Scheflen (1964:319), arguing for the importance of studying events in context, observes that "the chance to determine experimentally the function of an element is lost if the system in which it functions is scrapped."[42] The importance of natural data for the study of the hearer, one of the main subjects investigated in this study, has been emphasized by Kendon. For example, after reviewing some existing research on the hearer, Kendon (1974:150) states

> In all these cases, however, the investigator has studied only those features of the listener's behavior he has determined in advance. The listener is always giving a controlled performance, where what he does and when he does it has been decided upon beforehand, as part of the experimental design. We know remarkably little in a systematic way, about what it is that listeners ordinarily do, and how what they do is related to what speakers do.

Argyle (1969:22) notes that, even within the naturalistic approach, investigators have largely taken their data from psychotherapy sessions and laboratory groups, and he states that "it would be most valuable to have similar material on sequences of interaction in families, workgroups, etc."

An emphasis on the importance of natural data is not confined to analysts of human interaction. It has come to be recognized in linguistics—in large part through the work of Labov—that the study of language requires data drawn from the actual situations of everyday life. Thus, Labov (1972b:xiii) states that

> there is a growing realization that the basis of inter-subjective knowledge in linguistics must be found in speech—language as it is used in everyday life by members of the social order, that vehicle of communication in which they argue with their wives, joke with their friends, and deceive their enemies.

Labov's theories about the type of data appropriate for the study of speech were a strong influence on the naturalistic approach to data collection taken in this study.

The data for this study consist of conversations recorded in the following situations:[43]

---

[42] Schegloff (1972:432) makes a similar argument about the weaknesses of hypothetical data: "A central reason for frowning on invented data is that while it can be easily invented, it is invented only from the point at which it is relevant to the point being made, thereby eliminating a central resource members use in hearing it, i.e., its placement at some 'here' in a conversation, after X; in short, by eliminating its conversational context."

[43] One tape, a half-hour dinner conversation, was not recorded by me, but rather by George Kuetemeyer, and I am indebted to him and the parties on the tape for permitting me to use it.

- Members of a lodge of the Moose and their families at both an ice cream social and a picnic in southern Michigan (7 hr)
- A black extended family in the kitchen of one of their members in North Philadelphia, recorded on three separate occasions (10.5 hr)
- Butchers in an Italian-American meat market in South Philadelphia (2.5 hr)
- A teenage swim party in Tenafly, New Jersey (4.5 hr)
- Three midwestern couples drinking beer in a back yard, Central Ohio (3.5 hr)
- An Italian-American bridal shower in Northeast Philadelphia (3 hr)
- A bridge game in Tenafly, New Jersey (2 hr)
- Several middle-class women sitting on the lawn at a Fourth of July block party, suburban Pittsburgh (3.5 hr)
- Middle- and old-aged friends at a birthday party on Long Island (1 hr)
- Family get-together, Central Ohio (1.5 hr)
- Wall Street Bankers' Shipboard Cocktail Party (3 hr)
- A family reunion in Tenafly, New Jersey (5 hr)
- A young couple talking with a friend in their living room in Tenafly, New Jersey (1 hr)
- Middle-class family dinners with friends:
    Suburban Pittsburgh (1 hr)
    West Philadelphia (.5 hr)
    North Philadelphia (1.5 hr)

The situations in which data were collected have been described in terms of some standard and easily recognizable characteristics of the participants, events, and settings. Such a description has been provided to make more clear and specific the nature of the data utilized in this study. It is not, however, meant to imply either that the data were selected in terms of these characteristics or that such characteristics are necessarily relevant to the structure of the conversation taking place in these situations.[44]

[44] For further discussion of this issue, see Schegloff and Sacks (1973:291–292, including footnote 4). The work in Chapter 5 of the present study can be used to illustrate the difficulties that would be posed if particular attributes of the participants were assumed, in the absence of a demonstration of their relevance in the data themselves, to be ordering features of the conversation being examined. It is found in Chapter 5 that speakers differentiate their recipients in terms of whether the recipient already knows about the event being discussed by the speaker and that orientation to this feature produces utterances

Both the types of events that could be recorded and the usefulness of the material obtained were heavily constrained by the technical requirements of the recording process. Some consideration of this process will both clarify the nature of these constraints and provide a more precise description of the data utilized in this study.

All data were recorded on one-half inch videotape (EIAJ Type-1 standard) in black and white. Although film could have provided data suitable for the analysis in this study, tape was chosen for the following reasons: To begin with, one-half inch videotape equipment is much less expensive than a 16 mm film camera and tape recorder capable of recording a film with a synchronized soundtrack, and videotape is much less expensive than film. Furthermore, a comparatively long period of time (slightly over half an hour on the equipment I used) can be recorded without interruption; equipment capable of doing this in 16 mm is both expensive and bulky. However, it should be noted that, for work of the type done in this study, film is in certain respects a superior medium to tape. It provides greater resolution, thus permitting the recording of finer detail, is more permanent than tape, and is capable of being easily viewed at a great many different speeds. The decision to use black and white rather

---

with a characteristic structure when recipients with both states of knowledge are copresent. This feature is quite sensitive to other aspects of human social organization, serving, for example, to mark in moment-to-moment talk the distinction between parties who share much of their experience in common, such as spouses, and those who do not, such as acquaintances. It might thus seem that the organization of conversation should be analyzed in terms of social attributes of the participants such as their marital status. This approach would not, however, accurately characterize the phenomena under investigation. On the one hand, differential states of knowledge can be used to invoke the relevance of a very broad range of social attributes (for example, even in a situation where spouses are present, talk by army veterans about common service experience may locate them as parties who share knowledge of events that their spouses lack—description of the participants in terms of particular attributes thus does not necessarily indicate how the parties are being classified within the conversation); on the other, a particular ordering of information states is not consistent within specific social relationships (for example, when husband tells wife what happened at the office, the spouses' states of knowledge are not equivalent). The structure of this feature is thus independent of the particular social identities invoked by it within specific situations. Such considerations show the value of examining conversation in a broad range of situations and events (the generality and structural variety of its procedures can be more clearly investigated), but indicate that the attributes of such situations are not necessarily organizing features of the conversation occurring within them.

It should be noted that some work in sociolinguistics has followed a quite different approach. For example, Ervin-Tripp (1973:66) states that "for most sociolinguistic analyses the important features of participants will be sociological attributes. These include the participants' status in the society, in terms such as sex, age, and occupation; their roles relative to one another, such as employer and employee, a husband and his wife; and roles specific to the social situation, such as host–guest, teacher–pupil, and customer–salesgirl."

than color was made both for reasons of cost and because the recording equipment was more reliable and versatile. What was lost by not having color cannot be assessed. Smith's work on tongue displays (Smith, Chase, and Lieblich 1974) suggests that the color difference between the tongue and lips and the rest of the face might be an important signal in interaction, one that is quite possibly relevant to the work in this study.

Because of the focus of this study on conversation, securing a high quality record of the participants' speech was a primary concern in data collection. The video camera I used (a Sony AVC-3400) had a microphone built into the camera. This microphone was not, however, adequate for my purpose. It recorded a high-pitched hum generated by other electrical equipment in the camera, and, being at camera position, it was some distance from the participants. Tests at the time I was beginning to record data showed that the main influence on sound quality, even more important than the quality of the microphone used, was the distance of the microphone from the participants. The closer the microphone, the better the sound. The best sound is obtained by actually attaching a lavaliere microphone to the speaker. Because of the quality obtained, this method is regularly used by linguists to obtain samples of speech.

Such a procedure would, however, pose serious problems for the present study. It would necessitate attaching wires to the participants, which would severely constrain their movements within the group. Those wishing to leave altogether would have to disentangle themselves from the microphone, and any new participant would have to be wired-up before he could join. Furthermore, anyone looking at another participant would have his attention directed to the recording situation. This is quite different from the issue of the participants' awareness that they were being recorded. Gazing at the other is an integral part of conversational activity, and, indeed, one of the principal phenomena investigated in this study. To obtain good sound, the lavaliere microphone would be placed quite close to the mouth, constituting an unusual, noticeable, and distracting object just at the point when gaze at the other was initiated.[45] In view of these problems, it is not surprising that use by linguists of the lavaliere typically takes place in a special situation, the interview, where the single party wearing the microphone is confined to a restricted place and does not see anyone else so encumbered. In such circum-

---

[45] At one point in my data collection, I used a lavaliere, placing it on the prospective bride at a bridal shower. She reported being quite aware of the microphone and the attendant sitting next to her said that she was reminded of the fact that what she said was being recorded every time she looked at the bride. Both of these participants felt that the presence of the lavaliere constrained their talk.

stances, obtaining samples of other than formal speech styles is a difficult problem.[46]

Some of the liabilities of the lavaliere can be avoided by using a highly directional "shotgun" microphone which is capable of obtaining fairly good sound at some distance from the speaker. This is, in fact, the method used to obtain sound in natural situations by many documentary filmmakers. However, such a microphone would not be suitable for the present work. Precisely because it is so highly directional, its position must be constantly shifted to keep it pointing at the speaker of the moment. Further, it records the speech of the person it is being pointed at better than it records the speech of other participants. A microphone of this type would thus be both extremely intrusive and would produce a poor record of many basic conversational phenomena such as overlap.[47]

In view of these considerations, I recorded speech by positioning a stationary microphone with the participants but not attached to them. The microphone was centrally placed and located as close to the participants as possible without being excessively intrusive. The placement that produced perhaps the best results was over the center of the group, slightly above the heads of the participants. It seems that within conversation our eyes do not glance equally in all directions but gaze predominately in front of us or downward. Thus, though a microphone might be only a foot or so from a person, if it is overhead it will remain relatively unobtrusive. A standard microphone stand with a flexible gooseneck was capable of placing the microphone in this position; however, the arrangement was much less intrusive if a stand was not placed within the group. Outdoors, the best arrangement consisted in hanging the microphone from a tree and running the cable through the branches and along the trunk of the tree. Indoors, the microphone could be hung from some fixture on the ceiling or placed on a stand positioned on a high object such as a refrigerator.

This method of obtaining sound imposed strong constraints on the type of conversation that could be recorded. Most notably, because of

[46] The work of Labov (for example, 1972b:207–216) provides the best analysis of the constraints on speech imposed by the interview situation as well as some of the most productive attempts to overcome these limitations.

[47] Use of this microphone is in fact quite congruent with the behavior of listeners in conversation. For example, it shifts attention from participant to participant as speakership changes. Indeed, I have observed that a sound-man manipulating this device relies on many of the same conversational cues examined in this study; for example, moving to a new speaker after a restart, and thus producing a clear record of the sentence begun after the restart. It is precisely the ability of this microphone to adapt to conversational structures and human participation in them that makes it a poor tool for the analysis of such phenomena.

the cables, it was difficult to record people who moved from place to place. Recording was most successful when the conversation occurred in a fixed place of limited size, such as at a table. Moreover, because of the intrusion caused by hanging cables, it was desirable to have the microphones placed before the participants arrived. Thus, many conversations were chosen to be recorded, not on the basis of participants, who were not known when the choice was made, but rather, for technical reasons, on the basis of location.

To offset the limitations of being confined to a single location, three microphones were used.[48] Sometimes several microphones were placed in different locations so that the camera could move from one to another as circumstances demanded. More frequently, one microphone was hung in a fixed location while one or two of the others were mounted on stands so that they could be moved when needed. Although this arrangement provided some flexibility for moving from location to location, it did not make it possible to record moving groups.

The technical requirements for obtaining a picture of adequate quality also constrained the types of events that could be recorded. The most important factor governing picture quality was the amount of light available. The video camera used would produce a picture with ordinary room lighting. However, the picture was grainy, lacked some detail, and was not of sufficient quality to produce good copies. Although some early data were obtained under these conditions, whenever possible an attempt was made to provide sufficient light to produce a good picture. This could be done in a variety of ways. For some situations floodlights were directed toward the participants. However, such lights have the strong disadvantage of being quite intrusive, even when bounced off the ceiling. Some of the liabilities of floodlights can be avoided by placing higher powered bulbs (at least 200 watts) in the existing light fixtures of the setting. Although it changes the light level, this method does maintain the normal lighting arrangement of the setting and it is far less intrusive than movie lights. This arrangement works best when high overhead fixtures are available. It was used in preference to floodlights whenever possible. The least intrusive way of obtaining sufficient light consists of choosing a location where the existing lighting is adequate. Indoors, this can best be accomplished by choosing a room well illuminated by fluorescent lighting, but the best, as well as the least intrusive, lighting can be obtained by taping outdoors. For this reason, much of the data used in this study were recorded outdoors.

---

[48] Two of the microphones were medium quality electric condensors (Sony ECM 21's); a test before purchase showed that higher quality microphones did not produce a noticeable improvement in sound quality under field conditions. The third, which was used far less frequently, was a dynamic microphone (an Electro-Voice 644).

Other constraints on what could be recorded were imposed by the characteristics of the television camera I used (a Sony AVC-3400). Unlike a film camera, this camera averages all the light in a scene. Therefore, participants could not be recorded in front of a bright background, such as the sky or a window, without losing detail in their features. Further, any bright point of light in the picture produces a dark, permanent burn on the tube and must be avoided. In order to obtain the best picture, the lighting has to be comparatively even. All of these considerations limited what could be successfully taped. For example, when recording outdoors, it was desirable to have the participants in the shade and in front of some background other than sky.

Yet other limitations were imposed by the characteristics of the recorded image. First, its ability to resolve detail is limited. A great deal more can be seen about a face that fills the frame than about one that occupies only a corner of it. If the actions of several participants are to be observed simultaneously, information is lost about the finer actions of each. A choice must therefore be made. For the work being discussed here, the choice of what to include within the frame was governed by the research problems for which the data were being collected. For example, at one point, I wished to investigate how speakers animate characters within stories.[49] Therefore, whenever a story preface occurred, I filled the frame with the face of the speaker who had produced the preface.[50] However, most of my research focused on the process of interaction between speaker and hearer. For such analysis I needed information about the simultaneous action of all participants. Therefore, all participants were included within the frame.

In order to obtain maximum detail, the camera was panned and tilted, and a 12.5–75 mm zoom lens was adjusted, as the configuration of the group changed, or its members moved, so that the group just filled the frame. On a very few occasions, it was necessary to use an 8.5 mm wide-angle lens rather than the zoom in order to include all members within the group. The camera was still panned and tilted when this lens was used.[51]

---

[49] On this issue see Goffman (1974, Chapter 13, especially Section V).

[50] This work, which occupied less than an hour of tape, is not reported in this study.

[51] This method of taping thus does not conform to the "locked off camera" paradigm of Feld and Williams (1975:25). However, neither does it conform to their "researchable film" paradigm where "angle and focal length changes [are] justified by the triggering pattern of human response and intuition in relation to the structure of the event [p. 31]." In the present work, particular research interests, rather than the intuitions of the moment, determined what was to be included within the frame. I am in complete agreement with Feld and Williams when they state (p. 30) that "it is essential that the researcher, who has been trained in the observation of his subject, is also the filmer."

Seating arrangements posed a second technical problem for the recorded image. If someone was behind someone else he could not be seen. In many cases, this problem could be avoided or at least strongly limited by careful selection of camera position. An attempt was made to find natural seating arrangements—such as picnic tables with benches but no chairs—that would also provide an opening for the camera. When these were not available, chairs would sometimes be moved so that visual access to the group would not be blocked. The camera was mounted on a movable cart, allowing its position to be changed easily to provide the best view of all participants as circumstances changed. Only very rarely (on two occasions, a bridge game and a family dinner) were the participants arranged specifically for the camera. As people moved within the group, it frequently happened that someone was blocked, at least temporarily. Unless this occurred at the very beginning of taping, or involved a new person sitting down, it was not called to the attention of the group. If the camera could not be moved to a better position, the problems created by this situation were accepted.

Although the technical details of the recording situation can be specified with some exactness, it is difficult to calculate the consequences on the event of the fact that it was being observed. Heider (1976:80) notes that "normal, naturally occurring conversation . . . is a relatively low-energy, fragile sort of behavior, which is easily disrupted by the camera." Problems related to the process of observation have, in fact, emerged as important theoretical and methodological issues in several different fields. In linguistics, largely through the work of Labov, it is recognized that the most important source of data for the study of linguistic structure is the vernacular, "the style in which the minimum attention is given to the monitoring of speech [Labov 1972b:208]." However, "*any systematic observation of a speaker defines a formal context in which more than the minimum attention is paid* to speech [p. 209; italics in original]." The problem noted by Labov, far from being confined to linguistics, seems to arise in any inquiry in which precise information about natural human behavior becomes important. Thus, Eibl-Eibesfeldt (1974:21) states that hidden cameras are "a prerequisite for any documentation of natural undisturbed behavior." It should be noted, however, that considerable disagreement exists as to the extent of the problem. In contrast to Eibl-Eibesfeldt, Feld and Williams (1974:31) believe that the process of filming does not significantly alter the behavior being filmed.

For both technical and ethical reasons, hidden cameras were not used to collect any of the data for this study. Participants always knew that they were being recorded. The problems of observation are thus relevant to the data being used for analysis in this study.

Although most discussion of this issue has focused simply on the presence of the observer (or camera), such a concept in fact includes several different types of phenomena which must be distinguished analytically. To begin with, the behavior of the observer may organize the behavior being observed. Interviews provide a particularly clear example of this process. The actions of the interviewer shape the interaction into a particular pattern with a distinctive turn-taking structure providing different types of action for the interviewer and the party or parties being interviewed. Wolfson (1976:189ff) examines some of the problems posed by the use of such structures in linguistics. Some investigators have attempted to deal with such problems by making the actions of the interviewer, as well as the parties being interviewed, part of the final published record of the event (a particularly striking example is provided by Jean Rouch's *Chronicle of a Summer*). However, although such a strategy makes accessible the actions of the observer, it does nothing about the changes in the event itself wrought by the structure of his behavior.

The observer's actions may modify the structure of the event even though the observer does not cause any changes in the behavior of the participants. For example, after the event he can rearrange his record of it, as happens, for instance, when a film is edited. Further, the technology used to record the event in the first place will inevitably modify it in a systematic fashion. Any camera position or framing of participants involves a choice from a set of alternatives and any of the alternatives not selected would have produced a different record of the event. Similarly, using a category system, such as that of Bales (1970:92), to code the event will lose much information about the event and organize the information that remains in a particular fashion which is determined as much by the structure of the category system as by the events being categorized.

Analytically distinct from the behavior of the observer, is the observer as an addressee of the participants. People act differently toward different types of others,[52] and this will have consequences on their production of talk.[53] The implications for an investigator wishing to sample the speech behavior of different individuals are obvious. If the investigator is the addressee of the party he is observing, as is the case with interviews, what he will in general obtain are samples of how these different individuals talk to an academic stranger—rather than samples of how they talk to each other.

---

[52] For some discussion of the relevance of this for the conceptualization of culture, see Goodenough (1963:260–261).

[53] For some analysis of precisely how talk will vary in terms of its intended recipient, see Schegloff (1972).

An investigator can, however, systematically observe and record the speech of different groups of people without himself being the addressee of that talk.[54] In his early interviews in New York, Labov (1972b:89) observed that casual speech emerged when the party being interviewed began to talk to others present. In order to obtain better data about the vernacular, he therefore began to supplement formal interviews with group sessions. In these sessions, "the adolescents behaved much as usual, and most of the interaction—physical and verbal—took place between the members. As a result the effect of systematic observation was reduced to a minimum [p. 210]."

Analytically distinct from both the behavior of the observer and his status as an addressee of the participant's action are changes in the event caused by the mere fact that it is being recorded as well as by the observable presence of the recording equipment. The issue of how participants deal with observation is in fact a somewhat subtle one. Within conversation, participants never behave as if they were unobserved; it is clear that they organize their behavior in terms of the observation it will receive from their coparticipants. For example, a speaker does not simply "forget" a word; instead, he actively displays to the others present that he is searching for a word.[55] Thus the issue is, not what participants do when they are unobserved, but whether the techniques they use to deal with observation by a camera are different from those used to deal with observation by coparticipants. This is an empirical question requiring further research. It seems quite plausible that people may avoid discussing a variety of "sensitive" topics in the presence of a tape recorder (though the Watergate tapes provide some counterevidence), just as they avoid mentioning such topics in the presence of certain types of coparticipants.[56] It seems far less plausible that phenomena on the level being examined in this study would be changed—that, for example, restarts would act to bring the gaze of a recipient toward the speaker when the camera was present but not when it was absent—though this remains an empirical question.

It is frequently assumed and sometimes explicitly argued (for example, Wolfson 1976) that direct participant-observation is less disruptive of the phenomena being observed than recording that phenomena with a tape recorder. This does not necessarily seem to be the case. Consider the

[54] For a more detailed analysis of changes in speech that occur when someone other than the interviewer becomes the addressee, see Labov (1972a:207–212; 1972b:89–90).

[55] The techniques employed by speakers to signal "word searches" have been extensively investigated by Sacks and his students. Though most of this work is as yet unpublished, Jefferson (1974) analyzes some aspects of this process.

[56] For an analysis of such avoidance in an actual speech situation, see Thomas (1958:70–71).

problem of investigating the gaze of the hearer. The tool that a partic-ipant–observer would use to observe the gaze of others—his own gaze—is itself a relevant event in the interaction in which he is participating. If the observer employs his gaze in an inappropriate fashion, a noticeable event will occur which may well disrupt the process being observed. As noted by Scheflen (1973:88–89), gazing at a hearer is inappropriate: "One is to look at the speaker of the moment. . . . As a consequence we rarely get to observe the behavior of listeners and we do not ordinarily see the total bodily behavior of others in conversation." The camera, though intrusive and perhaps disruptive in other ways, does not focus attention on the gaze of either party (especially if it is not pointed at one participant in particular but includes both speaker and hearer within the frame) and is not itself an oriented-to feature of the process under observation. In this particular case, use of a camera is less destructive of the process being examined than direct participant-observation would be.

In gathering data, I tried to deal with the issues raised by the recording process in a number of different ways.

First, I attempted to limit as much as possible my interaction with the people I was taping. I could, of course, have chosen instead to become a member of the group myself. However, although such an approach would have provided a better record of my actions, it would have made more serious many of the other problems that have been discussed. For example, all the different groups I taped would have had a common addressee and my own behavior would have significantly organized the behavior of others in the group. Moreover, focus toward the camera would have been greatly increased unless I fixed it at a particular angle and focal length and left it. The strategy I chose to adopt was quite similar to that employed by Labov in recording group sessions. I ac-counted for my lack of engagement by displaying involvement in the technical details of recording. Thus were a participant to turn to me, he would find me studying the VU meter on the microphone mixer or checking the image in the viewfinder. I also wore earphones and gazed toward the viewfinder from a slight distance and at an oblique angle rather than pressing my eye to the camera. The camera was thus not presented as an extension of my face and body directed toward the participants but, rather as an object that was itself the focus of my attention (this was, of course, made possible by the fact that I was not peering through the lens, as is the case with a film camera, but rather looking at a very small television monitor). I was thus a person present at the event but not one immediately accessible for interaction, my involvement being directed to other tasks claiming my full attention.

Second, I tried to limit and make explicit, as far as possible, the organization imposed on the event by my recording of it. Thus, once the camera was set up and the participants were present, I tried to record them continuously until they left the scene. My reasons for not trying to select particular events are the same as those given by Goffman (1953:3) for his use of a similar strategy.

> While in the field, I tried to record happenings between persons regardless of how uninteresting and picayune these events seemed to be. The assumption was that all interaction between persons took place in accordance with certain patterns, and hence, with certain exceptions, there was no *prima facie* reason to think that one event was a better or worse expression of this patterning than any other event.

From a somewhat different perspective, Margaret Mead (1973:257) has noted that

> the future usefulness of field data for different kinds of exploitation, many of them unanticipated at the time the field work was done, is a direct function of the extent to which material can be collected in large, sequential and simultaneous natural lumps on which no analytical devices of selection have operated. . . . Long verbatim texts are more valuable than many short verbatim texts; tapes which contain many other kinds of information are more valuable than several hand-recorded verbatim texts. Only materials which preserve the original spatial-temporal relationships are virtually inexhaustible as sources for new hypotheses and ways of testing old hypotheses. The more material is codified by the method of selection, as when sample scenes, standard-length anecdotes, standard interviews, standard texts, are used the more immediately useful it may be in relation to some hypothesis and the less its permanent value.

The video recorder I used could record for slightly longer than 30 minutes before tape had to be changed. Except for the time lost when tape was being changed (approximately .5–1 minute), the recorder was run continuously, sometimes for more than 6 hours. In order to maintain a consistent and explicit approach toward the selection of what participants to include in the shot, the shot was framed (with several exceptions noted earlier) to include all present participants. The practice of shooting continuously for a long period of time might also have contributed toward obtaining samples of interaction in which the behavior of the participants was influenced less by the camera than by each other. This is, however, an empirical question which requires further investigation.

Transcription

Data were transcribed according to a system for capturing the auditory details of conversation designed by Gail Jefferson (Sacks *et al.* 1974:731–733) and a system for recording gaze direction devised by myself.[57] Both of these will be described shortly. All transcription was

---

[57] The system for coding gaze was suggested by that used by Kendon (1967) and was brought to my attention by Jefferson.

checked by at least two and frequently three transcribers. Some of the tapes used in the analysis were audio-transcribed by Gail Jefferson and I am deeply indebted to her for this.

Because the transcription system makes use of basic English orthography,[58] it might appear to the reader that sections of transcribed data can be read in much the same way as the basic text. Such material is, however, as different from the rest of the text as the statistical tables found in many journal articles. Both comprehension and evaluation of such data require that the material be attended to in quite specific ways. I will do several things to aid the reader in this task. First, relevant transcription devices, rather than being either assumed at the outset or relegated to an appendix, will be described initially here and then re-introduced progressively as the analysis develops. It is hoped that this will enable the reader both to see in detail the relevance of particular transcription conventions for the analysis and also to learn to use them before encountering new ones. Second, the transcription of the talk will be presented in a simplified fashion. Basically, only those distinctions necessary for the analysis being developed will be included. Though this does not provide the most accurate version possible of the talk as spoken, it will make the material far more accessible. Third, I have tried throughout to keep the examples as short as possible.

We will begin by examining some of the conventions used to transcribe speech. To facilitate subsequent reference to this section, symbols and key aspects of their meaning will appear in boldface. (For ease of reference a simplified version of the transcription system is also provided at the front of the book, immediately after the contents.) The following data fragment includes some of the conventions that are most important to the present study:

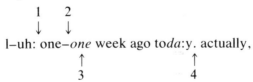

[58] Researchers who have utilized phonemic systems have found them almost useless for investigating conversational phenomena. Thus, Duncan (1974:300–301) transcribed his data in terms of segmental phonemes but found that "the segmental phonemes were the least important components of the study." The Jefferson system was constructed specifically to record phenomena in the stream of speech relevant to the organization of conversation. Thus, it not only notes such sequential phenomena as the precise location of both silence and simultaneous speech, but also records changes in duration which do not distinguish segmental phonemes in English and phenomena relevant to units larger than the sentence, such as differences in time between sentences or turns. Although this system does not capture all relevant distinctions in the stream of speech, it is the system most relevant to the issues being investigated in the present analysis. For discussion of some of the theoretical issues posed by the transcription process see Ochs (1979).

A **colon** (1) indicates that the articulation of the **sound preceding it is noticeably prolonged** (note that such a "sound stretch" also occurs within the word "to*da*:y"). Multiple colons would indicate even greater prolongation.

A **dash** (2) marks a **cut-off**; that is, it indicates that the sound in progress is noticeably and abruptly terminated. Very frequently, the sudden closing of the vocal cords produces a glottal stop.

Italics (3) indicate some form of **emphasis** which may result from increases in either pitch or amplitude. Thus, in these data, a cut-off occurs at the end of the first "one," and the second "one" is noticeably emphasized.

Punctuation marks (4) indicate **intonation**.[59] A falling contour is indicated with a period, a rising one with a question mark, and falling–rising contour (the kind of intonation that one finds, for example, after items in a list) with a comma. Thus, in these data, a full stop occurs before the end of the utterance, just after the word "to*da*:y." The fact that these symbols are being used to mark intonation and not traditional orthographic distinctions should always be kept in mind. For example, because of their characteristic intonation patterns, most wh-questions should be marked with a period. Were a question mark to be used, the rising contour thus indicated would in fact sound rather unusual.

In the following, **dashes within a parentheses** (5) indicate **tenths of seconds within a silence.** Each **full second** is marked with a **plus sign** (6).

How's uh, (––––––––– + ––) Jimmy Linder.
              ↑   ↑
              5   6

---

[59] The use of punctuation symbols to mark changes in pitch is not a recent development. Lieberman (1967:129, citing Hadding-Koch 1961:9) describes "a medieval rule for liturgical recitation from Munster which states that a fall in pitch corresponds to periods, a small rise to commas, and a large rise to interrogatives. . . ." The rule was written as shown here:

Sic can - ta com - ma, sic du - o punc - ta: sic ve - ro punc-tum.

Sic sig - num in - ter - ro - ga - ti - o - nis?

The silence can also be indicated with **numbers in parentheses**—for example, "How's uh, (1.2) Jimmy Linder"; the dashes and pluses will only be used when it is necessary to show something that happens at a specific place within the silence.

The conventions that have just been described are the ones that are the most important to the present analysis. As was stated earlier, for reasons of clarity, many details of the talk that can be captured by transcription have not been included. Thus the first fragment could be more accurately transcribed as follows:

I–uh: one–*one* week ago t'*da*:y. acshilly,

The nuances that have been omitted are certainly important for many types of analysis that could be developed from this fragment, and they should be included in any working transcript. However, they are not necessary for the presentation of the current analysis and the material is easier to follow if they are excluded.

Several other transcription symbols will also be used on occasion, though much less frequently than those already introduced.

A **bracket** connecting the talk of two speakers (7) indicates **the point at which overlapping talk begins:**

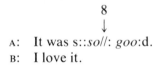

The same phenomenon can also be indicated with **double slashes** (8). In this case, the talk of the second speaker is placed at the beginning of the next line of the transcript.

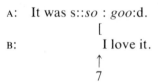

Double brackets before the talk of two speakers (9) indicate that they **start to talk simultaneously.**

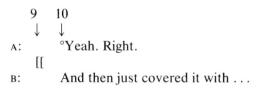

A **degree sign** (10) is used to show that the talk so marked is spoken with noticeably **lowered volume.**

A **less than sign** (11) is used to indicate a **hurried start**—that is, a push into the prior space:

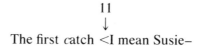

The first catch <I mean Susie–

An **equal sign** (12) indicates that **no break** occurs between two pieces of talk by either the same or different speakers:

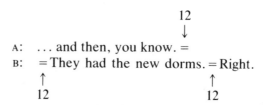

Thus, in this example, B's talk follows A's without any noticeable gap whatsoever. The second unit of the talk B then produces is also "latched" to the first unit without any visible break.

A **series of h's** (13) marks an **outbreath,** unless a **dot precedes the h's** (14), in which case an **inbreath** is indicated:

hhhh (0.4) ˙hhh *We* just want to get ...
↑   ↑
13   14

Thus, in this example, the speaker first produces an outbreath, then pauses, then produces an inbreath and finally begins to speak.

H's within parentheses (15) indicate **within-speech plosives:**

grease it wi(h)th va(h)selin(h)e
     ↑   ↑   ↑
       15

These plosives may be associated with phenomena such as laughter, crying, or breathlessness.

A **blank within parentheses** (16) indicates that the transcriber was **not able to recover what was said:**

She was (   )ing guys up to the ...
    ↑
   16

Words within parentheses (17) indicate **a possible hearing. Two sets of parentheses containing words** (18) show that **alternative hearings** are possible:

$$18 \rightarrow \genfrac{}{}{0pt}{}{\text{(Ours is)}}{\text{(this is)}} \text{ a hell of a discussion.}$$

$$\uparrow$$
$$17$$

The marking of multiple hearings might indicate either disagreement among cotranscribers, agreement to both possibilities by cotranscribers, or double hearings by a single transcriber.

Although many investigators have treated transcription as unproblematic and argued that different listeners should reach agreement on what is said in a particular passage (see, for example, Maclay and Osgood 1959:25), this does not appear to be either a realistic or an appropriate way to deal with the transcription of conversation. Not only do conversations in natural settings occur in locations that are far from ideal for either hearing or recording speech, but the speech signal itself may not be entirely unambiguous. Lieberman (1967:164–165) reports a series of experiments showing that words spoken in conversation and recorded under the very best of conditions cannot be reliably identified when heard in isolation. The regularity with which a request to repeat some item occurs in conversation provides some demonstration that accurately hearing what was said is a problem faced by participants within the conversation itself. In view of such phenomena, the goal of accurate transcription would seem better served by admitting the possibility of different hearings of the same stretch of speech. Accepting this possibility, as the Jefferson transcription system does, produces a more accurate record of the speech being transcribed than either settling disputed cases by flipping a coin (a method used by Buban [1976:285] to resolve differences between coders) or forcing transcribers to agree on a single hearing.

Transcription of nonvocal phenomena will be restricted to an extremely limited set of distinctions about the participants' gaze toward each other. This is not because these distinctions are thought to be the only ones relevant to the organization of the participants' interaction, but rather for just the opposite reason: specifically, because of a recognition of just how much the details of body movement are implicated in the organization of talk. Their importance is demonstrated by the research on kinesics discussed earlier and also became apparent whenever data were examined closely. It was nevertheless decided that if the scope of investigation were expanded, even the limited phenomena already included would not be dealt with either adequately or within a reasonable period of time. The work of McQuown and his associates (1971) demonstrates just how much time (well over 20 years) can be devoted to the intensive analysis of a very small strip of interaction.

Gaze will be transcribed as follows: The **gaze of the speaker** will be marked **above the utterance** and that of the **recipient(s) below it**. A **line** (19) indicates that the party being marked is **gazing toward the other**. The precise **place where gaze reaches the other** is marked with a **capital X** (20) tied to a specific place within the talk with a **bracket**. Thus, in the following, speaker (the party above the utterance) is gazing at recipient from the beginning of the talk transcribed, whereas recipient's gaze reaches speaker after the talk has begun:

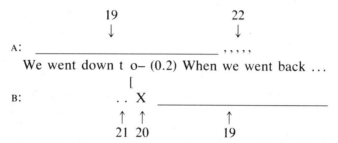

The **movement bringing one's party gaze to the other** is marked with **dots** (21), whereas the **movement withdrawing gaze** is indicated with **commas** (22). Thus, in this example, hearer begins to move toward speaker at the end of the word "down," whereas speaker's gaze leaves hearer at the beginning of the word "we." For a number of reasons, the termination of a withdrawal movement cannot always be accurately marked (for example, the movement may become part of another activity). Nonetheless, it is generally possible to capture both the beginning of this movement and the beginning and the end of the approach movement.

These are the most important transcription devices for recording nonvocal behavior that will be used in this study. However, on occasion some other phenomena will also be marked. In some multiparty situations it will be necessary to indicate who in particular is being gazed at. This will be done by putting a name above the gaze line (in such cases the name replaces the X marking gaze arrival). Thus, in the following, the speaker moves his gaze from Beth to Ann; one recipient, Beth, does not gaze at all; and another, Ann, moves her gaze from Beth to the speaker:

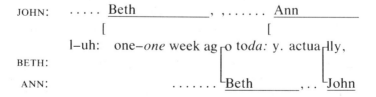

In Chapter 3, it will sometimes be necessary to show a **move toward another that does not culminate in full gaze.** This will be done by indicating its duration with **dashes** (23) rather than a line and marking the point of arrival with a **lower case y** (24) rather than a capital X. Thus, in the following, A moves toward B but stops that movement before his gaze actually reaches B:

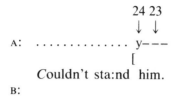

The meaning of particular transcription symbols for gaze will be noted again when the symbols are reintroduced in subsequent chapters. It is hoped that this will make the transcription as easy to follow as possible for the reader.

What exactly is being transcribed as gaze toward the other requires further discussion.[60] Because multiple participants were included on the screen, it was frequently impossible to distinguish individuals' eyeballs. Thus, what is being noted is the orientation of the head toward the other rather than the detailed behavior of the eyes. I am using the term "gaze" to refer to such orientation for a number of reasons. First, in view of the great number of times that I must refer to this event, a more cumbersome locution, such as "orientation of the head toward the other," would quickly become quite awkward and make the analysis more difficult to follow. More importantly, as will be demonstrated in some detail, the participants themselves do attend to precisely this distinction in the organization of their activity. For participants—and it is their distinctions that the analyst is concerned with—orientation of the head is one of the central components of the activity of gazing. It is of course recognized that gazing also includes many other phenomena which themselves merit extensive research.

---

[60] Despite the general acceptance of the phrase "eye contact," research indicates that participants do not, in fact, gaze into each other's eyes. Both Scheflen (1974:67–68) and Exline (1974:73–74) note that gaze toward another falls not precisely at the eyes but rather in a region about the face. However, as noted by Exline (1974:74), this does not pose serious problems for the analyst (or participants): "It is my belief that the validity problem is not critical, for our observations indicate that most people turn their heads and faces slightly away from the other when they break contact. Even if one looks into a zone of regard rather than the eye itself, the other reacts as if he were engaged in eye contact." Such a view is quite compatible with the approach to gaze being taken in the present study.

2

Achieving Mutual Orientation
at Turn Beginning

The Apparent Disorderliness of Natural Speech

Natural speech is frequently considered a poor source of data for the analysis of linguistic structure (see, for example, Chomsky 1965:3–4). Specifically, sentences produced within it are regularly found to be impaired in a variety of ways.[1] Thus, a sample of natural speech will contain not only well-formed grammatical sentences:

(1) JOHN: These egg rolls are very good.

(2) CURT: Al's a pretty damn good driver.

(3) MARSHA: *Chr*ist it was *just* go:rgeous.

but also sentences characterized by phrasal breaks, false starts, long pauses, and isolated ungrammatical fragments:

---

[1] Thus Chomsky (1965:58) argues that actual speech is of such "degenerate quality" that it is of limited usefulness for the study of linguistic competence. A similar view of speech production has been expressed by some psychologists, for example, Martin and Strange (1968:478), who argue that natural speech is so defective "that it is hazardous to guess at the exact constituent structure of any given utterance." It is also frequently argued that participants themselves do not perceive the restarts, pauses, and fragments in their talk (see, for example, Lyons 1972:58 and Mahl 1959:114).

(4) DEBBIE: Anyway, (0.2) um:, (0.2) we went t– I went to
                  bed really early.

(5) BARBARA: Brian you're gonna hav– You kids'll *have* to go
                  down *clo*ser so you can *hear* what they're gonna do.

(6) SUE: I come in t– I no sooner sit down on the couch in
                  the living room, and the doorbell rings.

THE USE OF RESTARTS TO CONSTRUCT
UNBROKEN SENTENCES

In contrast to the grammatically coherent Examples (1)–(3), Examples (4)–(6) manifest the supposed disorder of actual speech. However, note that, although Examples (4)–(6) contain fragments of sentences, they also contain coherent grammatical sentences.

(4) DEBBIE: I went to bed really early.

(5) BARBARA: You kids'll *have* to go down *clo*ser so you can
                  hear what they're gonna do.

(6) SUE: I no sooner sit down on the couch in the living
                  room, and the doorbell rings.

Furthermore, note that the fragment and the coherent sentence occur in a particular order: first the fragment and then the sentence. A single format is thus found:

[Fragment] + [Coherent Sentence]

This format defines a restart. Though it provides one demonstration of the possible disorder of natural speech, this format is a phenomenon that occurs repeatedly in actual talk and that has a specifiable structure in its own right—which, moreover, includes a coherent grammatical sentence.

This format will be investigated with respect to the possibility that its repeated occurrence is not haphazard but rather a regular product of the procedures constructing actual talk and, more specifically, that the format has the effect of systematically achieving something found within it: the occurrence of a coherent grammatical sentence in natural speech.

In order to investigate this possibility, one other aspect of the behavior of participants in conversation—their gaze—will also be examined.[2]

---

[2] The work of Kendon (1967) provides strong empirical support for the argument that gaze is a relevant feature of face-to-face talk as well as detailed investigation of its structure.

In most turns at talk in face-to-face conversation, the speaker is gazed at by some other party.[3] The following will be proposed as a gaze-related rule, implicated in the organization of the interaction of speaker and hearer in face-to-face talk.[4]

A speaker should obtain the gaze of his recipient during the course of a turn at talk.

Some actual utterances containing restarts will now be examined specifically with respect to the possibility that they are in fact systematic products of the orientation of participants to the feature specified by this rule. In transcriptions of these utterances, the gaze direction of the recipient will be marked below the utterance, as follows: A solid line will indicate that the recipient is gazing toward the speaker, with the letter "X" marking the precise point at which the recipient's gaze reaches the speaker; the absence of such a line will indicate that the recipient's gaze is directed elsewhere. For the sake of simplicity and clarity, only the beginnings of turns will be examined. Let us begin by considering Examples (4)–(6), discussed earlier:

(4) DEBBIE: Anyway, (0.2) Uh:, (0.2) We went t– I went ta bed

                                   [

CHUCK: X_____

(5) BARBARA: Brian you're gonna ha v– You kids'll *ha*ve to go

                                 [

BRIAN: X_____

(6) SUE: I come in t– I no sooner sit down on the couch

                       [

DIEDRE: X_____

---

[3] The ethnographic literature provides some striking exceptions to what will be said about gaze in this chapter. For example, Whiffen (1915:254) reports that "when he speaks, the Indian does not look at the person addressed, any more that the latter watches the speaker. Both look at some outside objects. This is the attitude also of the Indian when addressing more than one listener, so that he appears to be talking to some one not visibly present." See also LaFrance and Mayo (1976) and Erickson (1979), for differences between the conversational gaze behavior of blacks and whites.

[4] I find many problems with calling what is being talked about here a rule but am unable to locate the phenomenon to be focused on as clearly in any other way. Moreover, though the present wording is adequate as a point of departure for beginning to investigate gaze within the turn, subsequent analysis, both in this chapter and the next, will reveal that, although this feature is an operative feature of one type of turn, it is not found in every turn.

In each of these examples, the following may be observed:

1. Although the recipient is not gazing at the speaker at the beginning of his turn, he subsequently redirects his gaze to the speaker.
2. Without bringing his previous sentence to completion, the speaker begins a new sentence at the point at which he gains the gaze of a recipient.

The conjunction between a recognizable event in the utterance of the speaker and the place where the recipient's gaze reaches the speaker is consistent with the possibility that the gaze of the hearer is relevant to the speaker in the construction of his turn.[5]

The sequence of actions performed by the speaker produces a restart. The sentence being produced before the gaze of the recipient was obtained is abandoned without being brought to completion. When the speaker has the gaze of his recipient a coherent sentence is produced. To have the gaze of a recipient thus appears to be preferred over not having his gaze and this preference appears to be consequential for the talk the speaker produces in his turn. This is consistent with the possibility that gaze is one means available to recipients for displaying to a speaker whether or not they are acting as hearers to his utterance.[6]

---

[5] Within psychology and sociology, phrasal breaks in utterances, such as restarts and pauses, have received some attention (see, for example, Allen and Guy 1974; Argyle 1969; Beattie 1978b; Bernstein 1962; Cook 1971; Cook, Smith, and Lalljee 1974; Dittman 1974; Dittman and Llewellyn 1969; Goldman-Eisler 1961, 1972; Henderson 1974; Jones 1974; Maclay and Osgood 1959; Mahl 1959; Martin and Strange 1968; Mishler and Waxler 1970; Sabin et al. 1979; Siegman 1979). In these studies, two assumptions have been consistently made. First, as in contemporary linguistics, phrasal breaks are seen to be manifestations of defective performance. Second, phrasal breaks are assumed to result from processes entirely internal to the speaker, such as anxiety, cognitive difficulty, or problems in encoding the utterance. An alternative possibility is explored here: specifically, that the actions of the hearer as well as the speaker might be relevant to the production of phrasal breaks by the speaker. It certainly cannot be argued that processes internal to the speaker are irrelevant to the production of phrasal breaks or that the hearer is implicated in the production of all phrasal breaks. However, in cases where the speaker's phrasal break is coordinated with specific actions of the hearer, it would seem inadequate to attempt to specify either the distribution of phrasal breaks within the utterance, or the processes providing for their occurrence, without reference to the actions of the hearer.

[6] Though a hearer can signal his attentiveness in a number of different ways (see, for example, Wieman 1976:12), many investigators (for example, Argyle 1969:108–109, 202; Argyle and Cook 1976:212, 184; Goffman 1967:123; Kendon 1967:36; Philips 1974:143–144; Schelflen 1974:68–69) have noted the special importance of gaze as a display of attentiveness.

Argyle (1969:105) notes that in order to display proper attention to a speaker, a hearer may gaze at "some object with which they are both concerned" rather than the speaker. Though the present research will restrict itself to studying the gaze of the hearer toward

Sacks (10/26/67, Part II, p. 7)[7] has noted that "one wants to make a distinction between 'having the floor' in the sense of being a speaker while others are hearers, and 'having the floor' in the sense of being a speaker while others are doing whatever they please. One wants not merely to occupy the floor, but to have the floor while others listen."

In conversation speakers are thus faced not simply with the task of constructing sentences, but with the task of producing sentences for hearers. Suppose that a recipient begins to display proper hearership well after the speaker has begun to produce a sentence. If the speaker brings that sentence to completion, his utterance will contain a coherent sentence and no sentence fragment. However, when the actions of both speaker and hearer are taken into consideration, that complete sentence may in fact constitute a fragment, since only part of it has been properly attended to by a hearer:

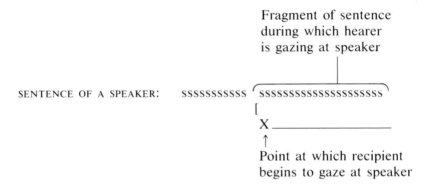

By beginning a new sentence when the gaze of the recipient is obtained, the speaker is able to produce his entire sentence while he is being gazed at by the hearer. In short, rather than providing evidence for the defective performance of speakers in actual conversation, restarts may provide some demonstration of the orientation of speakers to producing sentences that are attended to appropriately by their recipients.

---

the speaker, the situation described by Argyle is recognized as valid and not inconsistent with the analysis being developed here.

From a physiological rather than a social perspective, Diebold (1968:550–551) notes that facing the speaker optimizes a recipient's ability to actually hear the talk.

[7] Though much of the most important work of Harvey Sacks exists at present only in the form of unpublished lectures, many researchers do have access to these materials. I have therefore chosen to cite them as exactly as possible, giving a specific date and page number where relevant.

Procedures for Securing the Gaze of a Hearer

THE USE OF RESTARTS TO REQUEST THE GAZE OF A HEARER

Not all restarts exhibit precise coordination with the arrival of a recipient's gaze:

(7) ETHYL: So they st– their cla sses start around (0.2) in
                                [

     BARBARA: X _____

(8) LEE: Can you bring– (0.2) Can you
     RAY:

     LEE: bring me here that nylo n?
                               [

     RAY: X _

(9) JOE: My mother told me that– *We* had a col d water flat
                                     [

     PAT: X _____

Here the gaze of the recipient is obtained after the restart. These examples will thus not support the possibility that the speaker is awaiting the gaze of a recipient before proceeding to construct a coherent sentence. Further, in examples such as these, the point at which the recipient begins to gaze at the speaker is often rather distant from the restart. The argument that the restart and the movement into orientation by the recipient are performed with reference to each other, which seemed strong in the previous data because of the close coordination between the two events, here seems weak.

However, no consideration has been given to the time required for a recipient to move his gaze from some other position to the speaker. Examples (7)–(9) will therefore be reexamined to take into account the movement bringing the recipient's gaze to the speaker. This movement will be marked with a series of dots.

(7) ETHYL: So they st– their clas ses start around (0.2) in
                              [

     BARBARA: .... X _____

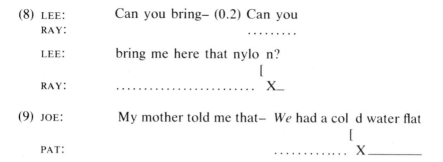

(8) LEE: Can you bring– (0.2) Can you
    RAY: . . . .

    LEE: bring me here that nylo n?
                                     [
    RAY: . . . . X_

(9) JOE: My mother told me that– *We* had a col d water flat
                                                   [
    PAT: . . . . X _____

In these examples the recipient's movement begins just after the restart. The argument that the restart and the gaze of the recipient toward the speaker might be performed with reference to each other seems once again tenable.

It has been frequently argued (for example, Allen and Guy 1974:171–172; Dittman 1974:175; Lyons 1972:58; Mahl 1959:114) that participants do not notice the phrasal breaks that occur in natural conversation. Thus Dale (1974:174) states that "subjects perceive the presence of hesitations but not their precise location." However, the close coordination between the actions of the recipient and the phrasal break in Examples (7)–(9) provides evidence that participants attend to the location of phrasal breaks with some precision.

These data also cast doubt on the accuracy of Martin and Strange's statement (1968:474) that "while . . . hesitations mark speaker uncertainty they have little utility for the listener."

The differences in the placement of gaze relative to the restart in the two data sets suggest that the restart may function to coordinate action between speaker and hearer in at least two alternative, but related, ways. First, as demonstrated in Examples (4)–(6), the restart allows a speaker to begin a new sentence at the point where recipient's gaze is obtained. Second, the recipient action just after the restart in Examples (7)–(9) raises the possibility that a restart may also act as a request for the gaze of a hearer. With respect to this possibility, note that the restart, containing as it does a marked phrasal break, is applicable to any sentence whatsoever. That is, because the flow of the utterance is interrupted in a quite noticeable fashion, a hearer can recognize the occurrence of a restart quite independently of the content of the particular utterance in which it occurs. Being widely usable and extremely noticeable, the restart is well suited to serve as a signal.[8]

[8] Indeed, on some occasions, a restart used to begin a new sentence at the point where a first recipient's gaze reaches the speaker might also have the effect of drawing the gaze

If the restart can in fact act as a request for gaze, the actions of speaker and hearer together would constitute a particular type of summons–answer sequence. Schegloff's (1968) study of the organization of summons–answer sequences provides analytic resources with which this possibility might be investigated further. In order to differentiate phenomena that participants orient to as sequences from events that merely happen to be adjacently placed, Schegloff (1968:1083) proposes that sequences have a property that he refers to as "conditional relevance." The occurrence of a first item in a sequence, such as a summons, establishes the relevance of a next item to it, with the effect that not only an answer, but also the absence of such an answer, can be treated as a noticeable event by participants. One way in which the absence of an answer to a summons might be noted is by repetition of the summons, though only until an answer to it is obtained, at which point the party making the summons proceeds to further talk.

If the restart–gaze pattern does in fact constitute a type of summons–answer sequence, it may therefore be expected that on some occasions a recipient's failure to gaze after an initial restart will be noted by the production of another restart which will have the effect of repeating the summons.[9] Further, the string of restarts thus produced will

---

of a second recipient. Note Examples (52) and (16) in the penultimate section of this chapter, p. 90.

[9] With respect to the insistent quality of such repetition, it may be noted that being gazed at by a recipient not only ensures that the channel between speaker and hearer is functioning, but also constitutes a display that the speaker is receiving from the hearer the respect owed him. Lord Chesterfield, writing to his son in 1752 (Letter CCLXXVIII) (1932:231–232) had the following to say about inattention in conversation:

> There is nothing so brutally shocking, nor so little forgiven, as a seeming inattention to the person who is speaking to you; and I have known many a man knocked down for (in my opinion) a much slighter provocation than that shocking inattention which I mean. I have seen many people who, while you are speaking to them, instead of looking at, and attending you, fix their eyes upon the ceiling, or some other part of the room, look out the window, play with a dog, twirl their snuff box, or pick their nose. Nothing discovers a little, futile, frivolous mind more than this, and nothing is so offensively ill-bred; it is an explicit declaration on your part that every, the most trifling, object deserves your attention more than all that can be said by the person who is speaking to you. Judge of the sentiments of hatred and resentment which such treatment must excite in every breast where any degree of self-love dwells, and I am sure that I never yet met with that breast where there was not a great deal. I repeat it again and again (for it is highly necessary for you to remember it) that sort of vanity and self-love is inseparable from human nature, whatever may be its rank or condition. Even your footman will sooner forget and forgive a beating than any manifest mark of slight and contempt. Be therefore I beg of you, not only really, but seemingly and manifestly, attentive to whoever speaks to you.

be terminated at a particular point—that is, when the gaze of the recipient is at last obtained.

Examination of the production of actual restarts at turn-beginning supports the possibility that such a process might be involved in their construction. First, multiple restarts are in fact found at the beginning of some turns. Second, this string of restarts comes to an end and a coherent sentence is entered when the recipient at last begins to move his gaze to the speaker. Examples (10)–(12) illustrate both these points.

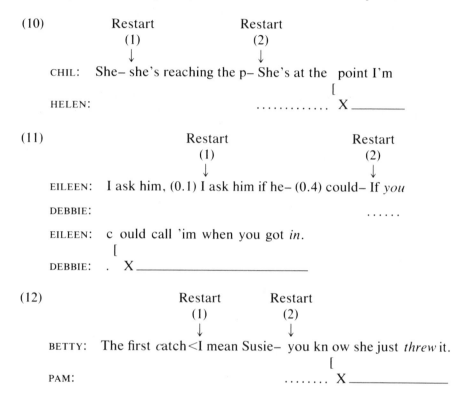

Each of these utterances contains not one but two restarts. (Subsequent analysis will reveal that the restart is not the only phrasal break that can request the gaze of a hearer. Analysis of Examples [10]–[12] in terms of such a possibility would reveal that some, such as [11], contain more than two requests for a hearer.) When the gaze of a recipient has been obtained, the speaker stops producing restarts and enters a coherent sentence.[10]

---

[10] This is not of course meant to imply that the sentence begun at this point will inevitably remain free of perturbations and phrasal breaks; these might subsequently arise from other

The data are thus consistent with the possibility that summons–answer sequences might function, not only to provide coordinated entry into a conversation as a whole (Schegloff 1968:1089), but also to establish the availability of participants toward each other within the turn itself.

It would thus appear that recipients have the ability to attend to restarts with precision, and that speakers in fact expect recipients to do this and systematically organize their talk with reference to such an ability by, for example, not only repeating the phrasal break, but also treating the recipient's failure to move after the initial phrasal break as the noticeable absence of relevant action.

WAITING FOR RECIPIENT TO RESPOND

The ability to recycle the phrasal break provides for the possibility of cases, such as (13)–(15), in which the beginning of the recipient's movement occurs after a slight delay:

(13) GARY: I know Freddy– (0.2) Freddy used to work over the plant.
                                                                [
      MIKE: .... X_____

(14) PAM: Why don't you go out– *What's* that one swin g doing up
                                                                  [
      BRUCE: .... X_____

(15) SARA: That's like– She tells me down there at the corner
                                                              [
      FLORA: .... X_____

Insofar as speakers have the ability to recycle their request for gaze, if a response is not immediately forthcoming they can wait briefly for that response. Further, it is possible that recipient's starting to move into orientation in examples such as these operates retroactively. By starting to attend, one may recognizably display that one has already heard some of the prior talk, and thus that it need not be redone.

Phrased differently, their ability to recycle the request for gaze makes it possible for speakers to treat the place where recipient's response is relevant and possible, not as an instantaneous point, but rather as a period of time with some duration. Thus, although recipients have the ability to attend to restarts with precision (and do in fact move immediately after the restart on many occasions), they are also given some

---

events in the interaction between speaker and hearer, as well as from the speaker's efforts to formulate his talk in an appropriate and relevant fashion.

leeway for the placement of their move relative to speaker's action by the larger framework of action within which such moves are given organization and made meaningful.

The processes that have just been examined provide some evidence for the possibility that a state in which a recipient is attending the speaker during the production of a coherent sentence is neither accidental nor automatic, but rather something toward the achievement of which the actions of the participants may be actively directed.

In sum, the restart constitutes one technique available to participants in conversation for coordinating the actions of the speaker and those of the recipient so that the recipient is attending the speaker during the time in which he is producing a coherent sentence.

AN ALTERNATIVE TO THE RESTART: THE PAUSE

In examining the restart as a request for the gaze of a recipient, it was found that the speaker did not require the gaze of his recipient from the absolute beginning of his sentence. Thus, if the speaker had a technique for obtaining the gaze of his recipient *near* the beginning of his first proposed sentence, he might be able to continue with the sentence without producing a restart.

Coherent Sentence

.X———————

However, consider a situation in which the speaker does not have the gaze of his recipient when he takes the floor, and in which, furthermore, it takes the recipient a considerable amount of time to bring his gaze to the speaker. In such a situation, by the time the recipient moves into orientation, the speaker's sentence would have advanced well toward its completion:

Coherent Sentence

. . . . X_

The length of time required for the recipient to move into orientation would pose no problem to the speaker if he had a way of holding the sentence at its beginning until he obtained his recipient's gaze. A very simple way the speaker might accomplish this task is by ceasing to speak near the beginning of his sentence, waiting until the gaze of his recipient is secured, and then continuing the sentence:

[Beginning] + [Pause] + [Continuation]

. . . . .X———————————

By using a pause to delay the onward development of his sentence in this fashion, the speaker would be able to secure the gaze of his recipient near the beginning of his sentence despite the fact that it takes his recipient some period of time to bring his eyes to the speaker.

The following provide possible examples of such a process. Dashes mark tenths of seconds within a silence, and plus signs mark each second.

(16) MICHAEL: *Who* know:s, 'hh (– – – –) nu:mbers and letters (huh),
                               [
     DON: . . . . X————————————————

(17) DIANNE: He pu:t uhm, (– – – – – – –) Tch! Put *crab*meat on
                                 [
     MARSHA: . . . . X————————————————

(18) MARSHA: (Ye–nd) uh, (– – – –) Muddy Ritz was saying that
                                 [
     DIANNE: . . . . X————————————————

In these examples, a pause is employed to hold the speaker's sentence near its beginning until the gaze of a recipient has been obtained. The use of a pause in this fashion is functionally analogous to the use of a restart to produce a new sentence beginning at the point at which a recipient's gaze has been secured.

These data also show that, in addition to silence, a speaker might use phenomena such as inbreaths, transcribed as "'hh" (see Example [16]), and filled pauses (the "uhm" and "uh" in Examples [17] and [18]) to delay the onward progression of his sentence while recipient's gaze is moving.

REQUESTING GAZE WITH A PAUSE BEGINNING

Terminating talk in the middle of a turn-constructional unit, as happens when a pause is begun, produces a noticeable perturbation in the stream of speech. Like the restart, this perturbation may be used to signal that the services of a hearer are being requested. In the following examples, nongazing recipients begin to move their gaze toward the speaker shortly after a pause is entered.[11]

---

[11] These examples raise one other issue. Hearer neither gazes nor even moves toward the speaker before the pause is entered. Yet the portion of the sentence spoken before the pause is not repeated. It thus appears that speakers may treat their hearers as having the ability to recover portions of the talk spoken before hearer showed any attention to the speaker. Chafe (1973:17) has argued that the human mind can retain sound briefly even if the sound was not consciously attended while actually being heard. The following data,

(19) ANN: When you had that big
     JERE:

     ANN: uhm:, (– – – – – – – – – + – –)
                                     [
     JERE: .... X̲̲̲̲̲̲̲̲̲

(20) BARBARA: Uh:, my kids. (– – – – – – – –) had all these blankets
                                   [
     ETHYL: .... X̲̲̲̲̲̲̲̲̲̲̲

(21) MIKE: Speaking of pornographic movies I
     CARNEY:

     MIKE: heard– (– – – – – – –) a while
                     [
     CARNEY: .. X̲̲̲̲̲̲̲

(22) ETHYL   I had a who::le:: (– – – – – – – – – – + – –) pail full of
                                [
     JIM: ...... X̲̲̲̲̲̲̲̲̲

It can also be observed that in many of these cases the visibility of the phrasal break, and thus its salience as a signal, is heightened by a range of other phenomena that cluster at pause-beginning, including

---

brought to my attention by Gail Jefferson, provide some demonstration that participants in conversation are in fact able to recover some piece of talk that they initially indicate has not been heard:

(A) RICK: So how'd you get home.
     LINNY: Hu:*h*,
     LINNY: Ben gave me a ri:de,
(B) RICK: What do you mean.
              (1.0)
     LINNY: Huh?
              (0.2)
     RICK: What d o you mean.
                 [
     LINNY: I mean I don't think I'm ready to take the exam.
(C) RICK: How have you been feeling lately.
     LINNY: Hu:*h*?
              (0.7)
     LINNY: How do *I* feel?

In these examples, by producing a "huh," a participant indicates that the last item of talk has not been heard in some relevant fashion and requests that it be repeated. However, before the repeat is provided (at least in complete form), the party who requested the repeat produces an utterance showing that the requested item has been recovered.

sound stretches (indicated in the transcript by colons), cut-offs, filled pauses, and marked changes in intonation (for example, the falling intonation indicated by a period following "kids" in Example [20]).

Like a restart, the beginning of a pause is able to signal that the services of a hearer are needed. However, with this same pause the speaker is also able to delay further production of his sentence until the gaze of his recipient is secured. In this sense, the pause is a more versatile tool than the restart: It can, if necessary, combine the functions of both classes of restarts, requesting the gaze of a recipient and delaying the production of the speaker's sentence so that the gaze of this same recipient is secured near the beginning of the sentence.

Criteria for Choice between Restarts and Pauses

The analysis so far presented reveals two different techniques available to a speaker for securing near the beginning of his sentence the gaze of his recipient. He can either begin a new sentence by producing a restart when his recipient reaches orientation or he can pause near the beginning of his original sentence and await the gaze of his recipient before developing the sentence further.[12] Given the structural and functional sim-

[12] Precisely where in his utterance the speaker places such a pause is an issue that is beyond the scope of the present analysis, but relevant for future study. A considerable amount of research has in fact been done on where pauses occur in utterances. First, a distinction is generally made between "juncture pauses" and "hesitation pauses." Juncture pauses occur at the boundaries between major units in the sentence (this argument has been made from the perspective of both structural linguistics [see, for example, Cook *et al.* 1974:15] and transformational grammar [for example, Lieberman 1967:125]). Juncture pauses are usually considered to be "essentially linguistic" phenomena, serving, for example, to demarcate units in the stream of speech, whereas hesitation pauses "are attributed to nonlinguistic or extra-linguistic factors [Boomer 1965:151, footnote 3]."

Most research has focused on hesitation pauses. As noted by Boomer (1965:148), "the linking hypothesis is that hesitations in spontaneous speech occur at points where decisions and choices are being made." Some early theories (for example, Maclay and Osgood 1959) argued that phrasal breaks occurred between words of high uncertainty. However Boomer (1965) found that pauses occurred most frequently after the first word of a phonemic clause. He argued (1965:156) that this finding provided evidence that speech was encoded in terms of the phonemic clause rather than the individual word (p. 148). Specifically, he proposed that the pattern he found demonstrated that speech encoding occurred in at least two stages, with hesitations occuring after a structural or grammatical decision had been made but before lexical selection (p. 156). Building on Boomer's work, Dittman (1974:172; see also Dittman and Llewellyn 1969) found that body movements tend to occur "at the beginning of fluent speech, be this when the speaker gets started on a clause or when he gets started after some nonfluency within the clause." The placement of both pauses and some relevant body movements early in the utterance in the present data is roughly consistent with the patterns described by Boomer and Dittman.

ilarities of the two techniques, one question that arises is why a speaker would choose one rather than the other to accomplish this task. Specifically, what criteria guide a speaker's selection between the two?

RELEVANT DIFFERENCES BETWEEN PROCEDURES

The choice of one procedure over another would be meaningless if the procedures did not differ from each other in some relevant fashion. One place to search for such difference might be in the phenomena constructed by such procedures. Restarts and pauses appear to be clearly distinguishable from each other:

> Restart: [Fragment] + [New Beginning]
>
> Pause: [Beginning] + [Pause] + [Continuation]

However, the distinctiveness of such phenomena, as well as their status as alternatives for securing gaze, is called into question by examples such as (8), (11), and the following, Example (23), in each of which the gaze of a recipient is secured through use of both a pause and restart:

(23) BARBARA: I– (– –) You know I think that's terrible.
                 [
     GORDIE: .... X———————————————————————————

These examples suggest that if the procedures considered earlier do in fact provide the speaker with a choice between meaningful alternatives, the criteria for that choice are not to be found simply in the difference between a restart and a pause. Because restarts and pauses are complex phenomena constructed through operations on more simple units, the nature of the choice available to the speaker might be obscured if the comparison is made between restarts and pauses as distinct, irreducible entities. Before being able to make the proper comparison, we must, therefore, briefly examine the process through which restarts and pauses are constructed as recognizable phenomena in the first place.

An event that occurs in the construction of both a restart and a pause is the self-interruption[13] of a turn-constructional unit after its beginning

---

[13] In some current work on the organization of conversation (for example, Zimmerman and West 1975), the term "interruption" is used as a technical term to refer to talk intruding into the talk of another. The term is being used here in a rather different way. What is at issue is not the placement of one party's talk relative to another's, but rather the way in which a unit that ceases before a recognizable completion to it has been reached can be seen as noticeably incomplete but still having the potential, though not the certainty, of being returned to and completed at some point in the future. The term is also intended to suggest that such a thing does not just happen, but, rather, is something that is actively being done by someone. Interruption in this sense can be performed by a single party on

but prior to a recognizable completion.[14] The talk that occurs after this interruption may either be a continuation of the unit already in progress or the beginning of a new unit. Only if it is the latter has a restart occurred. Thus, in the following example, whereas the talk after the first phrasal break constructs a restart, the talk after the second does not:

(24)   First   Second
                        Phrasal   Phrasal
                        Break   Break
                          ↓   ↓
      JERE: I have more– u I have– trouble keeping it clea:n.

After a unit has been interrupted, a period of silence—that is, a pause—may or may not occur before speech production is resumed. The talk after the period of silence may be either the beginning of a new unit, a restart (as in Examples [8], [11], [13], and [23]), or a continuation of the unit already in progress (as in Examples [16]–[22]).

One distinction in this process that may be relevant for the selection of one procedure over the other is whether the talk after the interruption continues the unit already in progress or begins a new unit.[15] Which of these events happens affects not only the talk after the interruption but also the talk that preceded it. If the talk following the interruption does not continue the speaker's initial unit, then the talk in that unit loses its status as a possible sentence beginning and becomes a sentence fragment. If, however, the talk following the interruption continues the unit that preceded it, then that original talk maintains its status as the beginning

---

a single unit and indeed is something that might be performed in activities other than talk, as, for example, when a person interrupts a task that is as yet uncompleted to perform another. Other available formulations, such as abandoning the unit in midcourse or delaying its further production, are inadequate in that they specify the outcome of possibilities that still remain open to the participants, who not only do not yet have the future history of the unit available to them, but might be actively using the range of possibilities it still provides as a resource for their current actions.

[14] The self-interruption is frequently but not always marked by a glottal stop (indicated in the present transcription system by a dash). The glottal stop results from the sudden closing of the vocal cords when speech production is abruptly terminated. Labov (1975) has argued that in English such a glottal stop constitutes a universal editing signal. For other relevant analysis see the discussion of repair initiators in Schegloff et al. 1977.

[15] The ability to recognize, first, that a unit has stopped at some place other than a possible termination for it, or, second, that some subsequent piece of talk is or is not a continuation of some prior unit, requires that the participants be able to determine from the part of the unit already produced what would constitute an appropriate termination or a continuation of it. As was noted in the last chapter, such a property is made explicit in the definition of turn-constructional unit provided by Sacks et al. (1974:702).

of the unit currently under construction by the speaker. In short, the procedures that have been examined provide a choice between continuing the unit that was in progress prior to the phrasal break and thus treating that initial talk as the beginning of the sentence still in progress, or beginning a new unit of talk and treating the talk originally begun as a fragment.

SPEAKER'S GAZE TOWARD HEARER

The basis for choice between the alternatives noted will now be investigated. This investigation will be restricted to criteria relevant to the process of negotiating a state of mutual gaze between speaker and hearer, although it is recognized that there are many other valid reasons for interrupting or abandoning an utterance prior to its completion.[16] One has only to look at the great number of false starts, hesitations, and pauses found in monologues, such as academic lectures, to realize that processes of interaction between speaker and hearer are by no means involved in the occurrence of all speech perturbations.

The analysis until this point has provided some demonstration that obtaining the gaze of a recipient within the turn is in fact relevant to the speaker. However, even casual inspection of a visual record of conversation reveals that the hearer does not gaze continuously toward the speaker. Rather, during the course of a turn, he gazes away from the speaker, as well as toward him. Given the regular presence of both alternatives, the absence of a hearer's gaze at a certain point cannot be definitively established. Either the speaker or an analyst could look at some specific place in a turn, find that the hearer is not gazing at the speaker, and yet not be able to establish that gaze is noticeably and relevantly absent, since the gaze appropriate to hearership might occur

[16] The work of Sacks and his colleagues on repairs (for example, Jefferson 1972, 1974a; Sacks 1974; Sacks *et al.* 1974; Schegloff 1972; Schegloff *et al.* 1977) analyzes many other processes that might lead to the interruption of a turn-constructional unit prior to its projected completion. Ways in which speech errors make visible underlying linguistic structures have been investigated by Fromkin (1971). The work of Goffman (1981) on the different aspects of the self generated through repairs examines yet other aspects of this phenomenon. Further, it cannot be claimed that the interaction of speaker and hearer is relevant to the production of all restarts and pauses. Processes internal to the speaker, such as those examined by Boomer (1965), Dittman (1974), and Mahl (1959), as well as social processes quite different from those being investigated here (see, for example, Beattie 1979:73; Brotherton 1979:200), are certainly relevant to the production of many phrasal breaks. Although the present analysis focuses on the social and interactive use of restarts and pauses, it is recognized that such phenomena may reflect actual difficulty the speaker is having in organizing what he is trying to say.

elsewhere in the turn. Nevertheless, the data already examined would indicate that speakers do in fact orient to the noticeable absence of a recipient's gaze at a specific point (for example, by requesting such gaze).

The issue thus arises as to where in the turn speaker is able to find that hearer's gaze is relevantly absent. When data are examined it is found that one place at which restarts requesting the gaze of a nongazing hearer systematically occur is just at the point when speaker's gaze reaches a nongazing recipient.[17] In the following examples, the gaze of the speaker is marked above the utterance.

(25) MARSHA: ..... X—————————— , , ,

                        [

       'N he c a– *he* calls me a Vassar sno:b.

                                      [

      DIANNE: .... X————————

---

[17] In many cases, such as in the examples provided, the restart occurs precisely at the point where the speaker's gaze reaches his recipient. However, in some cases, the restart is not produced until very slightly after the speaker has begun to gaze at his recipient:

(55) MARSHA: .... X—, ,

                                  [

        En a couple of gir ls–   *One othe* r girl from the:re,

                                       [

       DIANNE: .... X—————————

(9) JOE: .... X————————————————————

                                  [

        My mother told m e that–   *We* had a col d water flat

                                        [

       PAT: .... X—————————

Despite the nonsimultaneity of the speaker's gaze and the restart in these examples, their production seems compatible with a process of the type being described. First, the time between the arrival of the speaker's gaze and the production of the restart is brief: The phrasal break that begins the restart occurs in the syllable after the speaker's gaze reaches the recipient. Second, the units produced in this space, "ls–" and "that–" are marked by their pronunciation—by the glottal stop that occurs in each case—as defective. The space between where the speaker's gaze reaches the recipient and where the restart actually begins is retroactively marked as impaired. Thus, though the phrasal break in fact occurs a syllable later, it is displayed as getting started at the point where the speaker's gaze reaches the hearer:

                  MARSHA: .... X—

                                                [

                  En a couple of gir ls–

                  JOE: .... X—

                                                [

                  My mother told m e that–

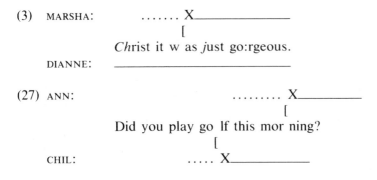

(8) LEE: ············ X_____

                      [

                 Can ya brin g– (0.2) Can you

    RAY: ·········

    LEE: _____

                 bring me here that nylo n?

                                      [

    RAY: ························ X__

(26) BETH: ······· X_____

                 [

             Terry– Jerry's fa scinated with elephants.

                            [

     ANN: ········ X_____

In these data, when speaker's eyes reach a recipient who is not gazing
at him, he treats the talk in progress as impaired by producing a restart,
an action that simultaneously has the effect of acting as a request for
the gaze of recipient. This raises the possibility that one basis for choice
between the procedures being examined might be found in the relationship between hearer's gaze and speaker's. Specifically, it suggests that
at least one place within the turn where hearers should be gazing at
speakers is when speakers are gazing at them.

One way to explore such a possibility further is to see what happens
when speaker's gaze reaches a gazing recipient. In general,[18] in such a
situation, rather than producing a restart, the speaker continues with the
talk in progress:

(3) MARSHA: ······· X_____

                 [

             Christ it w as just go:rgeous.

    DIANNE: _____

(27) ANN: ········· X_____

                         [

             Did you play go lf this mor ning?

                            [

     CHIL: ····· X_____

---

[18] Some quantitative description of this process will be provided in the next section of
this chapter.

(28) DIANNE: . . . . X_____
                                       [
                 It was pretty   ni:ce. It really wa:s,
     MARSHA: _____

Thus, talk produced when speaker's gaze arrives at a nongazing recipient
is treated as impaired, whereas talk in progress when speaker finds a
gazing hearer is not.

It may be noted that talk without recipient gaze is not treated as
impaired until speaker's gaze reaches the recipient. This has a number
of implications.

First, it suggests that there might be a preferred order for the sequencing of the participants' gaze at turn-beginning. If speaker's gaze
arrives first, he will be looking at a nongazing hearer, a situation that
may lead to the talk in progress being treated as impaired. However, if
hearer brings his gaze to speaker first, this situation is avoided:

Speaker Finds Gazing Hearer
SPEAKER: X_____
                                                 [
UTTERANCE: uuuuuuuuuuuuuuuu uuuuuuuuuuu uuuuuuuuuuuuuuuu
                                       [
RECIPIENT: X_____

Speaker Gazes at Nongazing Hearer
SPEAKER: X_____
                       [
UTTERANCE: uuuuuuuuuuu uuuuuuuuuuuuu uuuuuuuuuuuuuuuuuuuuuu
                    ╰────────────╯ [
HEARER: X_____

                     Place Where Speaker
                   Gazes at Nongazing Hearer

The order of hearer and then speaker is thus preferable to the order of
speaker and then hearer. To achieve an appropriate state of mutual gaze,
a hearer should move his gaze to the speaker early in the turn so that
it arrives before the speaker has begun to gaze at him. On the other
hand, in order to provide time for the hearer to make his move, the
speaker should avoid gazing at the hearer until the turn is well underway.[19]

[19] Such an ordering is consistent with the findings of Kendon (1967:33) and Duncan
(1974a) that, whereas hearer gazes at speaker at the beginning of his utterance, speaker
looks away at that point. These investigators did not account for this pattern in terms of

Second, if the speaker does not gaze at hearer anywhere in the turn, the relevance of the recipient's gaze toward the speaker is nowhere established. It is possible to have turns in which gaze between the parties does not occur.[20] Such turns are found within conversation, though typically in particular sequential environments, for example, during periods of disengagement; they will be examined in the next chapter.

Third, the finding that speakers produce restarts if they gaze at nongazing hearers whereas no problems arise when hearers gaze at nongazing speakers, suggests that the rights of speakers and hearers to gaze toward each other within the turn are not equivalent. Speaker should only gaze at a gazing recipient but does not have to gaze at him continuously, whereas a recipient can gaze either at a gazing or a nongazing speaker, but should be gazing at the speaker whenever he is being gazed at by the speaker.

Such a distribution of rights to look at the other is consistent with the finding made by a number of different investigators to the effect that hearers gaze at speakers more than speakers gaze at hearers (for example, Allen and Guy 1974:139–140; Argyle 1969:107; Exline 1974:74; Kendon 1967:26; Neilsen 1964). It is also compatible with the finding that, though eye contact regularly occurs between a speaker and hearer within a turn at talk, it is characteristically brief,[21] its occurrence frequently providing the occasion for its termination. Whereas a hearer may and should gaze frequently at the speaker, speaker himself is under no such obligation; his gaze toward hearer can be intermittent.[22] It is thus possible for there to be considerable variability in the amount of gaze that occurs within talk.

---

interactive procedures for the systematic achievement of particular, oriented-to states of gaze. Duncan did, however, find that one of the ways in which a participant's shift from hearer to speaker is marked is by movement of gaze away from his partner, and Duncan and Fiske (1977:215–221) found that presence or absence of such a move differentiated attempts to claim speakership from back channel vocalizations within the turn of another. Kendon (1967) accounted for the speaker's looking away at turn-beginning in terms of speaker being involved in planning what he was about to say. Such a possibility certainly cannot be discounted and, indeed, it rather neatly complements the processes being investigated in the present analysis.

[20] Now that the phenomena being pointed to in the rule proposed on p. 57 have been described in a more precise fashion, it can be seen that that initial formulation of these phenomena was indeed too broad.

[21] Thus Kendon (1967:27) notes that "mutual gazes tend to be quite short, lasting for little more than a second as a rule."

[22] Kendon (1967:27) notes that the looks of hearers toward speakers tend to be fairly sustained, whereas the glances of speakers toward their recipients are consistently broken by looks away from them. The structure being proposed here would provide for just such a pattern.

Fourth, the fact that an impairment is not located until speaker's gaze arrives raises the possibility that speaker might be able to request the gaze of a recipient who has not started to move without creating a situation where talk must be treated as impaired; that is, while requesting recipient's gaze, speaker might withold his own gaze. The phenomena initially examined as pauses provide resources for requesting gaze without locating the talk then in progress as impaired. The present line of reasoning suggests that, when the pause is used, speaker is not yet gazing toward his recipient. This is, in fact, what is typically found:

(17) DIANNE:　　　　　　　　　　　　　　　　................ X_____
　　　　　　　　　　　　　　　　　　　　　　　　　　[
　　　　　　He pu:t uhm, (– – – – – –) Tch! Put crabm eat on
　　　　　　　　　　　　　　　　　　[
　　MARSHA:　　　　　　　　........... X_____

(20) BARBARA:
　　　　　　Uh, my kids. (– – – – – – – –) had all these blankets,
　　　　　　　　　　　　　　　　　　　[
　　ETHYL:　　　　　　　　　.......... X_____
　　BARBARA:　　　　　　......... X_____
　　　　　　　　　　　　　　　[
　　　　　　and quilts and slee ping bags.
　　ETHYL:　　　　　　　　_____

(29) ANN:
　　　　　　When you had that big
　　JERE:

　　ANN:
　　　　　　uhm:, (– – – – – – – – – + – –) tropical fish tank.
　　　　　　　　　　　　　　　　　　　[
　　JERE:　　　　　　　..................... X_____

To summarize, speakers use a pause to request gaze if they have not yet gazed at their recipient and a restart if they have. Further, no perturbation in the talk occurs when speaker's gaze arrives at a hearer who is already looking at him. In essence, the present data suggest that when speaker's gaze reaches a recipient, that recipient should be gazing at the speaker.

Earlier sections of this chapter focused on the gaze of the hearer. In this section, those phenomena have been found to be but an aspect of a larger process through which the gaze of both speaker and hearer, including their avoidance as well as their contact, is organized.

Quantitative Description

One frequent request that has been made by readers of this analysis who are not themselves conversation analysts is for some quantitative measurement of the processes being investigated. I myself consider quantitative methodology not only premature but inappropriate to the type of phenomena here being investigated. However, to deal with questions that readers from other research backgrounds find both troublesome and legitimate, I will here attempt to provide at least some quantitative description.

In order to do this, a single 10-minute two-person conversation was examined in detail. This particular conversation was selected for a number of reasons. First, because of the limited number of participants, their seating configuration, and the outdoor setting which provided a great deal of light, the participants on this tape could be seen with a great deal of clarity.[23] Except for one brief sequence, both participants can be observed throughout the tape.[24] Second, the conversation was comparatively brief so that exhaustive analysis of it was possible. Third, there was available an audio-transcript of the conversation by Gail Jefferson, which had been checked against the original videotape by her and three other people.

All cases in which a party who was speaking brought her gaze to her coparticipant were noted, and the following frequencies were found:

		No restart	Restart
When speaker's gaze arrives hearer is	Gazing	97	2
	Not gazing	26	8

Quite clearly, restarts occur much more frequently when hearer is not

[23] For a clearer idea of how the participants were positioned, see Figures 3.1–3.5 in the next chapter. These figures are tracings from this conversation.

[24] This sequence (47 seconds long), in which someone else walked over and the camera zoomed back but still did not always include all participants, was excluded from analysis.

gazing that when she is.[25] When a chi-square is computed,[26] it is found to have a value of 13.888 and to be significant at the .01 level.

In 11 of the cases that were counted, the gaze of one party arrived during simultaneous speech.[27] In such a situation, who is to be treated as speaker and who as hearer may be at issue for the participants themselves.[28] In that this is one of the distinctions being used to organize the present data, these cases should perhaps not be included in the frequency distribution. When they are removed, the contingency table is found to have a chi-square value of 7.242 which is significant at the .01 level.

Our analysis in this chapter has focused specifically on turn-beginning. However, the frequencies just provided were for all cases in which a speaker's gaze reached a hearer. It might be argued that such a tabulation inflates the differences being examined, since it includes as separate events all of the looks a speaker gives her recipient during a long turn such as a story. The following are the frequencies found when analysis is restricted to gaze arriving at turn-beginning. The gazing–no restart cell includes two cases in which recipient's gaze was obtained through use of a pause.

		No restart	Restart
When speaker's gaze arrives hearer is	Gazing	24	1
	Not gazing	11	6

Again most restarts occur when a speaker gazes at a nongazing hearer.

[25] It should be emphasized that what I am trying to examine here is not every speech perturbation in the data (it is quite definitely *not* being argued that all speech perturbations are gaze related) but only the use of phrasal breaks in the specific interactive processes I am analyzing.

[26] Yates's correction for continuity was included in the computation of all chi-squares reported here.

[27] In six of those cases, the other party was gazing toward the party speaking; in five she was not. In no case was a restart produced just at the point of gaze arrival.

[28] Thus, in the following, both parties claim speakership when Marsha enters a new turn-constructional unit (note that neither party relinquishes within the overlap):

```
MARSHA:
           really a treat.    She was (      )ing guys to the room
                              [
                              O  h there were  always– dozens of tho:se,
                                                        [
    DIANNE:    _____, .............. X_____
```

For more detailed analysis of overlap, see Jefferson 1973.

When a chi-square is computed it is found to have a value of 5.059 which is significant at the .05 level.

One problem with the way in which statistical methodology is frequently used in the social sciences is that it provides a rationale for not engaging in detailed analysis of particular cases. Exceptions and examples that do not support the point being argued can be disregarded as "noise" if an acceptable level of significance is obtained. Despite the fact that the present frequency distribution supports my analysis, I find that it raises more questions than it answers. For example, though most restarts occur when hearer is not gazing, it is more likely that speaker will not produce a restart in such a situation than that he will. Of all the examples in the data, these 11 cases are the ones that would seem to provide the most interesting test of the analysis as well as the opportunity to learn something new about the phenomena being studied. Instead of treating these cases as statistically unimportant exceptions, one might therefore want to look at them carefully.

When the data are examined, it is found that in two of the cases where hearer is not gazing toward the speaker, she is none the less performing activities relevant to the talk in progress. In both cases, current speaker asks her recipient to remember something. One systematic component of the activity of searching for a word is looking into space rather than toward others present.[29] Indeed, in one of the examples, speaker displays explicit recognition of this activity and organizes her own talk with reference to it:

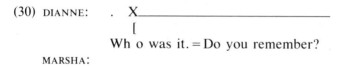

(30) DIANNE: . X_____
                      [
             Wh o was it. = Do you remember?
     MARSHA:

Here speaker talks about recipient being engaged in the task of remembering. Moreover, she does not even leave a space for her recipient to reply at the end of her first question. She is thus able to recognize in the course of her own talk that, rather than showing inattention, recipient's gaze aversion is involved in a specific activity which is relevant to the talk of the moment.

Quite clearly, recipient's lack of gaze in circumstances such as these is not a display of lack of hearership, and speakers do not treat it that way. Thus examples such as these highlight the fact that gaze toward the speaker is but one way of making visible proper hearership and that

[29] The practice of averting gaze while searching for a word has been frequently noted not only by students of gaze (Argyle and Cook 1976:122; Kendon 1967:41), but also by psychologists (Kinsbourne 1972) and ethnologists (Worth and Adair 1970:26).

participants have the competence to recognize that in some circumstances an activity that includes gaze aversion may be the most appropriate way to display involvement in the talk of the moment.

If these examples are removed from the no gaze–no restart cell of the contingency table, a chi-square of 6.104 which is significant at the .02 level is obtained.

When the remaining nine cases are examined, it is found that in four of them, though hearer is not yet gazing when speaker's gaze arrives, she is in the process of moving toward speaker. For example:

(31) MARSHA: .... X_____
              [
      A*no*ther interesting group were the one s from
                   [
  DIANNE: .... X_____

Recipients in these examples are thus visibly involved in activities relevant to hearership. The fact that no restarts occur suggest that speakers treat this activity as adequate to establish that proper hearership is present.

By paying attention to examples such as these we are able to refine our understanding of how the phenomena being examined are organized. Thus, though the sharp contrast between presence and absence of gaze is useful as an analytic point of departure, it appears that the distinctions the participants themselves make about what counts as gaze are somewhat more subtle. If these four examples are removed from the no gaze–no restart cell of the frequency distribution, a contingency table with a chi-square of 9.437 which is significant at the .01 level is obtained (the figure would of course be higher if these examples were counted as instances of hearer gaze).

When the remaining five cases are examined, it is found that in four of them speaker brings her gaze to hearer right at the beginning of the turn and that hearer starts to move her gaze very shortly after that:

(32) DIANNE: ... X_____ , , ,
        [
    (– –) We usetuh do some re ally a:wful things
              [
  MARSHA: .... X _____

(33) MARSHA: ..... X_____
       [
    But, a–another on e that went to school with me wa:s
          [
  DIANNE: .... X_____

(34) DIANNE: .... X_____

                      [
                      (– – –) Tch! *We* couldn't sta:nd her. so ba:dly we

                                                          [
MARSHA: .... X_____

(35) DIANNE: _____ , ,
                      Bro:colli pie I thin k that sounds grea:t.

                                           [
MARSHA: .... X_____

By moving right at turn-beginning, speaker has not allowed recipient
time to make her move first. In view of this, it is possible that recipient's
gaze can not yet be treated as relevantly absent. By moving quickly—
in a sense, as soon as can be reasonably expected—recipient shows that
she is in fact providing proper coparticipation in the turn.

One way to explore further the possibility that such cases are in fact
lawful exceptions would be to see what happens when speaker's gaze
is present early in the turn but hearer's movement does not begin until
the turn is well underway. Such cases would contrast with those we
have just discussed in that there would be a space of noticeable duration
in which speaker was gazing but recipient was not displaying coparticipation in any way. Under these circumstances, it could not be argued
that recipient was moving as soon as reasonably possible. When such
examples (which did not occur in the particular tape that is the current
focus of analysis) are examined, it is found that recipient's gaze-arrival
is marked with a restart:

(5) BARBARA: _____
                      Brian you're gonna ha v– You kids'll *have* to go

                                           [
BRIAN: ... X_____

(36) TOMMY: _____
                      You agree wi th– You agree with your aunt on

                                  [
PUMPKIN: X_____

(37) GARY: _____
                      He's a policeman in Bellview and he :, I guess he–

                                          [
MIKE: .. X_____

The data are consistent with the possibility that speakers do sometimes distinguish hearers who have not been given time to move from those whose coparticipation is visibly late.

It should be noted, however, that this is an area in which speakers do seem to have some range of choice as to how a particular case will be treated.[30] Note, for example, the similarity in the timing of recipient's movement in Example (36), where a restart occurs, and Example (34), where the sentence continues without perturbation.

In some cases, recipient's movement might be treated as not simply late but noticeably absent. In the data just examined, the restart was not produced until recipient's gaze actually arrived; recipient was able to begin her movement without visible prompting from speaker. However in the following, when recipient has not moved by the time that the turn is well underway, speaker interrupts the talk in progress to produce a restart which acts as a request for gaze:

(38) BETTY: _____
        I had about three different– I hear it <A bout three
                                                        [
      PAM: .... X_____

(12) BETTY: _____
        The first catch <I mean Susie– you kn ow she just
                                                   [
      PAM: .... X _____

In general, when gaze is requested with a restart, recipient's gaze arrival is not marked by another phrasal break—as is shown, for example, by (7)–(9). In (38), however, a second restart is produced when recipient's gaze arrives.[31] In (12), the transition movement of the recipient is covered with a "you know" so that the substantive beginning of the sentence does not occur until the recipient's gaze actually reaches the speaker.[32] It would thus appear that recipient's very noticeable delay in these examples is being treated as especially serious, getting both a request for gaze and a new sentence beginning when gaze arrives.

The data that we have been examining suggest that the longer recipient's movement is delayed, the more consequential its absence becomes

---

[30] Indeed, on some occasions, even early movement might lead to a restart (note Example [27]).

[31] Syntactically, the words spoken here could be a continuation of the prior talk. However, speaker's intonation makes it clear that a new unit is being begun.

[32] "Y'know" in this example may function analogously to the use of potentially deletable terms in positions of possible overlap as analyzed by Jefferson (1973).

for the talk in progress. If hearer is gazing when speaker's gaze arrives, no perturbation occurs in the talk. If recipient is moving when speaker's gaze arrives, or if the movement starts shortly after speaker is gazing but still near the beginning of the turn, the talk may proceed without interruption, though restarts might sometimes occur. If recipient's movement does not start until after a visible delay, a restart will be produced when gaze at last arrives. If recipient does not even begin to move within a reasonable period of time, speaker will not only interrupt the talk in progress to make a request, but might also place a second restart at the point of gaze arrival, something not done in other cases where the restart is used as a request. It thus appears that what is at issue is not simply absence of gaze but the timing of that absence relative to other events within the turn. In essence, if recipient's involvement in the turn can be seen as noticeably late or absent, then the talk in progress may be treated as impaired.

It may be noted that three distinct places where a restart might be placed have now been described. Two of these are at points where the gaze of one party reaches the other: First, when speaker's gaze reaches a nongazing recipient:

SPEAKER: ...... X_____

                                                 [

UTTERANCE: u u u u u u u u u Restart u u u u u

                                                          [

RECIPIENT   .... X_____

and, second, when the late-arriving gaze of a recipient reaches a gazing speaker:

SPEAKER: _____

UTTERANCE: u u u u u u u u u Restart u u u u u

                                         [

                                         X_____

RECIPIENT:

The third place where a speaker might produce a restart is when recipient's movement is noticeably delayed. The production of the restart in this latter situation is not coordinated with the gaze arrival of either speaker or hearer.

SPEAKER: _____

UTTERANCE: u u u u u u u u u u u u Restart u u u u u u u u u

                                                            [

RECIPIENT: ..... X_____

Restarts in the first and third positions act as requests.

Returning to the tape that has provided the basis for this discussion, there is one turn which has not yet been examined, Line 3 of the following, in which speaker gazed at a nongazing recipient but did not produce a restart.

(39) MARSHA: _____
1.   Yeah right.
     DIANNE: _____

     DIANNE: , , ,
2.   in Mount Pleasant.
     MARSHA: _____

     MARSHA: _____, ,
3.   r:Right.
     DIANNE:

It can be observed that this turn, which is extremely short, does not initiate a new activity or strip of talk, but rather performs a specific, limited operation on the just prior turn—that is, it shows agreement. By virtue of its length, sequential position, and retrospective—rather than prospective—orientation, this turn is quite different from most of the other turns that we have been examining. In many respects it is more like a "back channel" agreement than a substantive turn in its own right.

One other phenomenon, which was often present in both turns where a restart was produced and turns where it was not, was withdrawal of gaze from a nongazing recipient, frequently before that party's gaze arrived.

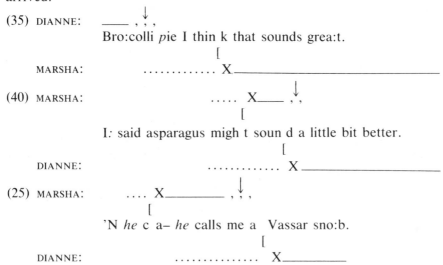

(35) DIANNE: _____ , ↓ , ,
                Bro:colli *p*ie I thin k that sounds grea:t.
                                    [
     MARSHA: .... X_____

(40) MARSHA: ..... X____ , ↓ , ,
                                          [
                I: said asparagus migh t soun d a little bit better.
                                              [
     DIANNE: .... X _____

(25) MARSHA: .... X_____ , ↓ , ,
                           [
                'N *he* c a– *he* calls me a Vassar sno:b.
                                        [
     DIANNE: .... X_____

Such an action both shows an orientation to the dispreferred status of gazing at a nongazing recipient and constitutes a way of minimizing that state of affairs.

The analytic gains that have been made by looking carefully at the cases that did not fit our original analysis would seem to lie less in the increases in statistical significance that have been obtained (indeed, if that were all that were at issue what has been done here would surely be overkill) than in the gains that have been made in our understanding of the detailed organization of the phenomena being investigated. For example, we now have a more precise understanding of what counts as gaze for the participants, when it can be seen as late, and some of the ways in which specific types of gaze aversion (for example that found in [30]) might constitute not signs of inattention, but rather displays of involvement in the talk of the moment.

In that the frequency distribution just examined was organized in terms of speaker's gaze arrival it did not capture cases where restarts were used to request gaze before speaker brought her gaze to recipient. This happened on seven occasions which seemed to fall into two classes. In one, the restart occurs right at turn-beginning:

(41) MARSHA:

But no:, uh–thut– uh the *Tex* ans were the ones that

[

DIANNE: .... X_____

(42) MARSHA:

But the– the yea r after we left they

[

DIANNE: ..... X_____

(43) MARSHA:

Bu:t.uh, but there– there was the Beth el Park– crew,

[

DIANNE: .... X_____

These restarts appear to be rather different from the restarts produced when a speaker's gaze reaches a nongazing hearer. First, they occur so early in the turn that almost no information is available about the substance of the speaker's initial sentence. The talk in progress is less marked as impaired than not fully begun. Second, the restart frequently occurs within a flurry of other hesitations and phrasal breaks. It would seem that in cases such as these, rather than making visible trouble in the talk so far produced, phrasal breaks are being used to indicate right at turn-beginning that gaze will be relevant to the talk about to be produced.[33]

---

[33] As was noted earlier (Note 19), turns with such a structure are not inconsistent with the presence of encoding processes that might be in progress when an utterance is begun.

In a second class of restarts without speaker gaze, failure by recipient to coparticipate appropriately in the turn is shown in other ways. In the following example, which will be considered in more detail in the next chapter, speaker leaves a pause after an initial phrasal break but recipient fails to move during the pause:

(44) MARSHA: .... X_____
                                                 [
              But I: uh, (0.9) Do:n uh: :, Don's fam ily moved,
                                              [
      DIANNE: ...... X_____

Here, even though speaker has not yet gazed, lack of appropriate coparticipation by recipient is shown by her failure to answer a request for gaze.

This tape also contains 19 turns in which no gaze between speaker and hearer occurs. As was noted earlier, such turns are not inconsistent with the present line of analysis and will be examined in more detail in the next chapter.

To summarize, detailed analysis of the tape examined here supports the line of argument that has been developed in this chapter and also provides the opportunity to conceptualize the processes involved in a more precise fashion.

Gaze Withdrawal in Midturn

For clarity, analysis of the achievement of an appropriate state of mutual gaze has so far focused on the beginning of the turn. However gaze is relevant throughout the turn. The same procedures utilized to establish an initial state of mutual gaze at the beginning of the turn can be employed to renegotiate an appropriate state of gaze between the participants later in the turn. In the following example, a speaker loses the gaze of her recipient in midturn. By producing an "uh" followed by a pause, she constructs a request for a hearer. The further development of her utterance is delayed through use of the pause until the gaze of her recipient is once again secured:

(45) MARGIE: _____
              And he put it a:ll the way up my ba:ck which was a
      ROSS: _____ , , , ,

      MARGIE: _____
              big uh (– – – – – – –) *help* on that.
                                   [
      ROSS: .... X_____

The following provides another example of such a process:

(46) TINA:
                      _____

You remember that– that white (1.0) that sweater
       [

MARLENE: ......X—— , , ,
TINA:
                      _____

sweate r with the (0.6) it was Earl's,
     [

MARLENE: .... X_____

The speaker thus has the ability to request and obtain the gaze of his recipient not just at turn-beginning, but throughout the turn.

It is, however, possible for gaze-withdrawal in midturn to be found acceptable. Note that such an act is not exactly the same as failing to gaze at turn-beginning. The party withdrawing has already displayed orientation to the speaker and the talk of the moment with the gaze so far provided within the turn. In this sense, subsequent positions within the turn differ from turn-beginning.[34]

In the following, recipient withdraws gaze in midturn, but, while doing so, performs other actions to show speaker that she is still acting as a hearer:

(47) MARSHA:
                      X_____
                  [

There was a   girl named Candy

DIANNE:
            _____
                Nod   Nod

MARSHA:
            _____

McCrady. who li ved over, in the ee–East
          [
        Mmhm,

DIANNE:
            _____ , , , , , , , ,
        Nod   *NOD*   *NOD*

MARSHA:
            _____ , ,

End. It was a very *ob*vious *dif*ference.
          [
        Mm
DIANNE: nod   Nod

[34] For more detailed analysis of how gaze withdrawal is performed with reference to the sequential structure of the talk of the moment, and of how both speaker and recipient orient to gaze withdrawal, see Goodwin (forthcoming).

As recipient withdraws, she uses both a vocal ''Mmhm'' and a very noticeable nod to show that she is still attending the talk in progress. Further, it appears that these actions constitute somewhat special displays of hearership. For example, vocal signs of attention do not occur until recipient withdraws her gaze; nods do occur while recipient is gazing, but the nods produced at the point of withdrawal are visibly accentuated. Thus, as she withdraws her gaze, recipient mitigates the reading of diminished hearership that might be made by performing other actions to show that hearership is still being provided.[35]

After gaze has been withdrawn, recipient sits with her eyes in front of her in a middle-distance look (this is indicated in the transcript with ''θ'').

(48) MARSHA: _____

Candy McCrady. who li ved over, in the ee–East End.

        [

        Mmhm

DIANNE: _____ , , , , , , , , ,

Nod   Nod   NOD   NOD   nod

————— , ,

MARSHA: It was a very *ob*vious *dif*ference. = And the girls

      [

      Mm

DIANNE: θθθθθθθθθθθθθθθθθθθθθθθθθθθθθθθθθθθθθθθθθθθθθθθθθθθθ

      Nod

MARSHA: .. X_____

   [

fro m Se*wick*ley were very *ob*viously different from

DIANNE: θθθθθθθθθθθθθθθθθθθθθθθθθθθθθθθθθθθθθθθθθθθθθθθθθθθθθ

MARSHA: ————— , , ,

the Bethel *P*ark group.

DIANNE: θθθθθθθθθθθθθθθθθθθθθθ

It can be observed that speaker returns her gaze to recipient while she is seated with this middle-distance look, but does not produce any request for gaze at this point in her talk. The middle-distance look is thus treated

---

[35] The way in which recipient withdraws her gaze here constitutes an instance of activity-occupied withdrawal, a phenomenon that will be examined in more detail in the next chapter.

as an acceptable display of hearership. However, at least in this data, such an action is not a free alternative to gaze toward the speaker, but rather something that has been made visible as a display of hearership for the current talk through the special sequential work done as gaze was withdrawn from speaker.

Participants thus orient to gaze-withdrawal as an act that may be interpreted as a display of diminished hearership. Speaker has the ability to request that gaze be returned by using the same procedures available for securing gaze at turn-beginning. However, recipient may establish that hearership is still being provided by performing other talk-relevant actions, such as nods and vocal displays of hearership, as gaze is withdrawn.

Securing the Gaze of Multiple Recipients

Such apparently minute events as phrasal breaks not only operate on a selected recipient, but are capable of coordinating the actions of several participants. Such coordination might be manifested in a variety of ways.

First, the gaze of several recipients may reach the speaker at the same point and at this point the speaker may produce a phrasal break:

(49) BEA: _____
             Well they've done away wi th (0.3) They've done away
                                     [
     JIM: . . . . X_____
                                     [
     ETHYL: . . . . X_____

(50) PAM: . . . . X_____
                     [
             So wha'ya nie–? Where you living now.
                         [
     TINA: . . . . X_____
                     [
     ED: . . . . X_____

Alternatively, in cases where the phrasal break acts as a request, several recipients may begin to move just after the phrasal break:

(51) CHIL:

    She– she's reaching the p– She' s at the point I'm

                                            [

    NANCY: .... X_____⌐_____

    HELEN: .... X_____

(9) JOE: .... X _____

                              [

    My mother told m e that– *We* had a col d water flat

                                      [

    PAT: .... X_____

                                 [

    GINNY: .... X_____

In other cases, a phrasal break that marks the arrival of one party might simultaneously act to request the gaze of a second party:

(52) GORDIE: What– *What* is uh: u h: Mitch   got anyway,

                            [

    ETHYL: ..... X ____⌐____

    BARBARA: .... └X_____

(16) MICHAEL: *Who* kno:ws, ˙hh (– – – – –) nu:mbers and letters (huh),

                           [

    DON: .... X ____⌐____

    ANN: .... └X_____

Finally, the procedures being examined might be applied repetitively throughout the turn. For example, in the following, a first pause has the effect of obtaining one recipient and a second pause obtains the gaze of a second recipient:

(53) CURT:

    How's uh, (– – – – – – – – –) Jimmy Linder. (– – – – – –)

                           [

    GARY: ...... X _____

    MIKE: ....

    CURT:

    He' ⌐s– he's   on the USAC, (0.1) trail isn't he?

    GARY: └_____

    MIKE: ..... └X_____, , , _____   _____

The procedures examined in this chapter for achieving an appropriate state of mutual gaze between speaker and hearer are thus available throughout the turn and are capable of coordinating the gaze of several recipients with the utterance of the speaker.

Modifying Gaze and Talk to Achieve Appropriate Mutual Gaze

Some basic resources for organizing gaze within the turn at talk have now been examined. On occasion, however, additional processes may be involved. The following provides an example of how a speaker might both modify her own nonvocal action and construct a variety of vocal actions addressed to different recipients in order to negotiate an appropriate state of mutual gaze at turn-beginning. The speaker, beginning to construct an utterance, starts to bring her gaze to its recipient. However, her chosen recipient does not move into orientation toward her. Just as her eyes reach this recipient, she pulls them away from him.

(54) KATE: .... X, ,
                              [
       You know Don Mas ters
  NED:

By modifying her emerging gaze movement, speaker manages to avoid gazing at a nongazing hearer.

However, the problem of securing the gaze of her recipient remains. In the examples so far considered, a phrasal break has been used to accomplish this task; in the present example, the speaker produces an explicit summons at this point. However, the summons is officially directed to someone other than the recipient she has just turned away from: As she begins to produce this utterance, the speaker is taking a Kleenex from her purse to give to her son who is eating a dripping ice cream bar. When she moves her eyes away from her first proposed recipient, she moves them toward her son and summons his attention with the word "Here!"

     KATE: .... N, , ... <u>Son</u>
                                 [[
     You know Don Mas ters = Her e!
  NED:

Despite the fact that the summons is officially directed to someone other than the speaker's first proposed recipient, as a marked break in the flow of an utterance, it may constitute a general signal that the services of a hearer are required (as has already been noted, several recipients may start to move after a phrasal break). And in fact the summons does secure the gaze of both the speaker's son and the original proposed recipient of her turn.

```
KATE:   ................... N, ....... Son
                            [          [
        You know Don Mas ters = Her e!
NED:                                   ... X
SON:                                   ...... X
```

In effect, the speaker is able to utilize this summons to secure the gaze of her original recipient while simultaneously arguing that in fact the summons is not directed to him but to someone else. Several purposes are served by such a structure of action. First, no problem in the state of mutual gaze between the speaker and her first proposed recipient is officially recognized. Second, mothers are entitled to perform certain actions to their children that they would not be permitted to perform to other adults. With this summons, the speaker chastizes her son for not being attentive to her and taking the Kleenex sooner. She is thus able to complain about a coparticipant's lack of attentiveness without officially lodging the complaint against the party whose failure to pay attention to her caused her to move to her son in the first place.

The subsequent course of the utterance provides some evidence that the speaker in fact recognizes the possibility that her summons might secure the gaze not only of her son but also of her first proposed recipient. Specifically, immediately after the summons, the speaker returns to the onward development of her original sentence:

```
KATE:   ................... N, , ..... Son
                            [            [
        You know Don Mas ters = Her e!  pi:tche d. hor:seshoe s a
                                           [
NED:                              ....... X _____
SON:                              ...................... X__
```

When the speaker's summons obtains the gaze of her original recipient, the possibility emerges that the turn can after all be constructed so that the speaker's gaze reaches her recipient only after her recipient has begun to gaze at her. After her recipient begins to move into orientation toward her, the speaker starts to shift her gaze to him:

KATE: .... N, , ... <u>Son___</u> ....
                                    [[
          You know Don Mas ters = Her e! pit:che d.
                                                          [
NED: .... X_____

KATE: .... <u>Ned_____</u>
                      [
          hor:seshoe s a week er so ago with Chuck?
NED: _____

When the speaker's eyes reach her recipient, she finds that she is already being gazed at by him. However, as we have seen, such a state of affairs is in fact the achieved product of rather careful work on her part: She first avoided looking at a recipient who was not looking at her by transforming the beginning of a look toward him into a look toward her son. She then added an explicit summons to her turn, also apparently addressed to her son. Only after this summons has obtained her original recipient's gaze does she return her gaze to him. The achievement of appropriate mutual gaze in this turn thus involves changes in the emerging structure of both the movement speaker is making and the utterance she is producing.

It may be noted that this example, as well as the other analysis developed in this chapter, strongly challenges recent work (Rutter *et al.* 1977; Rutter and Stephenson 1979) arguing that eye contact is simply a chance event.

Conclusion

In this chapter some procedures available to participants in natural conversation for coordinating the separate actions of speaker and hearer in the construction of the turn at talk have been investigated. It has been found that the gaze of both parties is a relevant feature of many turns in face-to-face conversation and that the participants have access to, and make use of, systematic procedures for achieving appropriate states of mutual gaze.[36] The use of these procedures produces characteristic phe-

[36] For some analysis of ways in which establishing mutual attention to some common

nomena in the speaker's utterance, including restarts, pauses, and hesitations of various types. These phenomena have usually been attributed to processes internal to the speaker and have been treated as performance errors on his part. The present analysis has shown that, though such phenomena can reflect difficulty the speaker is having in producing his utterance, they can also function interactively, and indeed demonstrate the speaker's attention to the construction of coherent sentences for his recipient.

---

phenomenon might be important to the language acquisition process, and the structure of a child's early utterances, see Atkinson (1979), Ochs, Schieffelin, and Platt (1979), and Scollon (1976, 1979).

It should also be noted that the structures that have been described here permit there to be variation in the amount of gaze that occurs within a turn (see, for example, p. 75). The systematic presence of such variability has a number of implications. On the one hand it suggests that quantitative measures of overall frequency (the method which has usually been used to study gaze in psychology and sociology) may not be an appropriate way to study the organization of gaze as an activity in its own right. Not only does summing the duration of separate events lump together phenomena that participants treat as quite distinct (for example, lack of gaze may mean quite different things at different places), but the possibility for considerable variation in the frequency of a particular type of event is built into the system itself. It is thus not at all surprising that attempts to use frequency to uncover the organization of phenomena such as eye-contact are able to come to the conclusion that they are just chance events. On the other hand, the possibility for variation provides the resources for gaze during talk to be turned to the service of a variety of other social processes such as establishing intimacy, dominance, or hostility (for a review of much of the research investigating the use of gaze in such processes, see Argyle and Cook 1976).

3

Notes on the Organization of Engagement

The phenomenon dealt with in the last chapter, a state of mutual gaze within a speaker–hearer relationship, is of course but one of many patterns of orientation that participants might assume toward each other during the course of a conversation. The present chapter will investigate some of the ways in which different structures of orientation are organized, how participants move from one of the alternatives open to them to another, and the consequences that such displays have for the organization of their talk. This analysis thus continues a line of investigation begun in the last chapter, but attempts to place within a broader framework the engagement structure that was studied there.

Engagement Displays

The present analysis will restrict itself entirely to events occurring during the time that a state of copresence that has already been established is being sustained.

Within such limitations, the fact that the participants are physically copresent is a constant. However, the form that their presence to each other takes is not. This can be seen most easily by comparing Figures 3.1 and 3.2, which are tracings from a videotape of a single conversation.

In Figure 3.1, A is noticeably gazing toward B.[1] A thus shows, first, that B is being publicly observed, and, second, that A herself is positioned to take account of what B is doing. In Figure 3.2, however, A is noticeably gazing away from B. B is thus not being publicly scrutinized by A, and A is not observably positioned to perceive all of the actions B might perform and thereby take them into account in the performance of her own actions.[2] For convenience such displays of orientation or non-orientation by one party toward another may be referred to as engagement displays.

It may be noted that a display of disengagement treats someone who is physically present as in a certain sense not relevantly present, that is, not the subject of observation or a locus for joint, collaborative activity. Displays about engagement thus permit the alternation between presence and nonpresence to be reestablished within a domain bounded by physical copresence and to become a relevant feature of activities occurring there.

One feature of engagement displays is that the display of one individual proposes something about the participation status of the other. For example, by displaying engagement toward another, one treats that other as available for such observation and coparticipation and not as someone then occupied with private activities that are not to be observed. Similarly, by displaying disengagement toward another, one treats that other as not then performing activities requiring the coparticipation of the disengaged party.

The engagement display of one party thus shows an orientation to the displayed engagement of the other. However, that other party is also performing a similar analysis with the effect that his display is simultaneously being organized with reference to the engagement state of the first. Each party's body thus displays an analysis of what the other is doing and by that very display constrains what the other can or should be doing if he is to organize his body in terms of a similar analysis. This raises the issue, to be examined later in this chapter, of how structures with such simultaneous organization can be changed. For the present, it is sufficient to note that the mutual orientation of the participants in Figures 3.1 and 3.2 is consistent with this line of reasoning—that is, their separate displays are compatible with each other.

---

[1] In this chapter, because references to individual participants are numerous, in order to simplify discussion, participants will be referred to by letters rather than names.

[2] As subsequent analysis will make more clear, what is at issue here are official displays about what is being perceived and attended to, rather than the actual limits of the participants' ability to monitor each other.

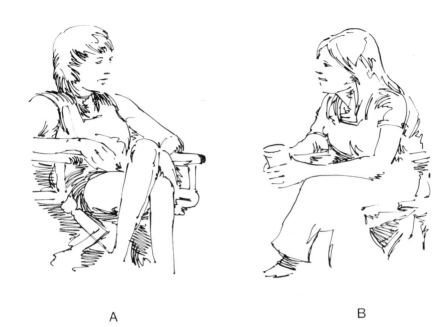

A

B

FIGURE 3.1

A

B

FIGURE 3.2

Disengagement

Displays of mutual disengagement, such as that found in Figure 3.2, characteristically occur during lapses in the conversation. This temporal embeddedness within an ongoing state of multiparty talk is in fact manifested spatially in the way in which the participants organize themselves relative to each other. First, unlike what happens when a state of copresence is broken,[3] the participants remain in close physical proximity to each other. Second, though the upper parts of their bodies, and especially their gaze, are directed away from each other, their lower bodies remain oriented toward each other.[4] When states of disengagement are examined closely, it is found that, despite their displayed lack of orientation toward each other, the participants are in fact monitoring each other's actions quite closely.

Just after the moment stopped in Figure 3.2, A sweeps her head past B (Figure 3.3). She ends the movement by recognizably looking toward something in another direction, at which point B moves her own gaze in the same direction and begins to noticeably search the scene (Figure 3.4). Thus, though B had not been officially gazing toward A, she notices, and reacts to, a movement of A. Moreover, her reaction shows, not simply a recognition that some movement has occurred, but an analysis of the activity being displayed with the movement: That is, rather than turning to the party making the movement, and thereby treating it as a movement to her, B interprets A's gaze as doing a distinct recognizable activity—making a noticing—an activity that B might also engage in by moving her own gaze in the same direction. Thus participants are not only monitoring each other's actions, but engaging in ongoing analysis of those actions, even as they carefully display lack of orientation toward each other.

When A's gaze sweep is examined in more detail, it is found to occur in two distinct stages. At the end of the first movement (Figure 3.5), A does not yet display involvement in an activity such as a noticing, but instead looks off into space with a middle-distance look. B does not respond to this movement but instead continues to display disengagement from A's activities.

[3] For detailed treatment of such phenomena, see Goffman (1963), Heath (1979a, 1979b), and Schegloff and Sacks (1973).

[4] The participants thus continue to collaboratively sustain what Kendon (1977:Chapter 5) has called an F-formation. In his analysis of the F-formation, Kendon demonstrates that the mutual orientation being displayed by the participants' lower bodies is actively and collaboratively sustained. From one perspective, the present analysis is an attempt to delineate some of the alternatives for copresence available within that framework and the ways in which these alternatives are organized and made relevant by the actions of the participants.

A   B

FIGURE 3.3

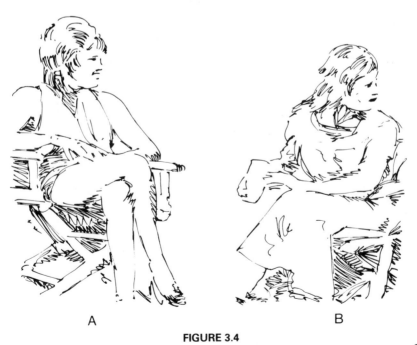

A   B

FIGURE 3.4

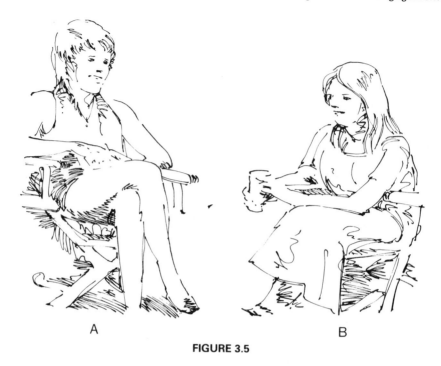

A   B

FIGURE 3.5

These data raise the possibility that one feature of the analysis B is engaged in is that of distinguishing actions of A that provide the possibility of coparticipation in them (such as a noticing) from actions (such as "staring into space") that do not permit such a possibility. Examining activities in terms of such features would seem to be relevant to the embedded sequential position within which the analysis is performed. First, even while displaying disengagement, the participants are situated within, and collaboratively sustaining, a framework proposing the relevance of collaborative activity such as talk. The absence of such multiparty activity is therefore a relevant and noticeable absence. Second, the resumption of collaborative activity will involve a change in the actions and participation status of the party doing the analysis. Such a distinction is therefore relevant to that party and consequential for what he is to be doing. Monitoring for the resumption of collaborative activity might therefore be one of the systematic activities that disengaged parties perform.[5]

[5] Analysis to be developed at a later point in this chapter will show that opportunities for returning to engagement are not evenly distributed throughout disengagement, but rather emerge with special salience at particular points within it, such as when various

Such phenomena shed further light on the events examined in the last chapter. Processes of reengagement do not operate in a vacuum, but rather build upon the types of analyses participants are already engaged in during disengagement (for example, monitoring for the possibility of reengagement) and the availability they manifest to each other by the collaborative framework of orientation being sustained by their lower bodies.[6] The use of an action such as a phrasal break to secure a co-participant's gaze succeeds in part by dealing with a possibility that is already being treated as a relevant one by participants.

During periods of disengagement, participants are explicitly displaying lack of orientation toward each other and nonparticipation in collaborative activities such as talk. However, the data examined so far support the possibility that such official displays of noncollaboration are in fact organized interactively and collaboratively sustained by the careful, systematic work of participants who maintain an ongoing monitoring of each other and an orientation toward the possibility of relevant changes in their mutual participation status.

Entering Disengagement

Analysis will now turn to investigation of how participants move from a state of engagement to a state of disengagement. To simplify the discussion, much of this analysis will focus on a single strip of conversation. The participants in this conversation, both of whom went to the same 2-year college, Marjorie Webster, have been discussing college days. We will first examine how the transition from talk to disengagement is accomplished at the end of Line 11. Next we will examine how talk is organized once disengagement has been entered, focusing in particular on Line 13. It will be found that the talk here is produced within an engagement framework quite different from that analyzed in the last chapter. Finally, we will look at how the participants might make use

---

activities come to recognizable completion. Insofar as this is the case, participants do not engage in uniform and homogeneous monitoring, but rather treat a strip of disengagement as a structured field of action.

[6] Thus Kendon (1973:37) notes that

each participant, by maintaining a spatial position, posture and orientation that is appropriate to his role in the gathering, signals to the others that he is committed to joint engagement with them. In so doing he signals that he is claiming certain rights as well as taking on certain obligations. He claims the right to listen and to speak, but he has an obligation also to attend and to speak when addressed. . . .

of the engagement possibilities available to them to manifest different types of coparticipation in the talk of the moment. This stretch of talk will thus provide the opportunity to examine in a systematic fashion a range of phenomena relevant to the organization of engagement.

(1)
```
 1.  A:  No I:, (we-) wouldn't of fit in there either I'm su:re
 2.      but it's (0.2) a hell of a lot better than uh, (0.8)
 3.      Marjorie Webster.
 4.          (0.4)
 5.  A:  The most ih- the most ama:zing thing was to see the
 6.      tuition we pai:d, hhh and to go over: and I was a
 7.      cheerleader (when I went) there, and we'd go over
 8.      to Mount Vernon? and play a ga:me? and see Mount Vernon.
 9.          (0.7)
10.  A:  Christ it was just go:rgeous. It was so beautiful.
11.      And our place was such a dump compared to it.
12.          (1.2)
13.  B:  It really was a dump.
14.          (0.5)
15.  A:  Yeah and I know we paid about the same a-amount of
16.      tuition. I think our tuition when I went there was
17.      one of the highest it was the highest in the country.
18.      for even (a) four year college it was incredible.
19.          (0.8)
20.  A:  And it went up, (0.2) the second year I was the:re.
21.          (2.0)
22.  A:  But I: uh,
23.          (0.9)
24.  A:  Do:n uh::, Don's family moved into (Serrano Park)
```

During the silence in Line 12, the participants display mutual disengagement toward each other. Analysis will begin by investigating how the transition from the talk preceding it to this state of disengagement is accomplished.

OPERATIONS BY RECIPIENT DURING TALK

One principal place where hearers display their understanding of a piece of talk, and where speakers can look to see if such understanding has been adequate and appropriate, is in a next utterance. The absence of an adjacently placed subsequent utterance to the talk in Line 11 raises the question of whether the work that such a next utterance does is absent. Thus one issue that may be posed by the occurrence of disengagement after a strip of talk is whether the talk that preceded it has been understood, attended to, and dealt with in a relevant fashion by its recipient.

When a visual record of this conversation is examined, it can be seen that, though recipient does not produce talk-relevant actions immediately subsequent to A's turn, she does perform operations on it while it is being spoken. Over the talk in Line 10 (beginning at the word "gorgeous"), she produces a series of nods. Moreover, these nods are not only seen by the speaker, but seem to be organized precisely so as to be seen. They begin just after the speaker, who has briefly turned her head away, returns her gaze to the recipient.

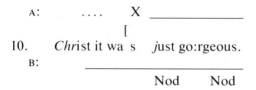

Because of their placement at particular points in the talk, actions such as these nods enable a recipient to display, not simply hearership, but some aspect of his understanding of the talk then being produced. Indeed, as the work of M. Goodwin (1979, 1980a) on mutual monitoring has shown, such displays may permit speakers to find even as they are talking that recipient's ongoing understanding of that talk is in some way inadequate. Speakers may then modify their talk to obtain more appropriate understanding. Thus, in this data, recipient's nods and speaker's acceptance of them permit the participants to collaboratively establish that recipient is operating on the talk in some systematic fashion and that speaker is finding no problems in her understanding of it. Insofar as this process provides some demonstration that the talk in progress has been attended to and dealt with in a relevant fashion by its recipient, some of the issues raised by the occurrence of silence after this talk are resolved; the talk has been ratified as a relevant event within the conversation through actions of recipient as well as speaker.

Nodding during a turn in no way precludes the possibility that recipient might produce subsequent talk to that turn or that speaker might expect such talk. Thus, although recipient's operations show that the talk has been attended to, they do not deal with the issue of whether the space just after the talk is or is not to be treated as a place where further talk is relevant.

Analysis will now turn to investigation of some of the systematic operations participants perform to collaboratively establish that at the termination of this turn further talk is not immediately relevant.

VISIBLE WITHDRAWAL FROM TALK BY SPEAKER

Further observation of the data reveals that, shortly after recipient begins to nod, speaker withdraws her gaze:

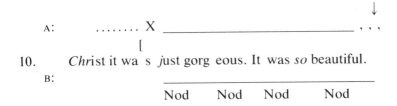

This raises the possibility that a speaker might use presence or absence of gaze toward recipient to display whether or not a next utterance is expected from recipient. However, speakers look away from their recipients quite frequently during talk without in any way proposing that their recipients may/should start to disengage from the talk. The silence in Line 9 of the present data provides a good example. Speaker withdraws her gaze from her recipient at the beginning of this silence and continues to look away from her until the word "was" in Line 10. However, during this silent look-away, speaker continues to produce her telling, performing an eye roll and head shake that provide a visual version of the assessment spoken in Line 10:[7]

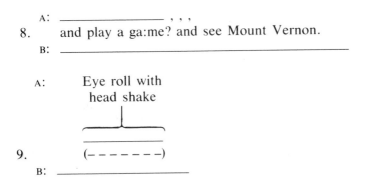

---

[7] For more detailed analysis of how participants utilize head shakes in the production of assessments, see M. Goodwin (1980a).

A: .... X_____

                  [
10.   *Ch*rist it wa s *j*ust gorgeous.

B: _____

Though speaker both withdraws her gaze and becomes silent here she is still actively involved in producing her talk.

If only some gaze withdrawals are disengagement-implicative, the issue arises as to how recipients recognize these and distinguish them from those that are not. The events just noted would suggest that recipients do not attend to the gaze withdrawal as an isolated event, but rather analyze it with reference to other activities the speaker is performing at that moment.

At this point in the conversation A has a lit cigarette in her hand. During the talk in Line 10, the cigarette is held slightly to the side of her face with its tip pointing upward. As speaker's head starts to move away from her recipient at the end of "beautiful," the hand with the cigarette is dropped to the front of her mouth and the cigarette pointed forward. Thus, as Line 11 is entered, the cigarette has been moved from a holding position to a preinhaling position. Such positioning of the cigarette makes the activity that A is performing here not simply gazing away from her hearer but rather withdrawal in preparation for another activity, one that does not involve the coparticipation (for example, through gaze) of the present recipient.

A's activities at this point thus have a rather distinctive character. She is still performing actions within the conversation, and in fact producing talk, but doing this with something less than full engagement, as shown by both the withdrawal of her gaze from her recipient (which is not offered as an event in the talk as the gaze withdrawal in Line 9 was) and her displayed preparation for engagement in another activity, smoking. Thus, in comparison with the talk that preceded it, the talk in Line 11 is done while speaker is manifesting diminished engagement in the conversation, which is no longer the exclusive focus of the activities her body is performing.

RECIPIENT WITHDRAWAL

The events described in the last section may constitute displays that recipient can attend to as relevant for the organization of her own actions. During the talk-relevant look-away in Line 9 recipient continued to gaze steadily at the speaker. However, just after speaker withdraws her gaze and repositions her cigarette in Line 11, recipient withdraws her own gaze from the speaker:

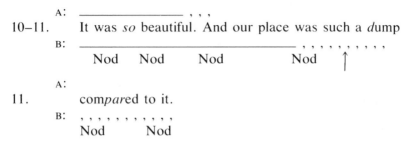

It was noted earlier that after speaker's gaze returned in Line 10, recipient began to nod. As recipient withdraws her gaze during Line 11 she continues to perform these nods. Recipient thus continues to co-participate in the turn, and perform specific actions relevant to the talk, even as she withdraws her gaze from the speaker; the withdrawal is occupied by talk-relevant activities.

Examining the data more closely it can be observed that the nods done during withdrawal are not performed in the same way as those done during full engagement; their pace and tempo are subtly but noticeably slowed (the transcription is not able to capture this distinction). Thus, though recipient's nods continue to perform actions relevant to the talk even as withdrawal is accomplished, these actions are performed in a way that is sensitive to the changes in engagement states that are occurring.

ACTIVITY-OCCUPIED WITHDRAWAL

The way in which recipient overlays talk-relevant acts with simultaneous moves away from talk is structurally analogous to what the speaker herself is doing at this point, that is, continuing to talk while withdrawing from her recipient and positioning herself for entry into a different activity. Organizing a withdrawal in this fashion has a number of consequences. First, the boundary between full engagement and mutual disengagement is not structured as a sharp, clear break. Instead, participants are afforded a space within which they can reorganize their bodies and actions in a way that both is relevant to the change and permits them to display to each other their proposals about and understanding of what is happening. Speaker is thus able to display upcoming disengagement in time for her recipient to organize her actions relative to it and does not find herself arriving at termination, or even beyond it, with the gaze of a hearer (a state of affairs that might well continue to propose the relevance of her identity as a speaker). Second, insofar as moves toward disengagement are overlaid with talk-relevant activities, the act of disattending each other never emerges for either party as a noticeable, recognizable activity in its own right. When each participant finishes her talk-relevant activities, she finds that she and her coparticipant are no longer in orientation toward each other, that state of affairs having been systematically achieved but never made visible as an explicit act of disaffiliation. Indeed, the transition itself never emerges as an explicit event in the talk.

Performing a withdrawal as a component of an action otherwise displaying involvement—frequently, heightened involvement—in the talk being withdrawn from is in fact one of the characteristic ways that this activity is done. This process may be used not only to achieve disengagement within an ongoing state of talk, but also to physically leave a conversational cluster without making that departure a noticeable event requiring the explicit coparticipation of the others present.[8] For example, in one departure recorded on videotape, one party withdrew from a conversational cluster while continuing to laugh loudly at a story that had just come to completion. Further, he initiated his move by walking away sideways so that the upper part of his body remained oriented toward the group he was leaving.

In the present data, recipient, finding that speaker is about to become disengaged, organizes her own actions so that she too enters a state of disengagement. By moving as she does, B displays her understanding of the change in participation status that A is proposing, the acceptability of that course of action to her, and her coparticipation in it.

Before proceeding further with the analysis, some of the disengagement-relevant actions of the participants will be summarized briefly. First, recipient has demonstrated her attention to, and coparticipation in, the talk in progress by performing operations on it in its course. Second, speaker has not only removed her gaze from recipient, but also made visible upcoming temporary withdrawal from the talk by noticeably positioning herself for entry into another activity. Third, after seeing this, recipient has withdrawn her gaze from speaker, but, while doing so, has continued to perform operations on the talk still in progress. The result of all this activity is that neither party is displaying orientation

---

[8] For more detailed analysis of phenomena relevant to such unilateral departure, see C. Goodwin (1979).

toward the other when the silence in Line 12 is entered. The lapse that follows is not entered through a recycling of turn-taking options (one possibility for entry into a lapse noted by Sacks *et al.* 1974:715) with first one party and then the other choosing not to exercise the opportunity to talk provided them by the turn-taking system. Rather, the identities of speaker and hearer are from the beginning of the silence no longer a relevant framework for the organization of the participants toward each other. Through their collaborative work, they have managed to construct a place immediately subsequent to a strip of talk where further talk is neither present nor absent but rather no longer being treated as either relevant or necessary.

Some Alternative Possibilities

The structure of the space the participants have managed to construct in the data just examined might be made more clear by comparing it with other examples in which different courses of action are taken. Three further pieces of data will now be examined. In the first, rather than withdrawing, speaker continues to gaze at recipient after his talk is brought to completion; recipient treats such gaze as proposing the continued relevance of conversation and puts aside another activity he was about to perform. In the second, speaker stops talking without displaying involvement in another activity; rather than either continuing to display engagement or moving immediately to disengagement, recipient adopts a transitional posture until the course of action that speaker is to pursue is clearly established. In the last, actions sufficient to provide for collaborative movement from talk to disengagement are performed right at the transition point, quite literally in the blink of an eye.

REFUSING TO WITHDRAW

In Example (2), as A's talk approaches completion, B is raising a can of beer to his mouth. When the turn ends and a silence ensues, B tilts the can, which is now just in front of his lips, to his mouth. A, however, continues to gaze toward B. B removes the can from his mouth without taking the almost accomplished drink and produces a next utterance to A's talk:

(2) A: ... er up on the back of his pickup truck with a, (0.4)

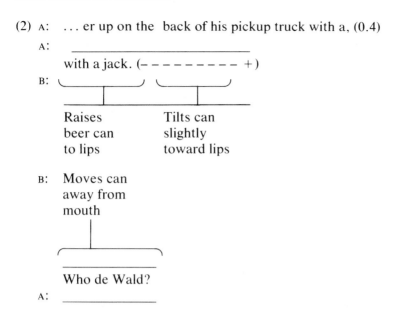

The actions occurring here, and in particular B's putting aside another activity which has already been begun in order to produce his talk, are consistent with the possibility that B sees A's continued gaze as proposing that further talk from him is relevant at that point.

In Line 11 of Example (1), when speaker started to move from talk to another activity, her recipient showed that such a change was acceptable to her by also withdrawing from the talk. Here, by way of contrast, one party counters the state of engagement being proposed by the other. B starts to perform private actions while A is talking. Instead of either permitting this during his talk, or withdrawing until B has finished, A performs actions that propose that B should be fully engaged in the conversation and B acquiesces by putting aside the competing activity.

MAINTAINING AVAILABILITY

In Example (3) A terminates her talk, without, however, displaying engagement in another activity. Just as A finishes her utterance, B withdraws her gaze from her. However, rather than immediately moving to a state of full disengagement, B quickly stops her move away and holds her head so that it is facing just to the side of the speaker (this position is indicated in the transcript by "#"). After a period of time during which A does not produce further talk, B drops this position and moves to a state of full disengagement:

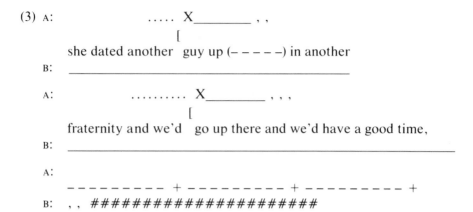

By moving away while remaining silent, B displays, first, that she will not become a speaker herself, and, second, that she is not now treating A as a speaker. However, by not moving to a position of full disengagement, she also displays that she remains ready to return as a recipient should A choose to resume speaking. B's body position thus shows an analysis not simply of what A is doing at the moment but also of the texture of possibilities still available at that point: A, though not speaking at the moment, *may continue* her talk, *but need not* do so; B, though not willing to become a speaker herself, demonstrates her availability as a recipient should A continue, without, however, treating A as a speaker. B's position displays a readiness for explicit collaborative action without requiring it. Insofar as from it one can move either to complete engagement or to complete disengagement, this position allows the party adopting it alternatives for dealing with and adapting to subsequent events in the interaction. When it becomes clear that A has chosen one of the possibilities open to her to the exclusion of the other, B moves from this position in a way that maintains the appropriateness of her body for the current state of the interaction.

MATCHING DISPLAYS

In Example (4), just as speaker's talk comes to completion, recipient performs a very visible action with her face, noticeably raising her brows. For convenience, this action will be called an eyebrow flash.[9]

[9] For analysis of how eyebrow flashes function as signals from an evolutionary and cross-cultural perspective, see Eibl-Eibesfeldt (1974).

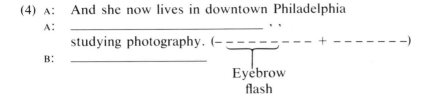

(4) A: And she now lives in downtown Philadelphia

Recipient's eyebrow flash does many of the same things as the nods performed during the phased withdrawal in Example (1). First, by making visible specific operations on the talk, recipient is able to display, not just attentiveness to the speaker, but also that she has in some way dealt with the particulars of the talk of the moment. Second, the eyebrow flash enables the recipient to perform an activity-occupied withdrawal from the talk in progress. When the action is examined in detail, it is found to have several distinct components: first, the actual raising of the brows; second, a hold of that position; and, third, the dropping of the brows. Although the raising and hold are done while recipient is displaying full orientation toward the speaker, the brows are dropped in such a way that, at the termination of the movement, recipient is no longer gazing at the speaker. By organizing the eyebrow flash in the way that she does, recipient avoids performing the withdrawal as an explicit, noticeable act in its own right.

Examining the data further, it can be seen that just after recipient's move (less than a tenth of a second), speaker also performs an eyebrow flash:[10]

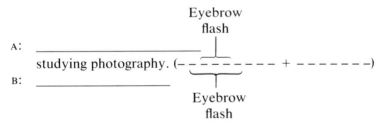

By each selecting the same display, the participants demonstrate to each other that they have come to the same analysis of the talk being produced and appreciate it in a congruent manner.

---

[10] It may be noted that even though speaker's eyebrow flash begins after recipient's, it is ended while recipient's is still being held. The participants thus arrange their actions so that even though speaker's eyebrow flash is placed as a response to recipient's, recipient, by holding her display longer, maintains orientation toward speaker until after speaker has withdrawn.

Such a display of congruent understanding may in fact be relevant to the issue of not providing further talk at this point. Insofar as recipient's action constitutes a type of response to speaker's talk, it may be examined by speaker to see whether recipient has dealt with the talk in an appropriate and relevant fashion. The selection by each party of the same action provides an economical but elegant demonstration that in fact their minds are together and that they have reached a common and congruent understanding of the talk.

It may be noted that the actions being examined here provide responses that do not themselves require further responses.[11] Given this characteristic, it is not surprising that matching displays are in fact found quite frequently at places where the transition from talk to disengagement is being accomplished. Further instances of this phenomenon will be examined later in this chapter.

[11] One might ask how an eyebrow flash in Example (4) can be seen as a response to this talk and, further, a response that speaker can and does readily treat as adequate. When speaker's actions at the beginning of this turn are examined, it is found that she performs another facial display there and that one component of this display is an eyebrow flash.

A: Another interesting group were the ones from Philadelphia.

       Eyebrow flash
    ┌──────────┴──────────┐

    Mainline Philadelphia.
         (0.7)
A: One of them was my roommate And she was unbelievable.
      S– Y'know.Very very wealthy.Came right out of (0.2)
      where'd she go (to wuh Magnus Erwin). And I was, a,
      course I was– at that point a public school girl.
         (0.2)
      very much different than she was. And she really changed
         (0.3)
      And she now lives in downtown Philadelphia studying photography.
         (1.7)

The preface of a multiunit turn is in fact a place where speakers regularly perform actions such as displaying what an appreciation of the talk to follow may consist of and in other ways providing their recipients with information about how to deal with the upcoming talk (Sacks 1974). In the present data, recipient has taken what speaker has provided her and used that to construct her own response. She thus ends up with a product that speaker not only finds acceptable as a response, but in fact herself selects for her comment on the talk.

It is also relevant to note that recipient *does not* do an eyebrow flash at the preface, before she has heard the talk to follow. Her actions are thus not the products of a simple stimulus–response reaction, or an instance of synchrony, but rather constitute recognizable acts that are produced and placed with reference to a sequential analysis of the talk then in progress and the tasks that talk sets for her at particular points.

Talk within Disengagement

Having examined some of the interactive work through which the transition from talk to disengagement is accomplished, we will now begin to explore what consequences such a change in coparticipation status has for the subsequent activity of the participants. Some of the ways in which a state of disengagement is organized have already been examined. It was noted at the beginning of this chapter that, though participants officially disattend each other during disengagement, they in fact pay close attention to each other, monitoring in particular for moves toward reengagement. We will now find that the interactive possibilities they might attend to are in fact more complex than has so far been suggested. Specifically, it will be seen that, once a state of disengagement has been entered, it is possible to produce talk that does not propose full engagement. It is thus not sufficient for participants to simply monitor for the resumption of talk. They must also determine what form of engagement is appropriate to a particular piece of talk. This will be found to have implications for the processes of reengagement examined in the last chapter.

Returning to the state of disengagement entered at the end of Line 11 in Example (1), it can be seen that, after over a second of silence, B produces further talk:

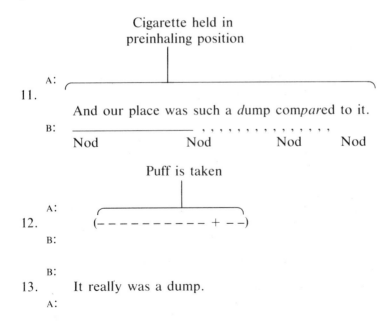

B:

14.   (– – – – –)

A:

The placement of the talk in Line 13 makes visible one further feature of the monitoring process participants are performing during disengagement. In Line 11, A accounted for her withdrawal from talk by showing that she was about to become engaged in smoking her cigarette. B begins her talk in Line 13 immediately after A withdraws the cigarette from her mouth. This suggests that the activity providing a warrant for the move to disengagement might also provide some organization for the strip of disengagement itself. Specifically, participants might attend to points of possible completion in that activity as opportunity places for the resumption of talk.[12]

Examining the actions of the participants during Line 13, it can be seen that speaker never moves her gaze to her recipient. Instead, she maintains the posture of disengagement assumed when the silence in Line 12 began. By not bringing her gaze to her recipient, speaker does not locate a place in her turn where recipient's gaze is relevantly absent (i.e., a place where speaker could be gazing at a nongazing recipient never arises). The displays speaker is making are matched by recipient, who does not in any way move toward the speaker during her talk. She does, however, produce subsequent talk, but only after a half second of silence.

The talk in Line 13 thus appears to be organized within an interactive framework quite different from that of a hearer attending a speaker who is addressing talk to her. Speaker makes her talk available but does not propose that the recipient should explicitly demonstrate that it is being heard. By producing her talk in this fashion, speaker also avoids dis-

---

[12] One of the strong currents in the contemporary social sciences is a push toward quantification whenever possible. One feature of interaction that apparently lends itself easily to precise measurement is the duration of various events such as silence, talk, and eye contact. However, it would appear that abstract clock time in seconds and tenths of a second is not an appropriate metric for the silence observed here. Participants appear to time the silence by attending to natural junctures in the activities in which they are engaged. Measuring the absolute duration of this silence with more and more precise instruments would produce no analytic gain (though observing what the participants are doing with greater detail might well be very fruitful). Indeed, the participants might treat two actions of quite different duration as functionally equivalent in terms of the possibilities for action they provide. This is not to deny the value of appropriate quantification, but merely to emphasize that the apparent rigor obtained with ever more precise measurement may be quite illusionary if one has not found the relevant objects to measure, that is, the natural units being used to organize the activity under analysis.

playing that she is awaiting a next utterance to it (for example, she is not gazing toward her recipient at and after the end of her turn), without however indicating that subsequent talk would be inappropriate.

The way in which the talk in Line 13 is treated by both its speaker and its hearer, and, in particular, their lack of explicit orientation toward each other, makes it relevant for us to examine its structure more closely.

Through the way in which it is constructed, the talk in Line 13 appears to be specifically designed to provide a next utterance to Line 11 without proposing that further talk need be tied to it. Thus, it is not only tied to the talk in Line 11, but, with the words "was a dump," literally repeats some of that talk. By using the same words her coparticipant has used, B not only shows the closeness with which she was listening to what A was saying even while she was withdrawing from her, but also shows that she is in agreement with the assessment made with those words. The parts of Line 13 that are not a repeat nonetheless operate in a similar fashion. Thus the pronoun "it" explicitly instructs a recipient to look to prior talk to find the item now being indexed, without, however, further transforming that item. The only place in Line 13 where new material is added to that available in Line 11 is the word "really." That term escalates the assessment made by prior speaker while at the same time arguing that such a view of the object being assessed is the result of an independent appraisal of it by second speaker.

The utterance is thus systematically constructed to demonstrate that the second speaker is in agreement with the first about what is currently under discussion.[13] Such an action permits but does not require a next utterance to it. Other ways of showing how the prior talk was understood—for example, constructing a next utterance that both transformed

---

[13] Though the operations B makes visible in Line 13 systematically argue for congruent understanding, they do not exclude the possibility that the understanding displayed might be found inadequate. Indeed, such a possibility might be systematically engendered by the very way in which the particular operations used to argue for congruence tie the talk that they produce so closely to the specifics of the immediately prior talk. Thus, in these data, A's assessment of "Marjorie Webster" is presented as something to be compared with "Mount Vernon"; in turn, this comparison is to be analyzed with reference to another phenomenon: "the tuition we paid" (Lines 5–6). By tying so closely and selectively (note, for example, that the focus on the comparison at the end of Line 11 is not picked up in Line 13) to the local details of the just-prior talk, the talk in Line 13 fails to demonstrate explicitly that its speaker agrees with the larger point that the assessment was intended to provide evidence for (the "amazingness" of the tuition) or even that she has analyzed the assessment in terms of the other issues raised by prior speaker's talk. Note that in Line 15, A, without in any way challenging the analysis B has made of her talk, nonetheless returns the conversation to the issue of tuition in a way which reinstates the comparison with "Mount Vernon." A thus revitalizes aspects of the prior talk not focused on in B's talk.

the prior utterance and added substantial new material to it (consider, for example, the phenomenon of second stories as analyzed by Sacks 1971)—might well have made relevant further talk. With the operations performed here, second speaker manages to transform the prior talk just enough to show that prior speaker's position is also her position, without changing it so much as to show that a new display of understanding from prior speaker is expected.[14]

In short, the speaker, by maintaining her posture of disengagement during this turn, shows that, though her talk is available to be heard, neither explicit hearership nor a next utterance is required. The structure of the talk itself—which systematically shows that it is a next utterance to the prior talk but does not require a subsequent utterance tied to it— is consistent with the nonverbal evidence.

It would thus appear that, though talk can be produced within a frame- work of disengagement, such talk is organized differently from talk pro- duced during full engagement. It has both a looser sequential structure at its boundaries and proposes a structure of coparticipation in its course that is quite compatible with the framework of mutual disengagement being maintained by the participants while it is being spoken.

It is sometimes convenient to think of talk in conversation as being produced by a speaker who addresses it to a hearer. However, in this data, one finds a range of participation structures within which the pro- duction of talk is possible.[15] These structures have consequences in detail for the organization of the talk, being relevant to such basic issues as whether or not the talk of the moment is to be treated as heard and sequentially implicative.

Selecting from Coparticipation Alternatives

The availability of alternative engagement frameworks for the orga- nization of coparticipation during talk has a range of consequences, some of which will now be examined. Analysis will first focus on how the

[14] It may be noted that in many respects this utterance is quite similar to recipient's matching eyebrow flash in Example (4). Both have a retrospective, rather than prospective, orientation; both display agreement and use actions already utilized by coparticipant. Such similarity is not surprising since the operations being performed are quite relevant to disengagement.

[15] For other analysis of talk produced beyond the framework of a focused speaker–hearer relationship see Goffman (1978). Also relevant is the concept of a "continuing state of incipient talk [Schegloff and Sacks 1973:325]."

possibility of talk with different types of coparticipation affects processes of reengagement. We will then look at how recipient might make use of resources provided by alternative engagement structures to display not just hearership but different types of coparticipation in the talk of the moment. This will be found to be consequential for speaker's own subsequent actions. Engagement alternatives permit participants to deal with the talk in progress in a differentiated fashion, and these resources become implicated in the organization of the talk.

The possibility of talk without gaze after a state of disengagement has been entered raises systematic issues for the types of analysis necessary for the achievement of reengagement. If all talk received the same type of coparticipation, the types of phenomena that a potential listener would have to attend to in order to satisfactorily achieve reengagement would be quite clear and straightforward. In essence, all that a listener would have to do would be to distinguish between talk and nontalk and, when talk occurred, move his gaze in a relevant fashion. With the present data we find, however, that such a movement is not appropriate to all talk. Rather, talk calling for gaze must be distinguished from talk where gaze is not relevant.

The issue arises as to how potential recipients make this distinction. Raising such an issue casts light on some possibly puzzling features of the analysis presented in the last chapter. Specifically, one might wonder why talk alone was not sufficient to secure recipient's gaze. Why were speakers found to place special signals, such as phrasal breaks, in their talk? The present analysis would suggest that such signals provide speakers with the ability to distinguish for their recipients talk where recipient gaze is relevant and expected from talk where it is not. In essence, after disengagement has been entered, a new speaker does not simply start to talk, but organizes the production of that talk so as to make visible to others present whether or not their explicit coparticipation is relevant. From the work that speaker does, a potential recipient is able to find whether or not the talk in progress is calling for his gaze.

In Chapter 2, phrasal breaks were found to be one set of signals that could be used to request the gaze of a recipient. However, other actions, such as the movement of speaker's gaze, might also be inspected for what they might propose about the participation status of the current talk. During Lines 13 and 14 of Example (1), A moves her head past B as part of the activity of flicking ashes to her side. This movement is done with lowered face and eyes, and B maintains her posture of disengagement even after A starts to talk again in Line 15. However, when A moves her head back, she sweeps her gaze past B, but hesitates in that movement just as her eyes reach B. She thus manages to glance at her recipient without constructing a full-fledged look. Just after this glance (which is marked in the transcript with a lower case "y" and dashes), B starts to move her gaze to A:

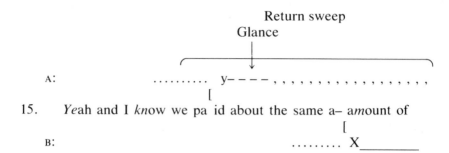

The placement of recipient's movement just after speaker's glance is consistent with the possibility that the glance is being treated as a signal that gaze is appropriate to this talk.

It would also appear that A is alive to the possibility that B might now start to gaze. For example, the place where B's gaze arrives is marked with a slight perturbation in A's talk.

After the glance, A immediately continues her sweep (indeed, the glance comes off as no more than a hesitation in her ongoing movement). Thus, when recipient's gaze arrives, she finds that speaker is not yet looking toward her. The preferred organization for the gaze of speaker and hearer relative to each other can therefore still be achieved. When speaker at last moves her gaze in officially, she finds that recipient is already gazing at her:

```
         A:  , , , , , , , , , , , ,            ......... X_____
                                                          [
15–16.       the same a–  amount of tuition. I think o ur tuition
                         [
         B:   ......... X _____
```

With her initial glance, speaker suggests that full engagement is relevant for the talk now in progress, but she then allows recipient to make the first official move into full engagement. Only after this has happened does speaker make her own move.

The following provides an example of how participants might use the resources just examined to negotiate the coparticipation status that a strip of talk is to have. After speaker uses a tentative movement toward recipient to suggest that gaze is relevant, recipient refuses to move her gaze to speaker. Rather than repetitively requesting that recipient move (one of the processes examined in Chapter 2), speaker, who has not yet herself assumed a posture of full engagement, acquiesces to recipient and subsequently treats her talk as talk that does not in fact require full engagement. To simplify presentation of this material we will begin with an audio transcript and then look at what is happening nonvocally.

(5)
1. B: and she didn't want to marry that guy (from)
2. (app(h)are(h)nt(h)ly?)
3. A: Yeah, right,
4. (1.0)
5. B: Couldn't sta:nd him.*I* don't wanna m(h)a(h)rry this guy.
6. °really, 'hh
7. (1.2)
8. A: But, a–an*o*ther one that went to school with me wa:s a girl

For most of Lines 1 and 2, the participants do not orient to each other. However, over "apparently," B brings her gaze to her recipient. A reacts to this by immediately bringing her own gaze to B. The two nod together[16] and then, during the silence in Line 4, withdraw from each other, occupying that withdrawal with a series of nods:

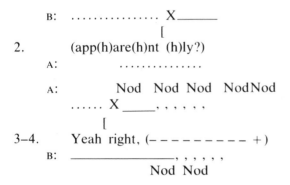

B now starts another utterance and after it is under way again moves

---

[16] Note that this is another example of participants performing matching displays in an environment where the transition from talk to disengagement is being accomplished.

her gaze toward A, but she stops this movement before she actually
gazes at A:

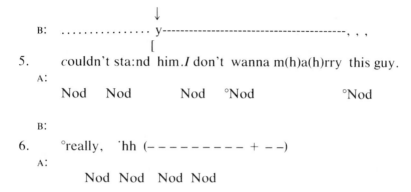

5.   couldn't sta:nd him.*I* don't wanna m(h)a(h)rry this guy.
A:

         Nod   Nod   Nod   °Nod   °Nod

B:
6.   °really, ˙hh (– – – – – – – – – + – –)
A:

              Nod Nod   Nod Nod

In Line 2, gaze movement toward recipient acted as a successful solicit
for recipient's gaze. This time, however, A does not move toward full
engagement. By not bringing her gaze to B in this sequential position,
A might be seen as not agreeing to provide the type of coparticipation
speaker is then proposing to be relevant. With respect to this possibility,
it may be noted that by continuing to nod recipient does do operations
on the talk the speaker is producing. It is thus not the case that coparticipation in the speaker's talk is absent, a situation that might be dealt
with by further attempts to secure coparticipation. Rather, recipient fills
the space provided for her coparticipation with relevant activity, but not
with the type of activity speaker has displayed to be preferred.[17] A refusal
to coparticipate in a particular way (as opposed to simply a failure to
achieve coparticipation) is thus visible. In the face of this, B, who has
stopped the movement of her head so that she is gazing not at A but
slightly in front of her, withdraws her gaze completely.

---

[17] There is one further subtlety in this process. In that the nods A performs over Line
5 continue an activity performed throughout the intervening silence, they might be seen
as continuing responses to the prior talk rather than actions specifically addressed to the
talk in progress. The way in which A organizes her nods may attend to such a possibility.
Just before the talk in Line 5 comes to an end, she stops her nods briefly and then begins
them again when B reaches termination. By breaking up the stream of nods in this fashion,
she is able to establish that at least some of them are specifically directed to B's later talk.
By not disrupting the stream of nods earlier, A may also be able to display that she is
treating the talk then occurring as continuing appreciation of the prior talk rather than as
the beginning of some new activity which requires new coparticipation from her.

These data thus provide support for the possibility that the engagement formation found to be operative over a stretch of talk may be the product of an active process of interaction between the participants and that the ability to formulate a piece of talk as not requiring mutual orientation between speaker and hearer constitutes a resource for the participants in their dealings with each other about the talk in progress.

The ability to display different types of engagement in the talk of the moment provides recipients with resources for making visible to speaker not only their alignment to that talk but also their enthusiasm for it. One possibility raised is that, by operating on a piece of talk but showing less than full engagement in it, a recipient might be able to close down a line of talk that speaker is prepared to develop further. This might be relevant to recipient's own projects. For example, in these data, after nodding for a while at the end of B's talk, A introduces a story of her own (Line 8).

Returning to Example (1), a refusal to coparticipate is found in Line 20. After her talk has begun, A moves her head, though with lids downcast, slightly toward B and then pauses briefly. B makes no move whatsoever toward A:

```
    A:          . . . . . . . .
20.      And it went up (– –)
    B:
```

A then moves her head slightly away from B, opens her eyes without looking in B's direction (indicated in the transcript with #), and produces further talk. When B still does not move, A withdraws her gaze sharply and completely from B's vicinity:

```
    A:          . . . . . . . .     ,#######, , , , , , , , ,
20.      And it went up (– –) the second  year I was *the*:re.
    B:
```

These data are consistent with the possibility that B is refusing to bring her gaze to A (note that both the beginning and end of the pause, as well as speaker's movement, might constitute requests for gaze) and that A, seeing this, first withdraws her own gaze prior to the point where it actually reaches B and then holds briefly in a ready position that maintains her availability should B choose to move after the pause is closed. When this does not happen, A withdraws her gaze entirely.

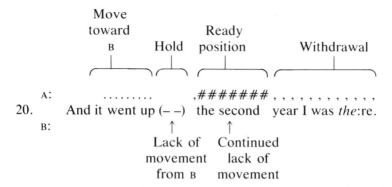

The effect of all this is that the turn is found to have a structure similar to Line 13: that is, it does not require the mutual orientation of speaker and hearer. The actions of the speaker suggest, however, that this formulation of what is happening is arrived at only after recipient is found to be unwilling to move to full engagement.

Two seconds later, in Line 22, A again starts to move toward her recipient while producing further talk. B, however, makes no move toward her, and A both stops her gaze movement before it reaches B and interrupts the talk she is producing in midunit:

```
         A:   . . . . . . . . . .
22–23.   But I: uh, (– – – – – – – – –)
         B:
```

It was seen in the last chapter that such phrasal breaks are frequently interpreted by recipients as requests for their gaze. Here, however, B continues to maintain her posture of disengagement. B's failure to move at a place where such a move is relevant raises in stronger fashion the possibility that she is actively refusing to coparticipate in A's current talk.[18]

When A starts to speak again, the talk she produces is quite different from the aborted talk just prior to it. Instead of the pronoun ''I'' this talk begins with the name of the speaker's husband. The sequence until this point has been concerned with female colleges. By producing a male name, A shows that the talk she is now proposing will be significantly

---

[18] When the data are examined in more detail it is found that just after the phrasal break B makes an almost imperceptible head movement toward A which she immediately stops. Such action both shows the coercive power of phrasal breaks as requests for gaze and provides further support for the possibility that B is actively refusing to attend to her coparticipant's current talk.

different from the talk that preceded it, that is, she makes visible a topic change. Such a move might, of course, be responsive to the possibility that B is refusing to coparticipate further in the prior topic. As soon as the name is produced, B starts to bring her gaze to A:

A:
22–24.   But I: uh, (0.9) Do:n uh: :, Don's family moved
                                    [
B: .. X_____

Accounting for Withdrawal

Analysis will now turn to the actions speaker performs after recipient fails to coparticipate in Lines 20–23. It was noted earlier that one way in which a speaker might account for her withdrawal from talk is by displaying that another activity is claiming her attention. Throughout the present sequence, speaker—but not recipient—continues to fill the silences between talk with other activity. The silence in Line 19 occupies just the time it takes for speaker to readjust a package of cigarettes sitting on her lap; during Line 21 speaker is adjusting her blouse; and, in the silence after Line 22, speaker turns to her side and flicks ashes from her cigarette into an ashtray:

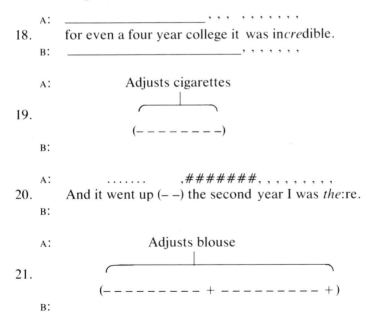

A: _____ , , , , , , , , , , ,
18.   for even a four year college it was in*cre*dible.
B: _____, , , , , , ,

A: Adjusts cigarettes

19.

B: (– – – – – – – –)

A: . . . .   ,#######, , , , , , , , ,
20.   And it went up (– –) the second year I was *the*:re.
B:

A: Adjusts blouse

21.   (– – – – – – – – – + – – – – – – – – +)

B:

```
      A:   . . . . . . . .
22.        But I: uh,
      B:


      A:                      Brings
                          cigarette to
                            ashtray

23.                    (– – – – – – – – –)
      B:
```

The timing of these activities relative to the talk makes visible reasons
for why speaker has withdrawn from the talk. It has been seen that Line
20 might be formulated as a turn not requiring explicit coparticipation
only after recipient fails to give speaker her gaze and that speaker's
interruption of her talk in Line 22 might be responsive to recipient's
failure to move toward her. By offering the activity in Lines 21 and 23
as accounts for her withdrawal from talk, speaker is able to argue that
she is leaving her talk, not because of her recipient's refusal to coparticipate in it, but because she herself has other matters to attend to. The
accounts thus provide A with the ability to display that the decision to
stop talking, rather than being responsive to her recipient's lack of interest, emerges from her own actions.

Conclusion

This chapter has explored some of the structures organizing coparticipation during the production of talk. Participants utilize both their
bodies and a variety of vocal phenomena to show each other the type
of attention they are giving to the events of the moment, and, recipro-
cally, the type of orientation they expect from others. Such phenomena
are not just responsive to the talk (or silence) in progress but consequential for its current structure and future possibilities, showing, for
example, what type of coparticipation is appropriate to the talk of the
moment, whether a next utterance is relevant, and whether the talk has
the full involvement of the participants. Of central importance is the fact
that the engagement displays of the separate participants are organized
relative to each other through an ongoing process of interaction.[19] This

---

[19] Since completing this analysis a paper by Heath (1980) on the display of recipiency
has come to my attention. Among the phenomena he examines are ways in which parties

can perhaps be most clearly seen at points where the transition from one type of engagement to another is being accomplished. However, even displays of mutual disengagement are collaboratively sustained through careful organization of the participants' bodies and their ongoing monitoring of what the other is doing. Insofar as engagement frameworks are interactively achieved and sustained, participants are able to negotiate even as the talk is being spoken the type of coparticipation it is to receive. For example, recipient may refuse to provide the type of orientation that speaker is proposing to be relevant, and speaker may acquiesce to recipient, with the effect that the utterance in progress is ultimately formulated as talk requiring only minimal coparticipation. This may be quite consequential for the continued viability of speaker's current projects and the directions that future talk will take. Indeed, what appears to be a change in topic by a single speaker may in fact be a response to the diminished coparticipation of the recipient in the prior topic, something that speaker is clearly able to see even though recipient does not say anything. The displays made by the participants' bodies also help shape the perceived meaningfulness of the events they are engaged in. Not only can particular reasons for why something is happening be made visible, but even withdrawal from talk can be embedded within heightened attention to it and thus not emerge as an act of disaffiliation. Engagement displays thus integrate the bodies of the participants into the production of their talk, and are important constitutive features of their conversation. They permit those present to display to each other not just speakership and hearership but differentiated attention to, and participation in, the talk of the moment.

---

might align themselves toward each other as speaker and hearer before the production of a strip of talk begins, a process that has a clear relevance to many of the phenomena examined in both this chapter and the last.

4

Modifying Units of Talk to Coordinate Their Production with the Actions of a Recipient

This chapter will investigate the ability of speakers to coordinate their utterances with the actions of their recipients by adding new sections to the units they are producing. Such analysis will both help make explicit some of the resources utilized by participants to achieve the fine coordination of action observed within the turn and provide some demonstration of how social tasks posed in the construction of the turn might be consequential for the talk being produced within it.

Lengthening Units by Adding to Their Ends and Middles

In the following, the speaker stops production of a fragment and begins a new sentence precisely at the point where the gaze of the recipient arrives:

$$\downarrow$$

(1) GARY: He's a policeman in Bellview and he :, I guess he's,
                                                [
                                         . X_____

(2) ANN: I think he : I think he even get it with the fir(h)st

PAT: .... X_____

(3) BARBARA: God that's: :, I don't want *that* life.

GORDIE: .... X_____

As is indicated by the colons in the transcript, the last sound in the fragment in all of these examples is prolonged in its pronunciation.[1] Were these sounds not prolonged the speaker would stop pronunciation of the fragment shortly before the arrival of the recipient's gaze:

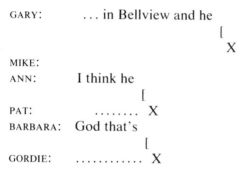

GARY: ... in Bellview and he

                                          [
                                          X

MIKE:
ANN: I think he

                           [
PAT: X
BARBARA: God that's

                           [
GORDIE: X

By elongating the terminal sound in a word they are constructing, the speakers in these examples are able to lengthen that word with the effect that the termination of the fragment occurs precisely when the recipient's gaze reaches the speaker. The ability of a speaker to pronounce certain sounds for variable lengths of time might thus be utilized to coordinate events in his utterance with the actions of a recipient.

In Examples (1)–(3), a unit that had come to a point of possible completion was extended past that completion. However, as is illustrated by Examples (4)–(5), it is also possible to delay an initial completion point by adding new material to the middle of the unit.

---

[1] The ability of speakers to vary the length of the sounds they are producing has received some study. For example, the work of O'Malley, Kloker, and Dara-Abrams (1973), Kloker (1975), and Macdonald (1976) demonstrates that "vowel and sonorant lengthening is an acoustic cue to the phonological phrase structure in spontaneous English speech [Kloker 1975:5]." Macdonald's work (1976) showed that changing the duration of sounds at constituent boundaries could change the perceived meaning of sentences with surface structure ambiguities. The work of Sacks and his colleagues (Sacks *et al.* 1974:707) has shown that lengthening sounds at the end of a turn-constructional unit provides one systematic basis for the occurrence of overlap.

$\downarrow \quad \downarrow$

(4) ESTHER: Wh::a : t (0.2) annoys me is they didn't (0.3) *t*ell us

                [

AMY: X_____

             $\downarrow$

(5) CARNEY: You know tha: t (0.4) first road off the bypass.

               [

PHYLLIS: . X_____

Here, by lengthening sounds in the middle of a word, speaker delays its completion until recipient's gaze arrives. Note that these words end in stops; they therefore could not be lengthened at their termination.

Many different types of phenomena, including silence (note the pauses in Chapter 2), can be added to a unit to increase its length. In the following, a glottal stop marking a phrasal break occurs well before the arrival of the recipient's gaze:

(6) ETHYL: *Y*eah. = Wher–

BARBARA: .... X_____

However, by adding an "uh" and an outbreath to the original cutoff, speaker manages to place the termination of the phrasal break precisely at the point where recipient's gaze arrives:

(6) ETHYL: Yeah. = Wher– uh hh Where *do* they register.

               [

BARBARA: .... X_____

The addition of these phenomena to the turn has the effect of delaying the beginning of a new sentence until the gaze of the recipient has been secured.

The procedures being examined operate on several different levels of organization. For example, coordination with a recipient might be achieved by adding an "uh" to a sentence. However, "uh" is in its own right a unit with a clear phonological structure and might itself be lengthened by the application of procedures appropriate to the phonological level of organization, that is, by a lengthening of its sounds. The following provides an example:

             $\downarrow$

(7) MARSHA: But I: uh, (0.9) Do:n uh: :, Don's family moved

               [

DIANNE: ...... X_____

An object such as "uh::" demonstrates the operation of the processes being examined on two different levels of organization.

In the following, speaker uses laughter (indicated in the transcript by "h" in parentheses) to extend the length of a word until the recipient's gaze arrives:

(8) BETTY: That wasn't any fa(h)(h)(h)i(h) (h)r.
                                              [
   PAM: .... X__

Note that the addition of a new segment to some particular unit has an effect on the length of some but not all other units as well. The speaker's laughter here increases the length of the word in which the laughter occurs, the utterance containing the word, and the turn in progress, but it does not increase the length of the speaker's sentence; that is, no new elements such as words or phrases are added to the sentence.

Changing the Emerging Structure of the Speaker's Sentence

In the preceding section, the techniques available to the speaker for coordinating his actions with those of his recipient were found to produce a range of characteristic phenomena in the turn. Analysis will now focus on how the use of such techniques might result in the addition of new elements to the speaker's sentence.

In the following, the speaker loses the gaze of his recipient in midutterance. When it has been regained, the speaker repeats the noun phrase that was spoken while his recipient was disattending him, this time adding a new adjective to it:

(9) RALPH: Somebody said looking at ⁀my:, son⁀ ⁀m y oldest son,⁀
                                                 [
   CHIL: _____ ,   .   X_____

Once again the speaker adds a segment to the unit he is constructing so that precise coordination between his actions and those of his recipient is maintained. By repeating the part of the sentence spoken as his recipient was turning away from him, the speaker succeeds in producing the entire sentence constructed in his turn while his recipient is gazing at him. However, the addition of the adjective to the second version of the noun phrase changes the sentence being constructed in the turn: If this segment had not been added, the word "oldest" would not have been part of the sentence eventually produced by the speaker.[2]

Analysis will now turn to investigation of examples in which a speaker adds a new section to his sentence without recycling an earlier portion of it. In the following, which will be examined in some detail, speaker obtains both gaze and a response from a first recipient but then, while continuing with the same sentence, moves his gaze to a second recipient, Beth:

(10) JOHN: .. , , ... Don , , ... Don
```
                            [                [
        I gave, I gave u p smo king  ci garettes::.
                            [
DON:                  ...... X_____

DON:     = Yeah,
                    (0.4)

JOHN:    ...... Beth_____
              [
        l–uh: one–one week ago toda:y.
BETH:
```

Beth, however, does not direct her gaze to John. The speaker thus finds himself in the position of gazing at a party who is not gazing at him.

Phrasal breaks occur just before and after John's gaze reaches Beth ("l–uh:" and "one–one"). Though these phrasal breaks do not secure the gaze of Beth, another party, Ann, does begin to attend the turn at his point. During the initial sections of John's sentence, and, indeed, for some time previous to it, Ann has displayed lack of orientation to the conversation, staring to her side with a fixed middle-distance look. However, shortly after the restart, Ann abruptly raises her head and moves her gaze to the recipient of the present utterance, Beth:

```
JOHN:    ....... Beth_____
              [
        l–uh: one–one  week ag ┌o toda:y.
BETH:                          │
ANN:              ......... └Beth____
```

[2] Bolinger (1975:19) notes that a speaker might add a new word to his sentence to coordinate the production of the sentence with the speaker's own actions. Goffman (1975:16) provides a similar analysis. For some analysis of how a speaker's reading that his recipient has not adequately understood the talk so far might lead to recycling of already produced material in the form of clarifications, see Erickson (1979).

Ann's abrupt movement of her gaze occurs in the standard position for a next move to a signal that the gaze of a recipient is being requested, that is, shortly after a restart. However, Ann directs her gaze, not to the speaker, but rather to another participant, Beth. John's sentence is projected to come to a possible completion point rather soon after Beth brings her gaze to the turn. "I gave up smoking cigarettes one week ago today" is an adequately complete sentence and such a unit could be projected[3] at the point Ann brings her gaze to the turn. If the floor were to pass to the speaker's addressed recipient at this point, Ann would be positioned to be gazing at the new speaker.[4]

Two different parties, John and Ann, are now gazing at Beth, who is returning the gaze of neither. If these two parties were gazing at each other instead of Beth, the speaker would be gazing at a gazing recipient. Because of Beth's failure to bring her gaze to him, John might now be prepared to seek the gaze of another party. Ann, who has just displayed her orientation to the turn by bringing her gaze to its field of action, is a possible candidate. However, although the task of securing a gazing recipient might lead John to switch his gaze from Beth to Ann, no comparable motivation exists for Ann to move her gaze to John, especially since she is not his current addressed recipient.

Less than a syllable after Ann begins to move into orientation, John withdraws his gaze from Beth. He then brings it to Ann, reaching her after she has demonstrated her coparticipation in the field of action

---

[3] Units of other length also could have been projected here. The sentence could have reached completion after "ago" if the speaker had begun this section of it with "a" rather than "one" ("I gave up smoking cigarettes a week ago"). However the idiom begun with "one" projects the inclusion of a specific time reference such as "today" after "ago" (though if spoken with a different intonation, for example with "week" stressed, the sentence "I gave up smoking cigarettes one week ago" would be perfectly appropriate). The speaker also might have specified the time with a still shorter phrase such as "last week" and, indeed, the cutoff "I–" at the beginning of this section provides some demonstration that such an alternative was in fact begun but changed (Jefferson 1974:186 provides evidence that participants in conversation do in fact orient to such bits of sound as possible word beginnings). If this is the case, the speaker in this example, faced with the task of securing a new recipient's gaze in this section, has gone from a short unit ("last week"), skipped the next longest ("a week ago") and found a longer one ("one week ago today"), providing more time in his sentence for his task to be accomplished.
I am indebted to Gail Jefferson for bringing this progression to my attention.

[4] This sentence will be examined from a somewhat different perspective in the next chapter. There it will be found that the portion of the sentence produced when John gazes at Beth is designed specifically for Beth and not for Ann, and that, by the time Ann begins to move, this has been displayed in the utterance in a number of different ways. Ann is provided with resources permitting her to locate, not only that she is not the current addressed recipient of the utterance, but also who that addressed recipient is, and this may also be relevant to her choice of a particular party to gaze at.

constructed through his turn by gazing at Beth, but before the turn has reached its next projected completion. Note that the time required to reach this completion point has been extended through the elongation of a sound within "to*da*:y."

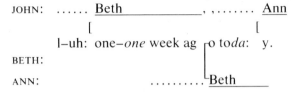

Though John is now gazing at Ann rather than Beth, he is still gazing at a recipient who is not gazing at him. His move has, however, made it relevant for Ann to bring her gaze to him: In that Ann is now being gazed at by the speaker, she should be gazing toward him. But, although John's shift in gaze permits Ann to recognize that she should bring her gaze to him, there is no time left within the turn for Ann to perform this action. As indicated not only by its grammatical structure but also by its falling terminal intonation (indicated in the transcript by a period), John's utterance has come to a recognizable completion.

If the length of the turn could be extended, Ann might have the time to move her gaze from Beth to John. However, providing the turn with such time for maneuvering requires that the sentence being constructed through it be extended past the completion point presently proposed for it. This is in fact what occurs, as John adds the word "actually" to his sentence:

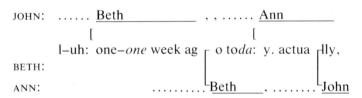

Appropriate mutual gaze is thus achieved by the collaborative action of speaker and hearer. While hearer brings her gaze to the speaker, speaker provides time in this turn for her to accomplish this task by adding a new word to his sentence. The turn now reaches completion with the speaker gazing at a gazing hearer. In this example, the sentence being produced by the speaker is modified by the addition of an extra word to it with the effect that a particular interactive task posed in the construction of the turn at talk can be accomplished.[5]

---

[5] An event that does not occur at this point is also relevant to the addition of this segment. "Actually" is not overlapped by any talk from Beth, though a turn transition

Further support for the possibility that speaker might adapt to actions of his recipient by adding new segments to an already complete sentence is provided by the following data. Here we will find speaker actively putting aside another activity, eating, so as to be able to produce further talk when recipient makes a relevant move. In this example, recipient does not bring her gaze to the speaker by the time his original sentence reaches a point of recognizable completion, and speaker starts to eat as soon as he finishes talking:

(11)

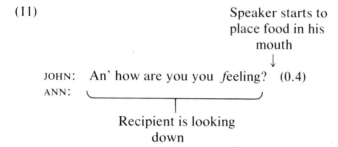

JOHN: An' how are you you *feeling?*   (0.4)
ANN:

Up until this point, the actions of both speaker and recipient are consistent with the possibility that the present turn is being treated as unsuccessful. First, it may be observed that the structure of the speaker's talk transfers the floor to its recipient at the end of his sentence. However, recipient does not produce any talk of her own and a gap occurs. The recipient thus shows that she is not treating the speaker's talk as sequentially implicative for subsequent talk on her part. Second, as soon as his sentence comes to completion, the speaker, rather than displaying that he is waiting for his addressee to start, begins to place an egg roll in his mouth.

At this point, the recipient belatedly begins to move her gaze toward the speaker:

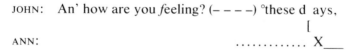

JOHN: An' how are you *feeling?* (– – – –) °these d ays,
                                                    [
ANN: . . . . X___

As soon as recipient acts, the speaker withdraws the uneaten egg roll from his mouth and produces with falling–raising intonation further talk:

---

point for the section of the utterance addressed to her has just been passed. Her lack of action here is consistent with the display of nonorientation to the talk provided by her lack of gaze. From this perspective, the addition of a new segment to John's sentence can be seen, not only as a way of providing time within the turn for Ann to move, but also as a means of avoiding the gap that would result from Beth's failure to take the floor from John.

"°these days,''. Note that these words with this intonation do not begin a new unit but rather constitute further development of the speaker's original sentence.

Tying this talk syntactically to the earlier talk has a number of consequences. First, the silence that was found after the speaker's initial completion now becomes a within-sentence pause rather than a gap. Second, recipient's arrival is placed within the boundaries of speaker's original sentence, rather than either after a noticeable gap or at the beginning of a new unit of talk. It may be that recipient's movement should be interpreted retroactively, as showing that, even though she did not display hearership during the course of the original talk, she did in fact hear it and is now prepared to deal with it. By continuing his original sentence, speaker shows recipient syntactically that he is treating her as someone who heard his initial talk and that he is interpreting the movement of her gaze as responsive to that talk and not as the beginning of an unrelated action. The ability to add a new section to his original sentence thus provides speaker with resources for making visible his understanding of recipient's gaze movement and with a way of adjusting his own action to it.

Adding Segments Repetitively

The following provides an example of how a speaker might repetitively add segments to a turn in order to deal with the gaze of her recipients in an appropriate fashion:

(12) ELSIE: See first we were gonna have Teema, Carrie, and Clara, (0.2) a::nd myself. The four of us. The four children. But then–uh:: I said how is that gonna look.

In the middle of her utterance the speaker moves her gaze from recipient to recipient. As she does so, she holds the onward development of the sentence she is producing in place by adding new sections to it in the form of appositives. This process will be examined in detail.

The recipient toward whom the speaker is gazing near the beginning of her turn disattends her midway through her utterance. Though the gaze of this recipient is regained, the speaker quickly shifts gaze to a different recipient:

ELSIE: <u>Ann_____</u>

                                                    [
            See first we were gonna ha ve Tee ma, Carrie and

                                                    [
ANN: . . . . X_____

BESSIE:

ELSIE: _____ , <u>Bessie_____</u>

                                                    [
            Clara, (0.2) a::nd myself.

ANN: _____ , , _____

BESSIE:

However, the new recipient, Bessie, is not gazing at the speaker. Rather
than advancing her utterance further the speaker holds it in place with
an appositive, "The four of us.", while Bessie moves into orientation:

ELSIE: _____ , <u>Bessie_____</u>

                                                    [
            Clara, (0.2) a::nd myself.   The four of u ⌐s.
ANN: _____ , , _____|
                                                                 |
BESSIE: . . . . ⌐X__

When Bessie finally does reach orientation, this segment of the speaker's
sentence is recycled yet another time, with a second appositive, making
clear why the four people being referred to constitute a single group:

ELSIE: _____ ,   <u>Bessie_____</u> ,   <u>Connie___</u>

                                [[
            a::nd myself.   ⌐The four of u ⌐s. The four children.
ANN: , , | |_____
                            | |
BESSIE: | . . . . ⌐X _____
                            |
CONNIE: . ⌐ X_____

Near the end of the second appositive the speaker shifts her gaze to
another recipient who has been gazing at her. Only then does she resume
the onward development of her utterance:

ELSIE: See first we were gonna have Teema, Carrie, and Clara,
          (0.2) a::nd myself. The four of us. The four
          children. But then–uh:: I said how is that gonna
          look.

The sentence eventually produced by the speaker in this turn is held in place, but changed by, the appositives she adds as she deals with her recipient's gaze.

In the examples considered until this point only a single turn has been at issue. However, the speaker might repetitively make use of his ability to modify his emerging utterance to negotiate a state of mutual focus with his recipients over several turns at talk. The following provides an example of such a process:

(13) ANN: The week before last it was cold in Washington.All week.
     CHIL: = Was it?
     ANN:
              = It was really cold and I'm thinking, 'h I was really
              thinking that summer was: finished,

When the speaker brings her eyes to her first intended recipient, Chil, she finds that he has not begun to gaze at her. The speaker covers a move to a different recipient by adding the words "All week." to her sentence:

ANN: .... Chil___ ,
                                                           [
             The week before last it was col┌d in Wash   ington.
CHIL: │
JERE: ... └X_____

ANN: ...... Jere
                  [
        All w eek.
CHIL:
JERE: _____

At that point Chil quickly constructs a next turn to Ann's:

ANN: The week before last it was cold in Washington.All week.
CHIL: = Was it?

Ann then begins to address a new utterance to Chil, but he does not move into orientation until after she has begun to gaze at him:

ANN: . Chil_____
                  [
        It was really cold and I'm thinkin g,
                                        [
CHIL: X
JERE: _____

The speaker is thus gazing toward a nongazing recipient, a situation that frequently leads to a phrasal break. Here the speaker covers a move to a recipient who has been gazing at her by recycling the last clause of her sentence, while changing its tense and adding an adverb to it:

ANN: .   Chil_____ , · · · · · · · · · ⌐Jere
                              [
            It was really cold   and I'm thinkin g, 'h I was reall⌐y
                                                    [
CHIL: · · · · · · · · · · · · · · X_____
JERE: _____

ANN: _____
               thinking
CHIL: _____
JERE: _____

As soon as this segment is complete, Ann returns her gaze to Chil:

ANN: .   Chil_____ , · · · · · · · · · · Jere
                              [[
            It was really cold   and I'm thinkin g, 'h I was reall y
                                                    [
CHIL: · · · · · · · · · · · · · · X _____
JERE: _____

ANN: _____ · · · · · · · · · ·   _Chil_____
                                                [
            thinking that summ er was: finished,
CHIL: _____
JERE: _____

This sequence provides some demonstration of how a speaker might regularly employ the ability to modify an emerging utterance so as to accomplish particular tasks posed in the construction of the turn at talk.

Although analysis has so far been restricted to the addition of segments to a sentence, units added to a turn to accomplish particular interactive tasks might also consist of whole sentences. In the following, Fred and Alice have been admiring a coat Elaine received from her husband as a Christmas present. Fred says "I love these cute dolls when they're well dressed." The following turn then occurs:

(14) ALICE: .... Fred_____

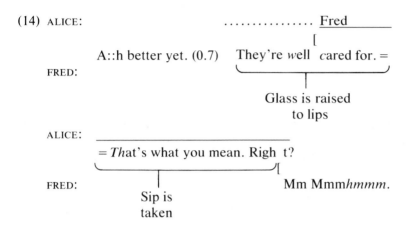

The first section of Alice's utterance—"A::h better yet."—projects that the next part of the utterance will provide an alternative to what Fred has just said. However, when Alice's gaze reaches Fred, he is not gazing at her but instead looking toward a glass that he is bringing to his lips. Despite Alice's talk, Fred does not interrupt this action and, when the first completion of Alice's turn arrives, has the glass to his lips. Alice then adds another sentence to her turn, explicitly locating Fred as its addressee and noting the relevance of what she has just said for what was said in his turn. At the end of this unit, the glass is just leaving Fred's lips. Alice then adds a first pair part explicitly requesting an answer from Fred to her turn.

Though now operating at the level of the sentence,[6] the procedures employed by speakers in these examples to achieve coordination with their recipients are structurally analogous to those examined earlier for synchronizing a phrasal break with the arrival of a recipient's gaze. In all of these situations the possibility can arise that the projected termination of a unit being constructed by the speaker will not occur at the point required for the achievement of appropriate coordination with a recipient:

---

[6] On yet another level of organization, Jefferson (1972) in her analysis of "side sequences" has examined how additional turns might be inserted into a sequence of turns.

(6) ETHYL: *Yeah.* = Wher–
    BARBARA: X

(3) BARBARA: God that's:
    GORDIE: X

(10) JOHN: one–*one* week ag o to*da*:y.
                                    [
     ANN: ... <u>Beth</u>

Though units on different levels of organization are at issue—in these examples, fragments, words, and sentences—in all cases the speaker has the ability to add a new section to the unit so that a new termination point, better suited to the immediate tasks posed in the interaction, is produced.

(6) ETHYL: Yeah. = Wher– uh hh Where *do* they register.
                                    [
    BARBARA: .... X_____

(3) BARBARA: God that's: :, I don't want *that* life.
                             [
    GORDIE: .... X_____

(10) JOHN: one–*one* week ag o to*da*:y. actua lly,
                              [[
     ANN: ... <u>Beth</u>   , ... <u>John</u>

Procedures with much the same structure thus operate on many different levels of organization to enable the speaker to coordinate his actions with those of his recipient.

However, when these procedures are applied at the level of the sentence, a different sentence from that originally projected by the speaker is constructed. Insofar as this is true, the procedures utilized by speakers in conversation to construct sentences are, at least in part, interactive procedures.

The Use of Repairs to Lengthen a Unit

It has been argued that the contingencies of the interaction producing a particular turn at talk may require changes in the length of the units being produced through the turn. Speakers have been found to be able to use many different types of phenomena to lengthen the units they are producing. Despite their diversity, many of these lengthening techniques—including repeats, pauses, "uh" 's, corrections, and clarifications—constitute instances of a single class of phenomena which Schegloff *et al.* (1977) have termed "repairs." Some properties of this class of phenomena which might make it useful for the tasks being investigated here will be briefly considered.

First, repairs are not limited to cases where some mistake or error has occurred. Schegloff *et al.* (1977:363) note that "repair/correction is found where there is no visible (or hearable) error, mistake, or fault."[7] If repairs could only occur after some "error" had been produced, they might not be useable for the tasks being investigated here. Suppose that a recipient turned away in midturn, as in Example (9). Were the production of repairs restricted, a speaker could not use one immediately in such a situation unless he happened to have made a recognizable "mistake" just before the recipient's gaze was lost. The lack of such restriction means that repairs are available to the speaker anywhere in the turn and thus can be employed whenever useful.

Second, the techniques available for signaling that repair is being begun (sometimes referred to as repair initiators) include phenomena such as speech perturbations, cutoffs, sound stretches, and "uh" 's. Many of these phenomena are not only units that can be added to an utterance to lengthen it, but also phrasal breaks with which tasks such as requesting the gaze of a hearer can be accomplished. Moreover, as Sacks (10/11/71:11) has noted, beginning a repair, such as a word search, may in fact invite recipients to help the speaker. Thus, quite apart from their function in requesting a recipient's gaze, repair initiators may request the recipient's collaboration in the talk of the moment and may locate that talk as something he should have been attending in special ways.

Third, repairs can operate on both items not yet produced and items that have already been produced. Repairs on items not yet produced provide, with a single structure, means for both requesting gaze and adding sections to the speaker's utterance until gaze has been obtained. Consider the following:

(15) DIANNE: .... X_____

                                         [

              He pu:t uhm, (– – – – – – –) Tch! Put crab   meat on

                [

    MARSHA: .... X_____

[7] Among the phenomena that make this possible is the fact that self-repair done in a single turn can, and overwhelmingly does, combine the operations of locating the repairable and doing a candidate repair (see Schegloff *et al.*, 1977).

Here the repair initiators provide phrasal breaks to request a hearer's gaze. The pause that follows provides time for the recipient to answer; and the retrieval of the item being sought—marked with a "Tch!"—warrants the speaker's continuing with her utterance. Repairs on items already produced, such as corrections, clarifications, and restarts, permit the speaker to add length to his turn by recycling a portion of his utterance.

Both types of processes may occur in a way relevant to the analysis being developed here in a single repair. Examples (1), (2), and (3) showed how a speaker might delay the beginning of a restart until the recipient's gaze had been secured by prolonging his pronunciation of the last sounds in the restart. Such lengthening can be heard as a repair initiation signaling, and preparing for, the upcoming restart.

Example (9) provides another example of how such processes might be used together in a way relevant to the present analysis:

(9) RALPH: Somebody said looking at my:, son m y oldest son,

                                                    [

    CHIL: _____ , ,   . X_____

Immediately after Chil's gaze is lost, Ralph elongates a word and produces a marked change in intonation. Such actions may be heard as displaying that the speaker is having difficulty in producing the next item in his utterance. In part because of the display of trouble they provide, these repair initiators function to request the gaze of a hearer. After Chil's gaze is regained, Ralph recycles the section of his utterance produced when Chil was not gazing by performing a repair upon the item his request for Chil's gaze has located as problematic. Thus, in this example, an appropriate state of mutual gaze between speaker and hearer is negotiated through the integrated use of both a display of trouble in an item yet to be produced and repair on that item after its production.

Maintaining Focus on Talk

Repairs provide an account for the actions the speaker is performing. Thus, repairs that recycle a portion of the utterance already produced, such as Example (9), generally use the repeated item to mark some change in the initial version of it, thereby displaying that a correction or clarification is being done. A similar account is provided when operations are performed on an item not yet produced. For example, the phrasal breaks, pause, and retrieval in Example (15) display that the speaker is involved in a word search. The aversion of speaker's gaze until recipient's gaze arrives is also accounted for by the word search. While producing the pause, speaker turns away and makes a face that is recognized as demonstrating that she is searching for the next word in her utterance.

In the present analysis, phenomena such as phrasal breaks have been argued to be produced, in some circumstances, with reference to the gaze of a recipient. The account provided by the process of repair—for example, that the speaker in Example (15) is engaged in a word search— does not, however, include the gaze of a recipient. The question might therefore be asked why, if the gaze of the recipient is relevant to the production of some repairs, it is not officially recognized in those instances.

Consider what would happen if speaker made an explicit request for gaze, for example, by saying "Look at me!" If this were to occur, the focus of the conversation, what was being explicitly talked about, would shift from the talk that the speaker had been attempting to produce in his turn to talk about his recipient's lack of proper orientation toward him.[8] Indeed, recipient might be given an opportunity to answer the charges against him so that speaker would even lose the turn itself.[9] If speaker wanted the activity of the moment to focus on the talk he was in the process of producing when recipient's inattention was noted, this would be a very poor way to do it.[10] In contrast, use of a repair, such as a word search, provides a structure that enables the participants to achieve an appropriate state of mutual orientation, without allowing this task to emerge as a noticeable event in its own right. Rather than being involved in the task of securing the gaze of a recipient, the speaker is officially involved in something else entirely—searching for a word. The attention of the participants thus remains directed to the talk that the speaker is producing. By using repairs to accomplish interactive tasks, a speaker manages not only to deal with potentially disruptive events but to have these dealings interpreted as events within his talk rather than as actions dealing with phenomena outside the talk. Because the speaker is able to transform the displayed meaning of his actions in this way, neither the intrusive act nor the work dealing with it ever emerges

---

[8] For more detailed discussion of the ritual consequences of such a shift, see Goffman (1967:125–126).

[9] On this issue see Sacks 10/10/67:12.

[10] Goffman (1953:34) has noted that "in conversational order, even more than in other social orders, the problem is to employ a sanction which will not destroy by its mere enactment the order which it is designed to maintain."

within the conversation as a noticeable event in its own right. Rather, the participants are constantly engaged in the details of the talk the speaker is producing.

Changing the Length and Meaning of Nonvocal Units

Participants have the ability to modify their nonvocal units in much the same way that they modify their vocal units. A very simple example of a task requiring for its accomplishment the coordinated nonvocal action of two participants occurs when one person lights another's cigarette. The cigarette held by one party and the match held by the other must be brought to the same place at the same moment in time.

An example of the performance of this task, (cited in the Appendix as Example [16]) will now be examined. Ann, finding herself with a cigarette but no matches, asks Ginny for a light. Ginny opens her purse and takes out a lighter. However, while Ginny is doing this, one of Ann's children demands her attention and Ann turns to him. Thus, when Ginny finally produces her lighter, she finds that the person who requested it is engaged elsewhere (see Figure 4.1). Ginny nevertheless brings her lighter forward; but when it reaches the place where her partner's cigarette should be, it meets empty air (see Figure 4.2). A failure to achieve coordinated action thus seems to have occurred.

However, the participants have the capacity to modify their emerging action so that precise collaborative action can nevertheless still be achieved. When Ginny, in the course of bringing the lighter to Ann, discovers that she will not be met by Ann's cigarette, she strikes the lighter awkwardly and it fails to light. She then brings the lighter back in front of her and attentively fiddles with the flint in a displayed attempt to fix it (see Figure 4.3). Ann terminates the exchange with her child and begins to turn back toward Ginny. Immediately after this happens, Ginny stops working on the lighter and brings it back to Ann (see Figure 4.4). The broken lighter thus suddenly becomes fixed just as Ann begins to return her attention to Ginny. The lighter lights perfectly on Ginny's first attempt, just before Ann's cigarette reaches it (see Figure 4.5).

Collaborative action is here achieved through modifications in nonvocal units, which are structurally equivalent to the modifications in vocal units considered earlier in this chapter. First, a segment is added to the action of bringing the lighter to the cigarette so that precise coordination between this act and the reciprocal act of a coparticipant—bringing the

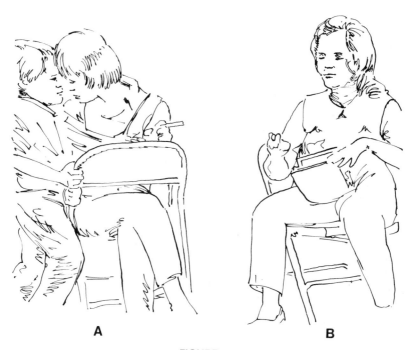

A   B

FIGURE 4.1

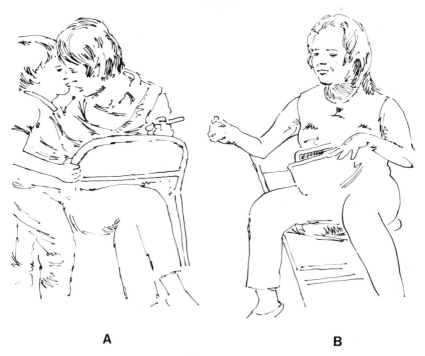

A   B

FIGURE 4.2

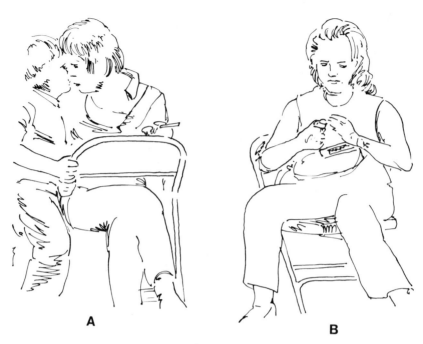

A

B

FIGURE 4.3

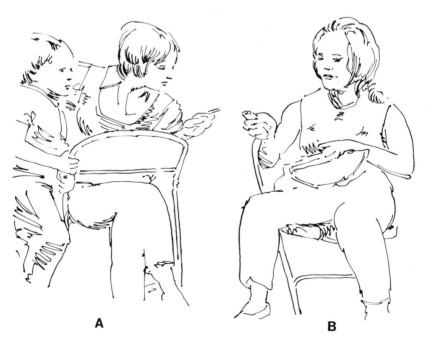

A

B

FIGURE 4.4

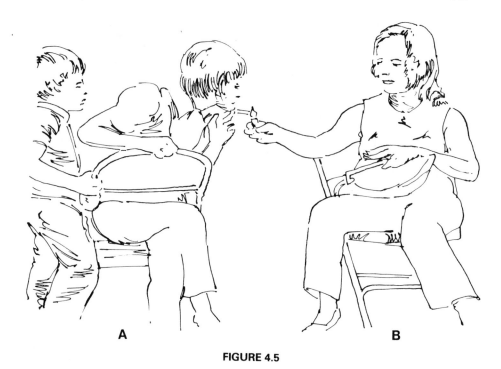

FIGURE 4.5

cigarette to the lighter—can be achieved. Second, this added segment
is displayed as added for reasons located within the original action:That
is, that the initially offered light would not have worked and needed to
be retracted in order to get it to work. It can be noted that this procedure,
display of necessity of repair, is a version of one of the major reasons
employed to warrant the addition of segments to vocal actions.

Summary and Conclusion

   In this chapter, the ability of participants in conversation to add new
sections to units they are in the process of constructing has been investigated. It was found that participants had the ability to do this to
units on many different levels of organization. Specific phenomena examined included the lengthening of sound articulation within an individual
speech sound, the addition of phrasal breaks of various types to an
utterance, the addition of new words and phrases to a sentence, the
addition of sentences to a turn, and, finally, the addition of new sections
to nonvocal action. The ability to add new sections to a unit was found

to facilitate coordination of the speaker's actions, including his utterance, with the actions of a recipient, and to be useful in the accomplishment of various tasks posed in the construction of the turn at talk. Some of the reasons displayed by a participant for the addition of a new segment to a unit were also examined. Particular attention was paid to repairs, a class of actions utilized quite frequently to provide an account for the addition of sections to a unit. Often the reason displayed for the repair does *not* include some of the interactive tasks facilitated by the lengthening of a unit. Some ways in which the absence of focus on this process might be functional were considered. Insofar as both the length and the meaning of units such as the utterance are capable of such systematic modification, it might be appropriate to say that they are not produced by the actions of either party alone, but rather emerge through a process of interaction between speaker and hearer as they mutually construct the turn at talk.

5

Designing Talk for
Different Types of Recipients

One of the most general principles organizing talk within conversation is recipient design.[1] In this chapter we will investigate some ways in which talk proposes specific characteristics for a recipient to it and the consequences this has for the organization of action within the turn. To do this, we shall examine a situation in which recipients with mutually exclusive attributes are simultaneously present. Analysis will focus on systematic methods and procedures available to the speaker for transforming an utterance appropriate to one type of recipient into one that also provides for the participation of the other.

Requesting the Aid of a Knowing Recipient

In the following, three parties—Pat, Jere, and Chil—are teaching a fourth—Ann—how to play bridge. Pat is explaining the bidding system to Ann. Analysis will begin with the talk in Line 5.

(1)
1. PAT: Now Ann you gotta count points.
2.   (1.0)

[1] See Sacks *et al.* (1974:727) and Garfinkel (1967).

3. ANN: Oh Okay.
4.   (15.8)
5. PAT: Now if you have thirteen *poi*nts:, (1.0)

It may be noted that Pat's utterance proposes an ordered, but unequal, distribution of information between the participants: that is, the speaker is engaged in the activity of telling the recipient something that the recipient does not yet know.[2] Specific characteristics are thus posited for both an appropriate recipient and an appropriate speaker. For convenience, a recipient who is proposed to lack relevant information that the speaker possesses will be referred to as an unknowing recipient; a recipient who is supposed to possess information that the speaker lacks will be referred to as a knowing recipient. This latter situation arises with many requests (e.g., "Where is Grand Central Station?"). Note that in such requests, as in the action being considered in the present data, the information states proposed for speaker and hearer are complementary to each other.

The utterance Pat constructs in the present data thus proposes criteria for a recipient to it that Ann, a party who has not yet learned the rules of bridge, meets. Ann, however, does not direct her gaze to the speaker. During the pause, Pat looks at her intended recipient and discovers that, rather than looking at her, Ann is continuing to gaze at her cards.

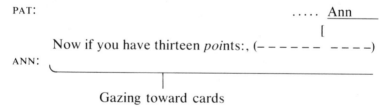

In Chapter 2 it was seen that speakers who find that they do not have the gaze of an addressed recipient have access to systematic procedures for requesting such gaze. However, in the present case, what the speaker finds is not simply that gaze is absent, but that her recipient is engaged in another recognizable activity relevant to the talk being produced, that of analyzing her cards. Further, this is an activity that might have to be brought to some sort of completion before the recipient will be able to

---

[2] Ways in which the analyses participants make of each other's information states are relevant to the organization of conversation have received considerable study. See, for example, Goffman (1974); Jefferson (1973); Labov (1970); Labov and Fanshell (1977); Sacks (1971 [especially his class lectures of 10/10/71 and 10/22/71], 1974) Sacks and Schegloff (1979); Schegloff (1972); and Terasaki (1976).

deal with the "then . . . " clause projected by the "if . . . " clause in the talk already spoken.

Rather than moving immediately to the projected "then . . . " clause, speaker at this point produces talk modifying the initial part of the utterance, that is, talk about how the counting being described, and being performed by Ann, is to be done. Further, rather than continuing to locate Ann as her addressed recipient, and thereby invoke the relevance of Ann's gazing at her, speaker moves her gaze to another recipient, Chil:

```
PAT:                                        ..... Ann
                                                  [
        Now if you have thirteen points:, (– – – – – –   – – – –)
ANN:
PAT:          , , , ...... Chil
        counting:
```

Unlike Ann, Chil knows how to play bridge. Explaining to a novice, such as Ann, the details of the bidding system is both necessary and helpful. Telling an experienced bridge player these same facts is either insulting or absurd.

Pat is thus faced with the task of reconstructing her utterance from one that proposes the ignorance of its recipient about the event discussed in the utterance to one that proposes that its recipient has knowledge of that event. She accomplishes this task of moving from an unknowing recipient to a knowing one by changing her intonation so that her statement becomes marked as problematic. The pronunciation of "voi:ds?", the place in her utterance where her eyes reach Chil, is characterized by both a slight rise in intonation and an elongation of the syllable being spoken:

```
PAT:                                        ..... Ann
                                                  [
        Now if you have thirteen points:, (– – – – – –   – – – –)
ANN:
PAT:      , , ...... Chil
             [
        counting: voi :ds?
```

Through this change in intonation, uncertainty is displayed about what Pat is saying. A new action is therefore embedded within the ongoing statement. This new action, a request for verification, proposes that its recipient is knowledgeable about something that speaker is unsure of.

In producing this action, Pat does not simply change the state of knowledge proposed for her recipient; by displaying uncertainty about some aspect of the same phenomenon that she is elsewhere presenting herself as informed about she changes her own state of knowledge.[3] The reciprocal changes of the states of knowledge proposed for both speaker and recipient have the effect of maintaining a complementary distribution of knowledge between them despite the fact that both action and recipient have been changed. Further, the speaker's display of uncertainty accounts for and warrants the changes in action, recipient, type of recipient, and state of speaker's knowledge that occur at this point in the talk.

It can also be noted that the talk to the knowing recipient continues to be relevant to the unknowing recipient. The talk addressed to Chil deals with how the activity of counting points—the activity Ann is performing—is to be done. It is thus inadequate to talk simply of this utterance as having an addressee; rather than being addressed to a single recipient, the utterance provides for the participation, not just of multiple recipients, but of recipients who differ from each other significantly in ways relevant to the talk in progress. Further, these different types of recipients are ordered relative to one another. Both the structure of the talk and the speaker's gaze locate one party as the current focal recipient and the other as nonfocal recipient.[4] Moreover, by combining shifts in gaze with modifications of her talk, speaker has the ability to change focal addressee and thus to reorder her recipients within a single utterance. The effect of all this is that an action to a knowing recipient can be embedded within an ongoing action to an unknowing recipient.

The knowing recipient Pat addresses here, Chil, fails, however, to attend her. Pat then brings her gaze to the last party present, Jere, who though he had briefly gazed at her, is discovered to have a glass in front of his face. Having failed to secure any of her three coparticipants as a recipient, Pat drops her eyes and escalates her action to the knowing recipients, adding to her utterance an explicit request for verification with full question intonation, "right?" Even this fails, and a gap over a second long follows:

[3] Of particular relevance to what Pat does here is Vološinov's argument (1973:86) that "orientation of the word toward the addressee has an extremely high significance. In point of fact, *word is a two-sided act.* It is determined equally by *whose* word it is and *for whom* it is meant. As word, it is precisely *the product of the reciprocal relationship between speaker and listener, addresser and addressee.* Each and every word expresses the 'one' in relation to the 'other.' I give myself verbal shape from another's point of view . . . [italics in original]."

[4] For other analysis of how different types of recipients might be distinguished see Goffman (1975:3).

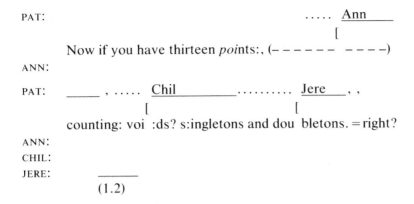

PAT: ..... __Ann____

                                                                  [
          Now if you have thirteen *poi*nts:, (– – – – – – – – – –)

ANN:

PAT: _____ , ... __Chil_____ .... __Jere___, ,

                         [[
          counting: voi :ds? s:ingletons and dou bletons. = right?

ANN:

CHIL:

JERE: _____
               (1.2)

Pat's failure to obtain a recipient generates the next item of talk. However, note that her recipients are chided, not for ignoring her, but for failing to attend to the tasks within which the talk is embedded:

PAT: Now if you have thirteen po*i*nts:, (1.0) counting:
        voi:ds? singletons and doubletons. = right?
              (1.2)

        You gotta *prompt* Ann as she goes alo*ng*. She's never
        gonna re*mem*ber all these things.

These data reveal one systematic procedure for specifying recipients with different characteristics within a single turn. As speaker moves her gaze from an unknowing to a knowing recipient, she displays uncertainty about something that she and the knowing recipient presumably know in common and asks him to verify its accuracy. The states of knowledge made visible in the talk for both speaker and hearer are thus changed; focal addressee changes from an unknowing to a knowing recipient, and speaker becomes uncertain. By operating on her initial statement in this way, speaker not only explicitly recognizes knowing recipient's special knowledge, but makes use of that knowledge for the organization of her talk.

There are in fact a number of systematic procedures that can be used to transform a statement, or a subordinate part of it, into an action appropriate to a knowing recipient. The following provides an example of two such techniques. As speaker moves her gaze to the party she is talking about, she asks that he verify what she has just said by adding the tag question "wasn't it?" to her initial sentence. While continuing to gaze at the knowing recipient, she provides further substantive information but finishes this talk with question intonation.[5]

(2) PAM: Well   I think what's funny is when he was in *gra:*de

    .... Curt _____

       [

    sch   ool. = wasn't it? And y– (0.2) you were up playing

    Curt _____

    poker with the other: little kids? (0.6) And, these
    kids: wouldn't have their lunch cause Curt's (0.7)
    getting their lunch money from them,

In the discussion of Example (1), it was suggested that the talk explicitly addressed to the knowing recipient was still being directed to the unknowing recipient as well. Further support for that possibility is provided by the present example. Note that the addressee of the sentence produced after the speaker's gaze leaves the knowing recipient is presumed to have heard that earlier talk. For example, the word "kids" in this subsequent talk is tied back to the earlier talk with the word "these," and the way in which Curt obtained the other kids' lunch money is not repeated but presumed to be already known. Thus, in the earlier talk, though the statements made are transformed (through intonation and the addition of a tag question) into statements appropriate to a knowing recipient, they are still being spoken for their unknowing recipients as well. Indeed, speaker organizes her subsequent talk on the assumption that unknowing recipient has made such a hearing.

Procedures for transforming a statement into a request for verification (for example, pronouncing the material to be marked as problematic with rising intonation) are available quite generally in conversation. It is there-

---

[5] In addition to the change in actions, the change in recipients in this example also requires a change in the pronouns utilized to identify Curt: When Curt is not being gazed at, and the proposed recipients of the story are unknowing recipients, Curt is referred to as "he"; however, when Pam brings her gaze to Curt and locates him as her recipient, he is referred to as "you." The same person is thus referred to with both second and third person pronouns within a single sentence. George Lakoff (1968) has examined some of the ways in which the same person might be different entities in the same sentence and the consequences this will have on features of the sentence such as its pronouns (see also Goffman 1974:524). In the data currently being examined, Curt is a present participant in one universe of discourse and a schoolboy in another. Pam's request for verification notes this distinction as well as the link between the two characters. Curt-the-present-participant can only be asked to verify the doings of Curt-the-little-boy because of some assumed relationship between them.

fore not surprising that such techniques are used frequently when the task of addressing a knowing recipient is posed. The following provide some examples:

(3) PAT: Jere had to help me. I gotta twist it. They told her to

PAT: .... Unknowing recipient
         [
         twist it co mpletely around like six times,

PAT: .... Knowing recipient (Jere)
         [
         (– – – – – – – –) three times a day or something?

(4) PAT: Unknowing recipient
         They just s:taple it.And the earring is in and you leave it

PAT: _____ .... Knowing recipient
         [
         in. (0.4) for:, (0.6) for :, (0.4) six weeks or something?

(5) BARBARA: ....
         Gordie bought some Orange Crush at

BARBARA: .... Unknowing rec..... Knowing recipient (Gordie)
         [[
         Rink's this morning. Six?   For *what*?

These examples provide support for the possibility that producing a request for verification in fact constitutes a systematic resource available to speakers for making visible the appropriateness of their talk for its current addressee as they move their gaze from one type of recipient to another.

Such procedures for including a knowing recipient in talk otherwise addressed to an unknowing recipient do of course provide a resource for dealing with interactive problems that might arise within the turn. For example, if an unknowing recipient fails to display proper hearership, speaker has the ability to change the talk in progress so that it can be addressed to another recipient (note Example [1]). However, not all such shifts in address are motivated by difficulties with a recipient's lack of attentiveness. In the conversation from which Examples (3) and (4) are taken, unknowing recipient was quite attentive. Nevertheless, speaker repeatedly used a request for verification with a concurrent gaze shift to include her knowing recipient in her talk. The regular presence of phenomena such as these requests in situations where both types of recipients are present makes it relevant for us to examine the interactive organization of such a situation more carefully.

Talk in the Presence of a Knowing Recipient

There are in fact sound reasons for why speakers repeatedly find themselves in the presence of both knowing and unknowing recipients.[6] For example, spouses regularly tell each other any new news that happens to one of them, but also attend many events, such as parties, together. At these events, some of the same news will be told, news that the spouse has already heard. In such circumstances, the knowing recipient might politely feign interest or even join a different conversation. However, it is also possible for such a party to systematically attend the talk. Instead of listening for the news that speaker is providing, the knowing recipient might monitor the adequacy of speaker's presentation. By comparing what he already knows with speaker's current description, a knowing recipient can find inaccuracies and omissions, and might even decide to provide his own version of the events being recounted.

The following provides an example of such a process.[7] Jim and Nadine have gotten married to each other on three separate occasions. Fred attended their third wedding. In this fragment Nadine tells the story of their three weddings. Both Jim (in Lines 6, 8, 11, 14, 17, 27–28, 31) and Fred (in Line 22) overlap her telling with their own versions of the events she is describing:

(6) (Simplified Transcript)
1. NADINE: You remember Father Denelland that mar– Well *yeah*
2.   we *were* married three times. Y ou knew that story.
                                                [
3. ANITA: I didn't know ever=
4. ANITA: hear that.
5. NADINE: Yeah well   we were married in–

---

[6] This paragraph draws heavily upon analysis developed in much greater detail by Sacks (10/19/71).

[7] Such phenomena are not of course unique to American culture. Thomas (1959:89–90), writing about the San of southern Africa, reports a dispute between two parties over the correct version of a story.

6. JIM: That's why I'm hooked!
                        [
7. NADINE: We–
8. JIM: I can't get out!
                    [[
9. NADINE: When we– When we were youngsters we elo:ped:,
10.   and were marr ied in *Ma*ryland:,
                                [
11. JIM: Went to Elkton.
12. NADINE: to Elkton Maryland,
13. NADINE: ˙hh
                    [[
14. JIM: Then we got married in Jamaica,
                            [
15. NADINE: The– the *se*:cond time we had
16.   all s orts of (0.1) property and everything =
                    [
17. JIM: Then we got married in Saint Pa:t's.
18. NADINE: = we thought we should be married again because
19.   of c:ivil papers and all that we were
20.   ma(h)rried in *Lo*ng Island.
                                [
21. ANITA: I never heard this.
22. FRED: And then in Saint Pat's.
                    [[
23. NADINE: ˙hh The *third* time when I converted, I was
24.   married in Saint Patrick's Cathedral. ˙hh And
25.   the priest who married us:, had to meet Jim
26.   before the wedding and he said ˙hh well I've been w–
                                            [
27. JIM: Find out whether
28. JIM: I was a Knights of Templar.
                            [
29. NADINE: He said–
30. NADINE: I'm certainly glad to marry a– t– t– m(h)– =
                                [
31. JIM: Or a Shriner.
32. NADINE: = to me(h)et a man who's willing to marry
33. NADINE: a wo(h)ma(h)n three(h) ti(h)(h)(h)(h)(h)(h)mes.
                            [
34. ANITA: ˙h Huh!

35. FRED: Eh ha ha ha
36. BOB: Eh ha heh heh

To illustrate in more detail the process through which a knowing party not selected as speaker monitors his partner's story for omissions and corrections one segment of the story will be examined more carefully.

Nadine's statement (Lines 24–26) "And the priest who married us:, had to meet Jim before the wedding" projects, in particular with the word "had," that a reason for the meeting existed. However, Nadine chooses not to include that reason in her version of the event; and indeed it is not required for the point she is making, which only involves what the priest said at the meeting. Jim's statement "Find out whether I was a Knights of Templar.", which competes with the ongoing development of Nadine's talk, provides a version of the omitted reason.

Jim's sequential placement of this item in the conversation is related directly to its status as an item of the original event that his wife has excluded in her description of it. Though this item could not have been placed before the meeting emerged in the story, and indeed becomes specifically relevant only after Nadine's projection of its existence, it could have been placed earlier than it was, after "wedding." However, at that point, Nadine could herself have produced the item. The fact of its exclusion in her version of the event only becomes explicit when she moves to a new segment of the story, what the priest said. Only then does the reason for the meeting gain the status of an item omitted in Nadine's description of the event. If Jim does not provide it, it will not be provided at all. However, if Jim does not provide it quickly, the place for telling it in conversation will be lost, as it is not relevant to the next and final segment of the story and there the participants will become involved in the task of appreciating the story.

Thus, both what Jim says and where he says it make visible the fact that he shared experience of the event being reported and that he is closely monitoring the details of its current telling. He locates a feature of the event known to him as a coparticipant but omitted from his wife's description of it; and he provides that item only after the fact of its omission has been displayed and before the relevance of that item to the present state of the conversation is lost.[8]

The problems Jim and Nadine encounter in describing their weddings are not the result of individual idiosyncracies or of the nature of their "relationship," but rather are systematic consequences of the ways in

---

[8] Note that insofar as Jim must wait until the omission has been displayed but must move before the next segment has been brought to completion, the beginning of his talk systematically occurs at some place other than a transition-relevance place.

which tellings are organized. Further, such problems are not confined to spouses; they emerge whenever parties who have experienced an event together are jointly in a position to describe it to someone else. As Sacks (10/19/71:9) notes, the difficulties spouses face in telling stories arise "not so much by virtue of being a spouse, but by virtue of the consequences of being a spouse."

The procedures being investigated in this chapter provide some techniques for dealing with the problems that emerge when both unknowing and knowing recipients are copresent. By producing a request for verification about a subordinate aspect of the event being described, a speaker can provide for the inclusion of a knowing recipient in a turn otherwise addressed to an unknowing recipient. A request for verification engages its recipient in many of the same operations that can lead to repeated correction and competition such as was found in Jim and Nadine's story. The knowing recipient is asked to monitor what the speaker is saying for its correctness, but his participation in the telling of the event is constrained by the form of the request. For example, a request for verification both provides a specific type of next turn—that is, an answer to the request (which might be a simple nod or "mm hmm")— and focuses the attention of its recipient not on items omitted by the speaker in his telling (such as the reason for the meeting with the priest in Nadine and Jim's story), but rather on the things he has actually said. Some of the potential for competitive talk is thus undercut. Moreover, such a request may also operate ritually, displaying deference to the other party present who could be telling the story and obtaining his approval of, and agreement with, the way in which it is being told.

The repeated forgetfulness that is sometimes found when spouses are in each other's presence might thus be socially engendered. Rather than reflecting cognitive difficulty, such uncertainty, because of its interactive organization, provides a resource for dealing with some of the consequences that sharing experience with another has for the organization of talk.

Discovering New News

In the data so far examined, the inclusion of a knowing recipient in a turn initially addressed to an unknowing recipient has been accomplished by producing an action, such as a request for verification, that changes the information states projected for speaker and hearer by the talk of the moment. An utterance will now be investigated in which the information states of speaker and hearer remain constant while the event being reported is transformed as the speaker moves his gaze from one type of recipient to another.

Analysis will focus on the following sentence (which has already received some attention, though from a different perspective, in Chapter 4): "I gave up smoking cigarettes one week ago today actually." The sentence was spoken during a dinner in the home of John and his wife Beth attended by their friends Ann and Don. While he is speaking, John directs his gaze to three different recipients during three different sections of the utterance. His gaze is directed to Don during "I gave up smoking cigarettes," to Beth during "one week ago today," and, finally, to Ann during "actually."

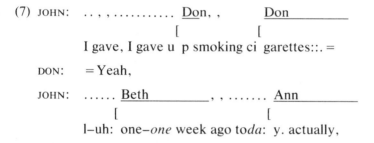

By plotting aspects of the speaker's gaze, it is thus possible to divide his sentence into three separate sections during each of which a different recipient is gazed at.

An attempt will now be made to demonstrate that each of these sections is designed specifically for the recipient toward whom the speaker is gazing at the moment. It will be argued, first, that each segment is appropriate to a specific recipient and inappropriate to other possible recipients and, second, that the recipient to whom it is appropriate is the recipient toward whom the speaker is gazing during its production.

The first section of John's sentence, "I gave up smoking cigarettes.", is a member of the class of actions that propose that the speaker has knowledge of an event about which the recipient is ignorant; it would be inappropriate to announce to someone that one had given up smoking when that recipient already knew it.[9] Don and his wife Ann are the dinner guests of John and his wife Beth. Neither has seen the speaker for some

---

[9] Sacks (1973:139) has noted the operation in conversation of a "general rule that provides that one should not tell one's co-participants what one takes it they already know." This rule is implicated in the organization of a range of different types of informings, including announcements, stories, and reports.

period of time before the present evening. John thus has reason to suppose that Don has not yet heard the news he is now telling.[10] He would
therefore be an appropriate recipient to an announcement such as that
made by John; and it is to Don that John directs his gaze during this
section of his utterance. At least one party present at the dinner would
not be an appropriate recipient of the first section of John's sentence.
Beth, the speaker's wife, has been living in the same house with him
for the past week and knows that he has given up smoking. Further,
this is something that the speaker knows that she knows and indeed the
others present can also legitimately see these things.[11] Insofar as John's
initial statement is appropriate to an unknowing recipient and Beth is
a knowing recipient, the present line of analysis implies that the event
described to Don should not be reported to Beth.

For the next section of the sentence, "I–uh: one–*one* week ago
to*da*:y.", John switches his gaze from Don, an unknowing recipient, to
Beth, a knowing recipient. With the addition of this section to the sentence, the news that John has stopped smoking cigarettes is transformed
into a different piece of news, that today is an anniversary of that event.
Such an anniversary is a new event that none of the parties present,
including Beth, need be expected to know about. By finding this new
news, speaker thus manages to reshape his talk so that it becomes appropriate to a knowing recipient.

The structure of an anniversary makes it particularly appropriate as
a solution to a problem such as that faced by John. An anniversary is
constructed via the lamination[12] of events at two separate moments in
time—an original event which becomes the object of celebration, and
the anniversary itself. The two are related by the occurrence of some
regular period of time between them.[13]

[10] Note that what is at issue is not the actual state of Don's knowledge, but rather the
speaker's analysis of what is known by his recipient. Further, participants in conversation
have access to systematic resources for affirming, denying, or negotiating that analysis
(on this issue see the work cited in Note 2). For detailed study of specific ways in which
participants analyze what their coparticipants know, display that analysis to each other,
and utilize that analysis in the detailed production of their talk, see Schegloff (1972).

[11] See Sacks (10/19/71).

[12] The analytic notion of lamination as a structural feature of events and actions is
discussed in Goffman (1974:82, 156–157).

[13] An interesting discussion of how measurements producing "round numbers" can
construct distinct cultural phenomena (a "four-minute mile" for example) is provided by
Lotz (1968). Jefferson (1973:65–66) gives an analysis of how participants in conversation
orient to, and utilize, this phenomenon in the construction of their talk. Gusfield (1976:20)
notes how numbers that are recognizably not round, such as percentages given in decimals,
may be employed by a scientist to demonstrate "meticulous attention to details . . .
thereby avoiding a judgement by the reader that he has been less than scrupulous."

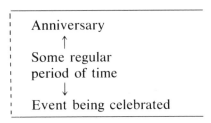

An anniversary is an appropriate object to call to the attention of someone who shared with the speaker the experience of the event that it celebrates. More precisely, interest in the anniversary is contingent upon interest in the event itself (for example, few other than a particular couple have any interest in the anniversary of their meeting). However, a party who knows of the original event need not be aware of the fact that a period of time appropriate for the location of an anniversary has passed. The laminated structure of the anniversary thus integrates items of common experience with novel information in a way particularly suited for the inclusion of a knowing recipient, such as Beth, in John's utterance.

Such a laminated structure also maintains the relevance of this section of the sentence for its original recipient. First, the initial report to him is incorporated within it as the lowest layer of the lamination. Second, the report of the anniversary continues to perform an action relevant to an unknowing recipient, the description of that original event. In particular, it specifies the time at which the event occurred, an item that a recipient presumed to be ignorant of that event would not be expected to know. Thus, though this section of the sentence is made appropriate to a new type of recipient, it maintains its relevance for its original recipient.

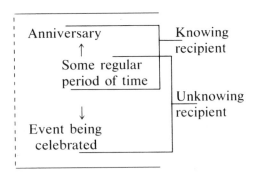

In essence, each layer of the lamination locates an alternative type of recipient. Thus, like the request for verification, this structure provides for the simultaneous participation of different types of recipients, one of whom is located as focal addressee. What happens here indicates that on some occasions a cultural object, such as an anniversary, might be selected for presentation at a particular moment because its structural properties permit the solution of interactive problems posed in the construction of the turn.

Other features of John's utterance provide support for the argument that he is reshaping his sentence in order to make it appropriate to a new type of recipient.

First, an alternative to the section of his sentence actually produced at this point is begun and abandoned:

> JOHN: l–uh: one–*one* week ago to*da*:y.

The word beginning, "l–", plus the hesitation, "uh:", plus the second word "one" correspond to what Jefferson (1974:186) has described as the Error Correction Format. The word begun by the initial fragment[14] constitutes an alternative to the second word, which corrects it. "Last week" and "last Monday" are possible alternatives to the section actually produced. An expression beginning with "last" in this position would do more than simply specify the time at which the event occurred; it would argue for the status of the speaker's statement as news to an unknowing recipient by explicitly telling the recipient that it happened since they were last in contact with each other.[15] In view of Don's "yea:h" after the first section of the sentence, which neither acknowledges the newsworthiness of the event[16] nor requests elaboration of it, warranting what has just been said in this fashion may be a relevant act for the speaker to perform.

Such an alternative differs, however, from the one eventually selected in that it does not construct an action appropriate to a recipient already informed about the event being described. Its rejection thus provides further support for the argument that John, faced with the task of making his utterance appropriate to a new type of recipient, reshapes the event being described through the utterance.

Other evidence that the anniversary, which redesigns the sentence for its new recipient, was not projected as an element of the sentence from its beginning is provided by the speaker's intonation, which locates sur-

---

[14] Jefferson (1974a: 185–186) provides evidence that participants in conversation do orient to such fragments as word-beginnings and analyzes the procedures utilized for such recognition.

[15] On this issue see Sacks (1974:341).

[16] The relevance of a recipient's acknowledging the newsworthiness of an event and ways in which this is done have been investigated by Terasaki (1976:4–9).

prise at the beginning of the section and places stress on the revelation of the anniversary:

> JOHN: I–uh: one–*one* week ago to*da*:y.

The discovery intonation at the beginning of the section is placed in contrast to a possible beginning without such stress. Specifically, the first and second "one" differ noticeably in their intonation so that the change in intonation is marked as the warrant for the restart. Such a structure both announces that something unanticipated has been discovered and locates where that discovery occurred. Recipients are thus informed not only that some new basis for listening is being offered, but also that this new information was discovered after the first section of the utterance. Such an announcement would be particularly important for a party, such as Beth, who has been located as an unlikely recipient to the speaker's sentence by its first section.

John's utterance thus provides some demonstration that a speaker in natural conversation has the capacity to modify the emerging meaning of his sentence as he is producing it with the effect that its appropriateness to its recipient of the moment can be maintained and demonstrated. Though the sentence originally begun proposed that its recipient had no knowledge of the event being described within it, by transforming that event and locating a new piece of news the speaker was able to make the sentence appropriate to one who shared experience of it with him.

Transforming the event being told in the way John does here is an unusual solution to the problem of including a knowing recipient in a turn otherwise constructed for an unknowing recipient. John could have employed the procedures examined earlier in this chapter to make his utterance appropriate to Beth. For example, on turning to Beth, John could have produced the time that the event took place (as he indeed began to do at the beginning of this section) but indicated that it was problematic by pronouncing it with rising intonation, that is, "last week?" or "last Monday?" In a certain sense a solution of this type would have been simpler than the one actually used since it would have involved less modification of the emerging utterance. John's choice of an atypical procedure for including a knowing recipient in his turn, and, further, a procedure that is not the most simple available for performing the tasks posed, invites speculation as to why his particular solution was chosen.

It is revealed several utterances later that John is taking a course on how to stop smoking from a group of Seventh Day Adventists. Seven days is of course precisely the time relationship necessary for the discovery of the anniversary. Sacks and his colleagues have shown that one feature systematically implicated in word selection in conversation is punning relationships of various types.[17] The availability of this particular name in the event being reported might thus be relevant to John's discovery of the anniversary. Moreover once the anniversary has been found it has a preferred status for telling since it is the latest news, the original event being news that is already a week old.

Despite John's careful and precise work to redesign his utterance for Beth, and, with his phrasal breaks, to signal that her gaze is needed, she does not bring her gaze to him. It was seen in the last chapter (pp. 131–133) that at this point John secures the gaze of a different recipient, Ann. In order to provide time within his turn for Ann to move her gaze to him, he adds to his sentence a new section, the word "actually":

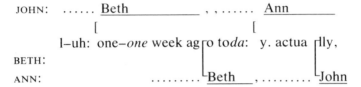

When John moves his gaze from Beth to Ann, the task of reconstructing his utterance so that it is made appropriate to his recipient of the moment is posed a second time. Unlike Beth, but like Don, Ann did not share with John experience of the event he is describing. Thus, a constraint on the segment to be added to the sentence to provide for her inclusion is that it make the proposed recipient of the sentence an unknowing recipient. "Actually" accomplishes this task. Through its addition the discovery of the anniversary is transformed into a report about it. Rather than being asked to recognize the anniversary, the recipient is told that in fact the event being marked by it did occur a week ago. The addition of "actually," thus again reconstructs the emerging meaning of John's sentence so that once more it becomes appropriate to its recipient of the moment.

In the course of its production, the unfolding meaning of John's sentence is reconstructed twice, a new segment is added to it, and another is deleted prior to its production but replaced with a different segment. The sentence eventually produced emerges as the product of a dynamic process of interaction between speaker and hearer as they mutually construct the turn at talk. The fact that a single coherent sentence emerges is among the more striking features of this process.

---

[17] See, for example, Sacks (1973), Jefferson (1974a: 189–190), and Sacks's first three fall 1971 class lectures.

Conclusion

In this chapter, analysis has focused on the ability of the speaker to differentiate particular types of recipients and to display in his talk the appropriateness of his utterance for its recipient of the moment. Though recipients may be relevantly distinguished from each other in many different ways, the present analysis has been restricted to a single feature, the state of the recipient's knowledge about the event being reported by the speaker. In examining situations in which the main addressee was an unknowing recipient but a knowing recipient was also present, it was found that when the speaker moved his gaze to a knowing recipient, he produced a display of uncertainty about what he was saying, thus constructing an action—a request for verification—appropriate to a knowing recipient. In order to maintain the appropriateness of his utterance for a recipient with a particular state of knowledge, the speaker changes his own state of knowledge. The ability to construct a turn capable of providing for the inclusion of both types of recipients was found to be useful both for the accomplishment of local tasks posed in the construction of the turn and because the copresence of knowing and unknowing recipients itself engenders particular structural problems. It was also found that a speaker might redesign his utterance for a knowing recipient by transforming the event being reported in it so that a new piece of news, appropriate to the knowing recipient, was provided. The analysis in this chapter provides further demonstration of the relevance of the hearer to the meaning and detailed construction of the utterance of the speaker.

6

Conclusion

This study has investigated some particular aspects of the interaction of speaker and hearer in the construction of the turn at talk in natural conversation. In Chapter 2, the negotiation of an appropriate state of mutual gaze at turn-beginning was examined. It was found that particular states of gaze were in fact relevant to the turn and that participants had access to systematic procedures for both achieving appropriate states of gaze and remedying the occurrence of inappropriate states. The use of these procedures produced characteristic phenomena, such as phrasal breaks, in the speaker's utterance. Chapter 3 examined some of the engagement alternatives available to participants, the ways in which particular engagement states are achieved through a collaborative process of interaction, and the consequences such engagement displays have for the organization of the talk in progress. Through use of such resources participants are able to make visible a range of different types of co-participation in the talk of the moment. In Chapter 4, the ability of participants to change the units they were in the process of producing by adding new sections to them was examined. It was found that vocal units on many different levels of organization, from within the phoneme to the sentence, as well as nonvocal units, were capable of such modification. It was further found that this ability constitutes a resource for the achievement of social organization within the turn, in essence enabling one participant to coordinate the units he is producing with the relevant actions of a coparticipant. This process leads to changes not only in the length of units being produced, but also in their meaning. The procedures investigated in this chapter were found to be relevant to the accomplishment of a number of tasks posed in the construction of the turn, including the tasks examined in Chapter 2. In Chapter 5, the ability of the speaker to modify his emerging utterance so that it remained appropriate to its recipient of the moment was investigated. A situation was examined in which two different types of recipients, a knowing recipient and an unknowing recipient, were both present.[1] It was found that a speaker who had been addressing his turn to an unknowing recipient could make it appropriate to a knowing recipient either by changing the states of knowledge projected both for himself and his recipient through a change in action, or by transforming the event being described so that it became appropriate to its new recipient. This study has thus described and analyzed specific procedures utilized by speaker and hearer to coordinate their interaction in the construction of the turn at talk.

The work reported here is relevant to research in several different fields. First, some empirical analysis of a basic and pervasive form of human communication, conversation, has been provided. It has been found that not only the exchange of turns, but the internal structure of the turn at talk itself, is constructed through a process of communication between speaker and hearer. Specific communication processes within the turn—for example, a speaker's request for his recipient's gaze and the answer to that request by the recipient—have been investigated and analyzed. It has also been found that this process of communication may systematically lead to the modification of phenomena such as sentences constructed within the turn. On the one hand, such findings cast doubt on the arguments of some communications researchers—for example, Coulthard and Ashby (1975:140) and Rogers and Farace (1975:226)—that communication is not present until an exchange of turns has occurred. On the other hand, they suggest that processes of communication may be far more deeply implicated in the production of language than has traditionally been recognized in linguistics. The present work has also provided some demonstration that the process of communication involved in the production of the turn at talk organizes not only the vocal behavior of the participants but also aspects of their nonvocal behavior, such as their gaze. Specific communications structures relating vocal to

---

[1] For other analysis of how the structure of a particular type of turn, a story, might provide organization for a range of different types of participants, see Goodwin (forthcoming). See also M. Goodwin (1980b) for analysis of how utterances with a particular syntactic structure might organize participants into a particular set of occasion-specific identities.

nonvocal actions have been investigated. This work thus supports both theoretically and empirically the argument long made by Birdwhistell (for example, 1970:162; 1973:93–94) that speech and body movement are integrated aspects of a single communications process. Some approach has also been made toward the analysis of communications processes from the perspective of models of the type Krippendorff (1969a) has termed discourse and communications models. Procedures through which essential variables in the turn—such as the appropriateness of an utterance for its recipient—are achieved and maintained in the face of changes in the relevant local environment—such as a change in recipients—have been specified and analyzed. Such procedures have been found to change the phenomena being constructed within the turn with the effect that the utterance eventually produced is both modified by, and a manifestation of, the constraints organizing the communication of the participants in the construction of the turn. The work in this study provides empirical analysis of specific communications behavior, such as utterances, sentences, phrasal breaks, and gaze; the codes organizing such behavior into relevant communicative messages, for example, a request and its answer; and the communications institution, the turn at talk, within which these phenomena are situated. A range of phenomena implicated in the organization of human communication are thus investigated.

Second, the work reported here is relevant to the study of human interaction and, in particular, to the analysis of conversation. Ties between the present work and other research into the structure of conversation have been made explicit throughout the analysis and no attempt will be made to summarize them here. At present I merely wish to note that some of the same sequential phenomena that have been found to be implicated in the organization of the exchange of turns— summons–answer sequences, for example—were also found to be operative within the turn itself. Further, such structures not only provide organization for the vocal behavior of the participants, but also organize aspects of their nonvocal behavior. It would thus seem that sequential structures of the type analyzed by Sacks and his colleagues operate quite generally and organize a very wide range of phenomena in conversation, and perhaps in human interaction in general.

Third, the work reported here is relevant to a number of different issues in linguistics, only some of which have been examined in the analysis. First, the process of communication between speaker and hearer as they mutually construct the turn at talk has been found to be capable of modifying both the length and the meaning of the sentence produced within the turn. Conversational structures are thus implicated not only in the relationships between sentences, but also in the internal organization of the sentence itself. Within linguistics, the sentence has traditionally been examined as a fixed, static object. However, both the work of Sacks and his colleagues, and some of the analysis here, provide some demonstration that sentences are in fact time-bound structures, emerging through and within a process of interaction. Insofar as this is the case, the procedures utilized to construct sentences are, at least in part, interactive procedures.

Second, as noted in Chapter 1, some linguists have argued that natural speech should not be employed as data for the analysis of linguistic competence because of the many errors and phrasal breaks found within it. Thus Chomsky (1965:4) states that "[performance] obviously could not directly reflect competence. A record of natural speech will show numerous false starts, deviations from rules, changes of plan in mid-course, and so on. The problem for the linguist, as well as for the child learning the language, is to determine from the data of performance the underlying system of rules that has been mastered by the speaker–hearer and that he puts to use in actual performance." This volume has provided some demonstration that the phenomena Chomsky dismisses as performance errors may result not from the actions of the speaker alone but rather might be emergent products of the interaction of speaker and hearer in the construction of the turn at talk. From such a perspective, objects such as phrasal breaks, rather than demonstrating the defective performance of a speaker, constitute manifestations of his competence to construct utterances and sentences that are in fact oriented to appropriately by a recipient.

If phrasal breaks are not simply noise in the system, but rather phenomena that participants attend to with precision, the possibility arises that they might in fact be relevant to the other issue Chomsky raises: the ability of an entity—child or linguist—to decipher from the data of performance the system of rules underlying a language he encounters. With respect to this possibility it may be noted that many (though not all) repairs involve the repetition, with some significant change, of something said elsewhere in the utterance. For example:

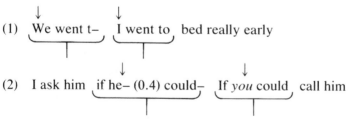

Such repetition has the effect of delineating the boundaries and structure of many different units in the stream of speech. Thus, by analyzing what is different and what is the same in these examples, one is able to discover, first, where the stream of speech can be divided into significant subunits; second, that alternatives are possible in a particular slot; third, what some of these alternatives are (in these examples different pronouns); and, fourth, that these alternatives contrast with each other in some significant fashion (or else the repair would not be warranted). In essence, these repairs provide a distributional analysis of relevant phenomena in the stream of speech, and, indeed, their form is in many respects analogous to techniques developed by linguists, such as elicitation frames and minimal pairs, for determining structure in the stream of speech.

Repairs in other examples not only delineate basic units in the stream of speech, but also demonstrate both the different forms such units can take and types of operations that can be performed upon them. Consider the following:

(3) Somebody said looking at ⎣my:, son⎦ ⎣my oldest son,⎦ he has

The repair in this utterance provides a range of information about structures utilized in the language. First, it separates out a relevant unit, a noun phrase, from the stream of speech. Second, it shows where that unit can itself be subdivided. Third, it provides an example of the type of unit, an adjective, that can be added to the noun phrase. Fourth, it locates at least one place in the noun phrase where such an addition is permitted. Finally, in the contrast between the first and second version of the noun phrase, the repair shows that such an addition is optional. Thus, insofar as repairs provide for significant differences in form to be displayed within a context of repetition, they give clear information about contrasts within the language that are significant to its users, as well as information about how the stream of speech is divided into appropriate units, the operations that are possible on those units, and the combinations they can form.[2]

Repairs further require that a listener learn to recognize that not all of the sequences found within the stream of speech are possible sequences within the language. Thus, in order to understand talk such as that found in the examples just noted, a hearer must distinguish between

---

[2] For some analysis of ways in which the process of repair is relevant to syntax, see Schegloff (1979). Fromkin (1971) analyzes some of the ways in which speech errors reveal basic structures being utilized in the production of language, and Labov (1975) describes some of the syntactic operations involved in repair. Cazden (1972:106) reports unpublished work of Snow (1971) which suggests that partial repetition may be useful in the language acquisition process in that it provides information about the boundaries of grammatical units.

an utterance and another unit manifested within the utterance—that is, a sentence—which does not contain all of the words spoken by the speaker. Similarly, in order to properly interpret the speech in the following a hearer must be able to recognize that "you kids" is not a next element in the sentence which had been in progress until that point, but that a discontinuity has occurred and "you kids" marks the beginning of a new sentence:

(4)   Brian you're gonna hav– You kids'll *ha*ve to go down closer

In order to deal with repairs, a hearer is thus required to make one of the most basic distinctions posed for anyone attempting to decipher the structure of a language: He is called upon to distinguish between what are and are not possible sequences in the language, that is, between grammatical and ungrammatical structures. The fact, in itself, that this task is posed may be extremely important for any learning process. If a learner did not have to deal with ungrammatical possibilities, if, for example, he were exposed only to well-formed sentences, he might not have the opportunity to determine the boundaries or even the structure of the system. For example, in order to both test and formulate their rules, linguists have found it necessary to systematically produce sentences not permitted by the language. The opportunity to deal with ungrammatical structures may be an essential component of the process through which the language is learned.

Chomsky (1957:13) has formulated the basic goals of linguistic analysis as follows: "The fundamental aim in the linguistic analysis of a language L is to separate the *grammatical* sequences which are the sentences of L from the *ungrammatical* sequences which are not sentences of L and to study the structure of the grammatical sequences." Repairs are one place where the distinction between grammatical and ungrammatical sequences is in fact made by native speakers of the language and, indeed, utilized by them in the conduct of their talk. Further, this process provides materials relevant to the systematic analysis of many aspects of a language's structure, with the effect that someone attempting to learn the language is given a great deal of information by repairs. The argument that the repairs found in natural speech so flaw it that a child (or linguist) hearing it is faced with data of very "degenerate quality" (Chomsky 1965:58) does not appear warranted. Rather it might be argued that, if a child grew up in an ideal world where he heard only well-formed sentences, he would not learn to produce sentences himself because he would lack the analysis of their structure provided by processes such as the repair process.

In conclusion, the analysis of the turn at talk in natural conversation provides the opportunity to investigate in detail a diverse and important range of phenomena. First, the turn is a principal locus of human linguistic activity, one of the central places where sentences emerge in the natural world. Second, the turn requires for its achievement the collaborative work of both a speaker and a hearer and thus provides an elementary instance of the achievement of social order. Further, this type of social organization is extraordinarily pervasive, occurring not only in many different human societies, but also in a wide variety of institutions within a single society—from the play of children, to the conduct of business in the workplaces of tailors, salesmen, scientists, and heads of states, to the intimate encounters of lovers, the disputes of enemies, the daily activities of families, etc. Though very little attention has yet been paid to the turn as an institution in its own right, the pervasiveness of its occurrence, the range of phenomena achieved within it, and the clear but intricate data it makes accessible to detailed study, would seem to make it a crucial locus for anyone attempting to develop a general theory of how human beings coordinate their actions with each other and thus organize themselves socially. Third, within the turn participants are faced with the cultural task of displaying to each other the meaningfulness of their utterances and actions, and of maintaining this meaningfulness as relevant events change through time. The investigation of the turn at talk thus permits the analysis of basic social, linguistic, and cultural phenomena as elements of a single integrated process.

Data Sources

The first number in each of the following citations identifies the tape that the example is taken from; the remaining numbers locate where that example is found on the tape.

Chapter 1

(1) G.50:3:25   Suburban Pittsburgh Block Party
(2) G.26:9:00   Philadelphia Dinner

Chapter 2

(1) G.26:3:30   Philadelphia Dinner
(2) G.84:7:00   Midwestern Backyard Picnic
(3) G.50:7:00   Suburban Pittsburgh Block Party
(4) G.126:330   Suburban Pittsburgh Family Dinner
(5) G.76:652   Midwestern Moose Picnic
(6) G.58:410   New Jersey Teenage Swim Party
(7) G.76:652   Midwestern Moose Picnic
(8) G.90:475   Midwestern Moose Picnic
(9) G.103:544   New Jersey Family Reunion

(10)	GA.8:0.6	Long Island Family Reunion
(11)	G.126:297	Suburban Pittsburgh Family Dinner
(12)	G.91:520	Midwestern Moose Picnic
(13)	G.87:160	Midwestern Backyard Picnic
(14)	G.82:618	Midwestern Backyard Picnic
(15)	G.78:115	Midwestern Moose Picnic
(16)	G.26:13:25	Philadelphia Dinner
(17)	G.50:3:50	Suburban Pittsburgh Block Party
(18)	G.50:4:00	Suburban Pittsburgh Block Party
(19)	G.23:124	New Jersey Friends
(20)	G.75:614	Midwestern Moose Picnic
(21)	G.86:510	Midwestern Backyard Picnic
(22)	G.76:620	Midwestern Moose Picnic
(23)	G.76:108	Midwestern Moose Picnic
(24)	G.23:149	New Jersey Friends
(25)	G.50:5:30	Suburban Pittsburgh Block Party
(26)	G.26:18:45	Philadelphia Dinner
(27)	G.23:180	New Jersey Friends
(28)	G.50:03:05	Suburban Pittsburgh Block Party
(29)	G.23:124	New Jersey Friends
(30)	G.50:8:40	Suburban Pittsburgh Block Party
(31)	G.50:7:40	Suburban Pittsburgh Block Party
(32)	G.50:2:10	Suburban Pittsburgh Block Party
(33)	G.50:8:30	Suburban Pittsburgh Block Party
(34)	G.50:0:04	Suburban Pittsburgh Block Party
(35)	G.50:3:40	Suburban Pittsburgh Block Party
(36)	G.140:352	North Philadelphia Family Get-together
(37)	G.84:06:30	Midwestern Backyard Picnic
(38)	G.91:550	Midwestern Moose Picnic
(39)	G.50:4:20	Suburban Pittsburgh Block Party
(40)	G.50:3:43	Suburban Pittsburgh Block Party
(41)	G.50:0:15	Suburban Pittsburgh Block Party
(42)	G.50:2:40	Suburban Pittsburgh Block Party
(43)	G.50:8:20	Suburban Pittsburgh Block Party
(44)	G.50:6:15	Suburban Pittsburgh Block Party
(45)	G.79:540	Midwestern Family Reunion
(46)	G.140:345	North Philadelphia Family Get-together
(47)	G.50:8:20	Suburban Pittsburgh Block Party
(48)	G.50:8:21	Suburban Pittsburgh Block Party
(49)	G.75:122	Midwestern Moose Picnic
(50)	G.91:385	Midwestern Moose Picnic
(51)	GA.8:0.6	Long Island Family Reunion

(52) G.76:090	Midwestern Moose Picnic
(53) G.84:7:15	Midwestern Backyard Picnic
(54) G.78:150	Midwestern Moose Picnic
(55) G.50:7:25	Suburban Pittsburgh Block Party

Chapter 3

(1) G.50:5:45	Suburban Pittsburgh Block Party
(2) G.84:3:45	Midwestern Backyard Picnic
(3) G.50:7:30	Suburban Pittsburgh Block Party
(4) G.50:8:00	Suburban Pittsburgh Block Party
(5) G.50:8:50	Suburban Pittsburgh Block Party

Chapter 4

(1) G.84:6:30	Midwestern Backyard Picnic
(2) G.98:690	New Jersey Friends
(3) G.76:584	Midwestern Moose Picnic
(4) G.34:222	Midwestern Moose Ice Cream Social
(5) G.86:352	Midwestern Backyard Picnic
(6) G.76:659	Midwestern Moose Picnic
(7) G.50:6:15	Suburban Pittsburgh Block Party
(8) G.91:512	Midwestern Moose Picnic
(9) GA.4:302	Long Island Family Reunion
(10) G.26:8:50	Philadelphia Dinner
(11) G.26:19:15	Philadelphia Dinner
(12) G.34:05.5	Midwestern Moose Ice Cream Social
(13) G.23:202	New Jersey Bridge Game
(14) GA.4:018	Long Island Family Reunion
(15) G.50:4:00	Suburban Pittsburgh Block Party
(16) G.91:055	Midwestern Moose Picnic

Chapter 5

(1) G.23:490	New Jersey Bridge Game
(2) G.75:290	Midwestern Moose Picnic
(3) G.99:385	New Jersey Friends
(4) G.99:380	New Jersey Friends
(5) G.75:290	Midwestern Moose Picnic

(6) GA.4:257   Long Island Family Reunion
(7) G.26:8:50   Philadelphia Dinner

Chapter 6

(1) G.126:330   Suburban Pittsburgh Family Dinner
(2) G.126:297   Suburban Pittsburgh Family Dinner
(3) GA.4:302   Long Island Family Reunion
(4) G.75:668   Midwestern Moose Picnic

References

Allen, Donald E., and Rebecca F. Guy

1974 *Conversation Analysis: The Sociology of Talk*. The Hague: Mouton.

Argyle, Michael

1969 *Social Interaction*. London: Methuen.

Argyle, Michael, and Mark Cook

1976 *Gaze and Mutual Gaze*. Cambridge: Cambridge University Press.

Argyle, Michael, and Janet Dean

1965 Eye-Contact, Distance and Affiliation. *Sociometry* 28:289–304.

Atkinson, J. Maxwell, and Paul Drew

1979 *Order in Court: The Organisation of Verbal Interaction in Judicial Settings*. London: Macmillan.

Atkinson, Martin

1979 Prerequisites for Reference. In *Developmental Pragmatics*. Elinor Ochs and Bambi B. Schieffelin, eds. Pp. 229–249. New York: Academic Press.

Bales, Robert Freed

1950 *Interaction Process Analysis: A Method for the Study of Small Groups*. Reading, Mass.: Addison-Wesley.

Bales, Robert Freed

1970 *Personality and Interpersonal Behavior*. New York: Holt, Rinehart and Winston.

Bar-Hillel, Yehoshua

1954 Indexical Expressions. *Mind* 63:359–379.

Beattie, Geoffrey W.

1978a Floor Apportionment and Gaze in Conversational Dyads. *British Journal of Social and Clinical Psychology* 17:7–16.

Beattie, Geoffrey W.

1978b Sequential Temporal Patterns of Speech and Gaze in Dialogue. *Semiotica* 23:29–52.

Beattie, Geoffrey W.
1979   Planning Units in Spontaneous Speech: Some Evidence from Hesitations in Speech
and Speaker Gaze Direction in Conversation. *Linguistics* 17:61–78.
Beattie, Geoffrey W., and P.J. Barnard
1979   The Temporal Structure of Natural Telephone Conversations (Directory Inquiry
Calls). *Linguistics* 17:213–229.
Bernstein, Basil
1962   Linguistic Codes, Hesitation Phenomena and Intelligence. *Language and Speech*
5:31–47.
Birdwhistell, Ray L.
1970   *Kinesics and Context: Essays on Body Motion Communication.* New York: Bal-
lantine Books.
Birdwhistell, Ray L.
1973   Kinesics. In *Social Encounters: Readings in Social Interaction.* Michael Argyle,
ed. Pp. 93–102. Chicago: Aldine.
Bloomfield, Leonard
1946   *Language.* New York: Henry Holt and Company.
Bolinger, Dwight
1975   *Aspects of Language* (Second ed.). New York: Harcourt Brace Jovanovich.
Boomer, Donald S.
1965   Hesitation and Grammatical Encoding. *Language and Speech* 8:148–158.
Brotherton, Patricia
1979   Speaking and Not Speaking: Processes for Translating Ideas into Speech. In *Of
Speech and Time: Temporal Speech Patterns in Interpersonal Context.* Aron W.
Siegman and Stanley Feldstein, eds. Pp. 179–209. Hillsdale, New Jersey: Law-
rence Erlbaum Associates.
Buban, Steven L.
1976   Focus Control and Prominence in Triads. *Sociometry* 39:281–288.
Cazden, Courtney B.
1972   *Child Language and Education.* New York: Holt, Rinehart and Winston.
Chafe, Wallace L.
1973   Language and Memory. *Language* 49:261–281.
Cherry, Colin
1971   *World Communication: Threat or Promise? A Sociotechnical Approach.* New
York: Wiley-Interscience.
Chesterfield, Philip Dormer Stanhope
1932   *The Letters of the Earl of Chesterfield to His Son.* Charles Strachey, ed. London:
Methuen.
Chomsky, Noam
1957   *Syntactic Structures.* The Hague: Mouton.
Chomsky, Noam
1965   *Aspects of the Theory of Syntax.* Cambridge, Mass.: MIT Press.
Cole, Peter, and Jerry L. Morgan, eds.
1975   *Syntax and Semantics, Vol. 3: Speech Acts.* New York: Academic Press.
Condon, W.S., and W.D. Ogston
1966   Sound Film Analysis of Normal and Pathological Behavior Patterns. *Journal of
Nervous and Mental Disease* 143:338–347.
Condon, W.S., and W.D. Ogston
1967   A Segmentation of Behavior. *Journal of Psychiatric Research* 5:221–235.

Condon, W.S., and L.W. Sander
 1974 Neonate Movement Is Synchronized with Adult Speech: Interactional Participation and Language Acquisition. *Science* 183:99–101.
Cook, Mark
 1971 The Incidence of Filled Pauses in Relation to Part of Speech. *Language and Speech* 14:135–139.
Cook, Mark, Jacqueline Smith, and Mansur G. Lalljee
 1974 Filled Pauses and Syntactic Complexity. *Language and Speech* 17:11–16.
Coulthard, Malcolm, and Margaret Ashby
 1975 Talking with the Doctor. *Journal of Communication* 25:140–147.
Cullen, J.M.
 1972 Some Principles of Animal Communication. In *Non-Verbal Communication*. Robert A. Hinde, ed. Pp. 101–125. Cambridge: Cambridge University Press.
Dale, Philip S.
 1974 Hesitations in Maternal Speech. *Language and Speech* 17:174–181.
Diebold, A. Richard
 1968 Anthropological Perspectives: Anthropology and the Comparative Psychology of Communicative Behavior. In *Animal Communication*. Thomas A. Sebeok, ed. Pp. 525–571. Bloomington: Indiana University Press.
Dijk, Teun A. van
 1977 *Text and Context: Explorations in the Semantics and Pragmatics of Discourse.* New York: Longman.
Dittman, A.T.
 1974 The Body Movement–Speech Rhythm Relationship as a Cue to Speech Encoding. In *Nonverbal Communication*. Shirley Weitz, ed. Pp. 169–181. New York: Oxford University Press.
Dittman, A.T., and L.G. Llewellyn
 1967 The Phonemic Clause as a Unit of Speech Decoding. *Journal of Personality and Social Psychology* 6:341–349.
Dittman, A.T., and L.G. Llewellyn
 1969 Body Movement and Speech Rhythm in Social Conversation. *Journal of Personality and Social Psychology* 11:98–106.
Duncan, Starkey, Jr.
 1974a Some Signals and Rules for Taking Speaking Turns in Conversations. In *Nonverbal Communication*. Shirley Weitz, ed. Pp. 298–311. New York: Oxford University Press.
Duncan, Starkey Jr.
 1974b On the Structure of Speaker-Auditor Interaction During Speaking Turns. *Language in Society* 2:161–180.
Duncan, Starkey Jr., and Donald W. Fiske
 1977 *Face-to-Face Interaction: Research, Methods, and Theory.* New York: Wiley.
Eibl-Eibesfeldt, I.
 1974 Similarities and Differences between Cultures in Expressive Movements. In *Nonverbal Communication*. Shirley Weitz, ed. Pp. 20–33. New York: Oxford University Press.
Ekman, Paul, and Wallace V. Friesen
 1974 Nonverbal Leakage and Clues to Deception. In *Nonverbal Communication*. Shirley Weitz, ed. Pp. 269–290. New York: Oxford University Press.

Erickson, Frederick
  1979 Talking Down: Some Cultural Sources of Miscommunication in Interracial Inter-
        views. In *Nonverbal Behavior: Applications and Cultural Implications*. Aaron
        Wolfgang, ed. Pp. 99–126. New York: Academic Press.
Ervin-Tripp, Susan
  1973 An Analysis of the Interaction of Language, Topic and Listener. In *Social En-
        counters: Readings in Social Interaction*. Michael Argyle, ed. Pp. 65–75. Chicago:
        Aldine.
Exline, Ralph V.
  1974 Visual Interaction: The Glances of Power and Preferance. In *Nonverbal Com-
        munication*. Shirley Weitz, ed. Pp. 65–92. New York: Oxford University Press.
Feld, Steven, and Carroll Williams
  1975 Toward a Researchable Film Language. *Studies in the Anthropology of Visual
        Communication* 2:25–32.
Frake, Charles O.
  1972 How to Ask for a Drink in Subanun. In *Language and Social Context*. Pier Paolo
        Giglioli, ed. Pp. 87–93. Baltimore: Penguin.
Fries, C.C.
  1952 *The Structure of English*. New York: Harcourt, Brace and World.
Fromkin, Victoria A.
  1971 The Non-Anomalous Nature of Anomalous Utterances. *Language* 47:27–52.
Garfinkel, Harold
  1967 *Studies in Ethnomethodology*. Englewood Cliffs, N.J.: Prentice-Hall.
Garfinkel, Harold, and Harvey Sacks
  1970 On Formal Structures of Practical Actions. In *Theoretical Sociology*. J.D.
        McKinney and E.A. Tiryakian, eds. Pp. 337–366. New York: Appleton-Century
        Crofts.
Goffman, Erving
  1953 Communication Conduct in an Island Community. Ph.D. dissertation, Sociology
        Department, University of Chicago.
Goffman, Erving
  1963 *Behavior in Public Places: Notes on the Social Organization of Gatherings*. New
        York: Free Press.
Goffman, Erving
  1964 The Neglected Situation. In *The Ethnography of Communication*. John J. Gum-
        perz and Dell Hymes, eds. Special Publication of American Anthropologist 66,
        6, pt. II:133–136.
Goffman, Erving
  1967 *Interaction Ritual: Essays in Face to Face Behavior*. Garden City, New York:
        Doubleday.
Goffman, Erving
  1971 *Relations in Public: Microstudies of the Public Order*. New York: Harper and
        Row.
Goffman, Erving
  1974 *Frame Analysis: An Essay on the Organization of Experience*. New York: Harper
        and Row.
Goffman, Erving
  1975 Replies and Responses. *Centro Internazionale di Semiotica e di Linguistica,
        Working Papers and Prepublications* num. 46–57, serie C. Urbino. Italia: Univ-
        ersita di Urbino. [Later published in *Language in Society* 5:257–313, 1976.]

Goffman, Erving
1978 Response Cries. *Language* 54:787–815.
Goffman, Erving
1981 *Forms of Talk*. Philadelphia: University of Pennsylvania Press.
Goldman-Eisler, Frieda
1961 A Comparative Study of Two Hesitation Phenomena. *Language and Speech* 4:18–26.
Goldman-Eisler, Frieda
1972 Pauses, Clauses, Sentences. *Language and Speech* 15:103–113.
Goodenough, Ward H.
1963 *Cooperation in Change: An Anthropological Approach to Community Development*. New York: Wiley.
Goodenough, Ward H.
1965 Rethinking 'Status' and 'Role': Toward a General Model of the Cultural Organization of Social Relationships. In *The Relevance of Models for Social Anthropology*. Michael Banton, ed. Pp. 1–24. London: Tavistock.
Goodwin, Charles
1979 Unilateral Departure. Paper presented at the 74th Annual Meeting of the American Sociological Association, Boston.
Goodwin, Charles
Forth- Notes on Story Structure and the Organization of Participation. To appear in
coming *Studies in the Organization of Conversational Interaction* (Vol. II). Jim Schenkein, ed. New York: Academic Press.
Goodwin, Marjorie
1979 Vocal and Nonvocal Interaction in Assessment Sequences. Colloquium given at Oxford University.
Goodwin, Marjorie
1980a Processes of Mutual Monitoring Implicated in the Production of Description Sequences. *Sociological Inquiry* 50:303–317.
Goodwin, Marjorie
1980b He-Said-She-Said: Formal Cultural Procedures for the Construction of a Gossip Dispute Activity. *American Ethnologist* 7:674–695.
Grice, H.P.
1969 Utterer's Meaning and Intentions. *Philosophical Review* 68:147–177.
Gunter, Richard
1974 *Sentences in Dialog*. Columbia, S.C.: Hornbeam.
Gunter, Richard
1976 Review of *Intonation, Perception and Language* by Philip Lieberman. *Language in Society* 5:390–401.
Gur, Racquel E.
1975 Conjugate Lateral Eye Movements as an Index of Hemispheric Activation. *Journal of Personality and Social Psychology* 31:751–757.
Gusfield, Joseph
1976 The Literary Rhetoric of Science: Comedy and Pathos in Drinking Driver Research. *American Sociological Review* 41:16–34.
Hadding-Koch, K.
1961 *Accoustico-Phonetic Studies in the Intonation of Southern Swedish*. Lund, Sweden: C.W.K. Gleerup.
Halliday, M.A.K., and Ruqaiya Hasan
1976 *Cohesion in English*. London: Longman.

Harris, Zellig
1951 *Methods in Structural Linguistics.* Chicago: University of Chicago Press.
Heath, Christian
1979a Breaking Co-Presence. Manuscript.
Heath, Christian
1979b Establishing Co-Presence and the Display of Recipiency: Some Preliminary Observations. Manuscript.
Heath, Christian
1980 The Display of Recipiency: An Instance of a Sequential Relationship in Vocal and Nonvocal Action. Manuscript.
Heider, Karl G.
1976 *Ethnographic Film.* Austin: University of Texas Press.
Henderson, Alan I.
1974 Time Patterns in Spontaneous Speech—Cognitive Stride or Random Walk? A Reply to Jaffe *et al.* (1972). *Language and Speech* 17:119–125.
Hiz, Henry
1969 Referentials. *Semiotica* 1:136–166.
Hymes, Dell
1971 Sociolinguistics and the Ethnography of Speaking. In *Social Anthropology and Language.* Edwin Ardener, ed. London: Tavistock.
Jaffe, Joseph, and Stanley Feldstein
1970 *Rhythms of Dialogue.* New York: Academic Press.
Jefferson, Gail
1972 Side Sequences. In *Studies in Social Interaction.* David Sudnow, ed. Pp. 294–338. New York: Free Press.
Jefferson, Gail
1973 A Case of Precision Timing in Ordinary Conversation: Overlapped Tag-Positioned Address Terms in Closing Sequences. *Semiotica* 9:47–96.
Jefferson, Gail
1974 Error Correction as an Interactional Resource. *Language in Society* 2:181–199.
Jefferson, Gail
1979 A Technique for Inviting Laughter and its Subsequent Acceptance Declination. In *Everyday Language: Studies in Ethnomethodology.* George Psathas, ed. Pp. 79–96. New York: Irvington Publishers.
Jones, Pauline A.
1974 Elaborated Speech and Hesitation Phenomena. *Language and Speech* 17:199–203.
Kendon, Adam
1967 Some Functions of Gaze-Direction in Social Interaction. *Acta Psychologica* 26:22–63.
Kendon, Adam
1973 The Role of Visible Behavior in the Organization of Social Interaction. In *Social Communication and Movement: Studies of Interaction and Expression in Man and Chimpanzee.* Mario Von Cranach and Ian Vine, eds. Pp. 29–74. New York: Academic Press.
Kendon, Adam
1974 Movement Coordination in Social Interaction: Some Examples Described. In *Nonverbal Communication.* Shirley Weitz, ed. Pp. 150–168. New York: Oxford University Press.
Kendon, Adam
1977 *Studies in the Behavior of Social Interaction.* Bloomington: Indiana University Press.

Kendon, Adam
  1978   Looking in Conversation and the Regulation of Turns at Talk: A Comment on the Papers of G. Beattie and D.R. Rutter *et al. British Journal of Social and Clinical Psychology* 17:23–24.

Kinsbourne, Marcel
  1972   Eye and Head Turning Indicates Cerebral Lateralization. *Science* 176:539, 541.

Kloker, Dean
  1975   Vowel and Sonorant Lengthening as Cues to Phonological Phrase Boundaries. Paper presented at the 89th Meeting of the Accoustical Society of America.

Krippendorff, Klaus
  1969a   Models of Messages: Three Prototypes. In *Analysis of Communication Content.* G. Gerbner, O. Holsti, K. Krippendorff, W. Paisley, and P. Stone, eds. New York: Wiley.

Krippendorff, Klaus
  1969b   On Generating Data in Communication Research. Paper presented at the 17th Annual Conference of the National Society for the Study of Communication.

Labov, William
  1970   *The Study of Nonstandard English.* Champaign, Ill.: National Council of Teachers of English.

Labov, William
  1972a   *Language in the Inner City: Studies in the Black English Vernacular.* Philadelphia: University of Pennsylvania Press.

Labov, William
  1972b   *Sociolinguistic Patterns.* Philadelphia: University of Pennsylvania Press.

Labov, William
  1975   On the Grammaticality of Every-Day Speech. Paper presented at Current Trends in Linguistics, SUNY at Binghamton.

Labov, William, and David Fanshel
  1977   *Therapeutic Discourse: Psychotherapy as Conversation.* New York: Academic Press.

LaFrance, Marianne, and Clara Mayo
  1976   Racial Differences in Gaze Behavior During Conversation: Two Systematic Observational Studies. *Journal of Personality and Social Psychology* 33:547–552.

Lakoff, George
  1968   *Counterparts, or the Problem of Reference in Transformational Grammar.* Bloomington: Indiana University Linguistics Club.

Lakoff, George
  1971   Performative Antinomies. *Foundations of Language* 8:569–572.

Lieberman, Philip
  1967   *Intonation, Perception, and Language.* Cambridge: MIT Press.

Lindenfeld, Jacqueline
  1971   Verbal and Non-Verbal Elements in Discourse. *Semiotica* 8:223–233.

Lotz, John
  1968   On Language and Culture. In *Language and Culture.* Patrick Gleeson and Nancy Wakefield, eds. Pp. 101–105. Columbus, Ohio: Charles E. Merrill.

Lyons, John
  1969   *Introduction to Theoretical Linguistics.* Cambridge: Cambridge University Press.

Lyons, John
  1972   Human Language. In *Non-Verbal Communication.* R.A. Hinde, ed. Pp. 49–85. Cambridge: Cambridge University Press.

Macdonald, Nina H.
  1976 Duration as a Syntactic Boundary Cue in Ambiguous Sentences. Paper presented at the 1975 IEEE International Conference on Acoustics, Speech, and Signal Processing, April 12–14, 1976, Philadelphia.
Maclay, Howard, and Charles E. Osgood
  1959 Hesitation Phenomena in Spontaneous English Speech. *Word* 15:19–44.
McQuown, Norman A., ed.
  1971 The Natural History of an Interview. Microfilm Collections of Manuscripts, 15th Series n. 97' Joseph Regenstein Library, University of Chicago.
Mahl, George F.
  1959 Exploring Emotional States by Content Analysis. In *Trends in Content Analysis.* Ithiel de Sola Pool, ed. Pp. 89–130. Urbana: University of Illinois Press.
Martin, James G., and Winifred Strange
  1968 Determinants of Hesitations in Spontaneous Speech. *Journal of Experimental Psychology* 76:474–479.
Mead, Margaret
  1973 The Art and Technology of Field Work. In *A Handbook of Method in Cultural Anthropology.* Raoul Naroll and Ronald Cohen, eds. Pp. 246–265. New York: Columbia University Press.
Miller, G.A.
  1963 Speaking in General. Review of *Universals of Language,* J.H. Greenberg, ed. *Contemporary Psychology* 8:417–418.
Mishler, Elliot G., and Nancy E. Waxler
  1970 Functions of Hesitations in the Speech of Normal Families and Families of Schizophrenic Patients. *Language and Speech* 13:102–117.
Nielsen, G.
  1964 *Studies in Self-Confrontation.* Copenhagen: Munksgaard.
Norwine, A.C., and O.J. Murphy
  1938 Characteristic Time Intervals in Telephonic Conversation. *Bell System Technical Journal* 17:281–291.
Ochs, Elinor
  1979 Transcription as Theory. In *Developmental Pragmatics.* Elinor Ochs and Bambi B. Schieffelin, eds. Pp. 43–72. New York: Academic Press.
Ochs, Elinor, Bambi B. Schieffelin, and Martha L. Platt
  1979 Propositions across Utterances and Speakers. In *Developmental Pragmatics.* Elinor Ochs and Bambi B. Schieffelin, eds. Pp. 251–268. New York: Academic Press.
O'Malley, Michael, Dean R. Kloker, and Benay Dara-Abrams
  1973 Recovering Parentheses from Spoken Algebraic Expressions. *IEEE Transactions on Audio and Electroacoustics* Vol. Au-21, No. 3, June 1973:217–220.
Philips, Susan U.
  1974 The Invisible Culture: Communication in Classroom and Community on the Warm Springs Reservation. Ph.D. dissertation, Anthropology Department, University of Pennsylvania.
Pike, Kenneth L.
  1945 *The Intonation of American English.* Ann Arbor: University of Michigan Press.
Pomerantz, Anita
  1978 Compliment Responses: Notes on the Co-operation of Multiple Constraints. In *Studies in the Organization of Conversational Interaction.* Jim Schenkein, ed. Pp. 79–112. New York: Academic Press.

Rogers, L. Edna, and Richard B. Farace
  1975   Analysis of Relational Communication in Dyads: New Measurement Procedures. *Human Communication Research* 1:222–239.
Rutter, D.R., G.M. Stephenson, A.J. Lazzerini, K. Ayling, and P.A. White
  1977   Eye-Contact: A Chance Product of Individual Looking? *British Journal of Social and Clinical Psychology* 16:191–192.
Rutter, D.R., and G.M. Stephenson
  1977   The Role of Visual Communication in Synchronizing Conversation. *European Journal of Social Psychology* 7:29–37.
Rutter, D.R., and G.M. Stephenson
  1979   The Functions of Looking: Effects of Friendship on Gaze. *British Journal of Social and Clinical Psychology* 18:203–205.
Sabin, Edward J., Edward J. Clemmer, Daniel C. O'Connel, and Sabine Kowal
  1979   A Pausological Approach to Speech Development. In *Of Speech and Time: Temporal Speech Patterns in Interpersonal Contexts*. Aron W. Siegman and Stanley Feldstein, eds. Pp. 35–55. Hillsdale, New Jersey: Lawrence Erlbaum Associates.
Sacks, Harvey
  1963   Sociological Description. *Berkeley Journal of Sociology* 8:1–16.
Sacks, Harvey
  1967   Unpublished class lectures.
Sacks, Harvey
  1970   Unpublished class lectures.
Sacks, Harvey
  1971   Unpublished class lectures.
Sacks, Harvey
  1972a   On the Analyzability of Stories by Children. In *Directions in Sociolinguistics: The Ethnography of Communication*. John J. Gumperz and Dell Hymes, eds. Pp. 325–345. New York: Holt, Rinehart and Winston.
Sacks, Harvey
  1972b   Unpublished class lectures.
Sacks, Harvey
  1973a   On Some Puns with Some Intimations. In *Report of the Twenty-Third Annual Round Table Meeting on Linguistics and Language Studies*. Roger W. Shuy, ed. Pp. 135–144. Washington, D.C.: Georgetown University Press.
Sacks, Harvey
  1973b   The Preference for Agreement in Natural Conversation. Paper presented at the Summer Institute of Linguistics, Ann Arbor.
Sacks, Harvey
  1973c   Lectures at the Summer Institute of Linguistics, Ann Arbor.
Sacks, Harvey
  1974   An Analysis of the Course of a Joke's Telling in Conversation. In *Explorations in the Ethnography of Speaking*. Richard Bauman and Joel Sherzer, eds. Pp. 337–353. Cambridge: Cambridge University Press.
Sacks, Harvey
  1978   Some Technical Considerations of a Dirty Joke. In *Studies in the Organization of Conversational Interaction*. Jim Schenkein, ed. Pp. 249–269. New York: Academic Press.
Sacks, Harvey, and Emanuel A. Schegloff
  1979   Two Preferences in the Organization of Reference to Persons and Their Interaction. In *Everyday Language: Studies in Ethnomethodology*. George Psathas, ed. New York: Irvington Publishers.

Sacks, Harvey, Emanuel A. Schegloff, and Gail Jefferson
  1974 A Simplest Systematics for the Organization of Turn-Taking for Conversation. *Language* 50:696–735.
Scheflen, Albert E.
  1964 The Significance of Posture in Communication Systems. *Psychiatry* 27:316–331.
Scheflen, Albert E.
  1973 *Communicational Structure: Analysis of a Psychotherapy Transaction.* Bloomington: Indiana University Press.
Scheflen, Albert E.
  1974 *How Behavior Means.* Garden City, New York: Doubleday.
Schegloff, Emanuel A.
  1968 Sequencing in Conversational Openings. *American Anthpologist* 70:1075–1095.
Schegloff, Emanuel A.
  1972 Notes on a Conversational Practice: Formulating Place. In *Studies in Social Interaction.* David Sudnow, ed. Pp. 75–119. New York: Free Press.
Schegloff, Emanuel A.
  1976 *On Some Questions and Ambiguities in Conversation.* Pragmatics Microfiche 2.2:D8. Department of Linguistics, University of Cambridge, England.
Schegloff, Emanuel A.
  1979 The Relevance of Repair for Syntax-for-Conversation. Manuscript.
Schegloff, Emanuel A., and Harvey Sacks
  1973 Opening Up Closings. *Semiotica* 8:289–327.
Schegloff, Emanuel A., Gail Jefferson, and Harvey Sacks
  1977 The Preference for Self-Correction in the Organization of Repair in Conversation. *Language* 53:361–382.
Scollon, Ronald
  1976 *Conversations with a One Year Old: A Case Study of the Developmental Foundation of Syntax.* Honolulu: The University Press of Hawaii.
Scollon, Ronald
  1979 A Real Early Stage: An Unzippered Condensation of a Dissertation on Child Language. In *Developmental Pragmatics.* Elinor Ochs and Bambi B. Schieffelin, eds. Pp. 215–277. New York: Academic Press.
Searle, John R.
  1970 *Speech Acts: An Essay in the Philosophy of Language.* Cambridge: Cambridge University Press.
Seigman, Aron Wolfe
  1979 Cognition and Hesitation in Speech. In *Of Speech and Time: Temporal Speech Patterns in Interpersonal Contexts.* Aron W. Seigman and Stanley Feldstein, eds. Pp. 151–178. Hillsdale, New Jersey: Lawrence Erlbaum Associates.
Simmel, Georg
  1950 *The Sociology of Georg Simmel.* Translated by Kurt Wolff. Glencoe, Ill.: Free Press.
Simmel, Georg
  1969 Sociology of the Senses: Visual Interaction. In *Introduction to the Science of Sociology.* R.E. Park and W. Burgess, eds. Pp. 356–361. Chicago: University of Chicago Press.
Sluzki, G.E. and J. Beavin
  1965 Simetria y Complementaridad: Una Definicion Operacional y una Tipologia de Parejas. *Acta Psiquiatrica y Psyiocologica de American Latina* 2:321–330.

Smith, W. John
  1974 Displays and Messages in Intraspecific Communication. In *Nonverbal Communication.* Shirley Weitz, ed. Pp. 331–340. New York: Oxford University Press.
Smith, W. John, Julia Chase, and Anna Katz Lieblich
  1974 Tongue Showing: A Facial Display of Humans and Other Primate Species. *Semiotica* 11:201–246.
Snow, C.E.
  1971 Language Acquisition and Mothers' Speech to Children. Ph.D. dissertation. McGill University.
Sommer, Robert
  1959 Studies in Personal Space. *Sociometry* 23:247–260.
Sommer, Robert, and Franklin Becker
  1974 Territorial Defense and the Good Neighbor. In *Nonverbal Communication.* Shirley Weitz, ed. Pp. 252–262. New York: Oxford University Press.
Soskin, W.F., and U.P. John
  1963 The Study of Spontaneous Talk. In *The Study of Spontaneous Talk.* R.G. Barker, ed. New York: Appleton-Century Crofts.
Taylor, William R.
  1970 Research on Family Interaction I: Static and Dynamic Models. *Family Process* 9:221–232.
Terasaki, Alene
  1976 *Pre-Announcement Sequences in Conversation* (Social Science Working Paper 99). School of Social Sciences. Irvine, California: University of California.
Thomas, Elizabeth Marshall
  1958 *The Harmless People.* New York: Random House.
Trager, G.L., and H.L. Smith
  1951 *An Outline of English-Structure.* Norman, Oklahoma: Battenburg.
Vngve, Victor H.
  1970 On Getting a Word in Edgewise. In *Papers from the Sixth Regional Meeting, Chicago Linguistic Society.* M.A. Campbell *et al.,* eds. Pp. 567–578. Chicago: Department of Linguistics, University of Chicago.
Vološinov, Valentin Nikolaevic
  1973 *Marxism and the Philosophy of Language.* Translated by Ladislav Matejka and I.R. Titunik. New York: Seminar Press. (First published 1929 and 1930.)
Wiemann, John M.
  1976 An Experimental Investigation of Communicative Competence in Initial Interactions. Paper presented at the International Communication Association Convention. Portland, Oregon.
Wiffen, Thomas
  1915 *The North-West Amazons: Notes on Some Months Spent among Cannibal Tribes.* London: Constable.
Wolfson, Nessa
  1976 Speech Events and Natural Speech: Some Implications for Sociolinguistic Methodology. *Language in Society* 5:189–209.
Worth, Sol, and John Adair
  1970 Navajo Filmmakers. *American Anthropologist* 72:9–34.
Zimmerman, Don H., and Candace West
  1975 Sex Roles, Interruptions and Silences in Conversation. In *Language and Sex: Difference and Dominace.* Barrie Thorne and Nancy Henley, eds. Pp. 105–129. Rowley, Mass.: Newbury House.

Subject Index